About the author

Dr. Jack Child is professor of Spanish and Latin American Studies in the Department of Language and Foreign Studies of The American University, Washington, DC. He was born of American parents in Buenos Aires, Argentina, and lived in South America for 18 years before coming to the United States in 1955 to attend Yale University. Following graduation from Yale, he entered the U.S. Army, and served for 20 years as an Army Latin American Specialist until his retirement as a lieutenant colonel in 1980. His M.A. and Ph. D. are from The American University.

In 1980 he joined The American University's School of International Service as Assistant Dean. Two years later he moved to the Department of Language and Foreign Studies, where he teaches a variety of courses (in both English and Spanish) dealing with translation, conflict, and Latin American studies. He has a special interest in using literature and art to teach history, and has authored several Macintosh computer programs.

His principal research interests have focused on conflict and its resolution in Latin America and Antarctica. He has worked with the U.S. Institute of Peace and the International Peace Academy (associated with the United Nations in New York), on issues dealing with peacekeeping and confidence-building measures in Central and South America, and the Antarctic Quadrant of South America. His interest in high latitudes has taken him to Alaska, and on seven trips as staff lecturer aboard expedition cruise vessels to Antarctica and various sub-Antarctic islands, including the Malvinas/Falklands and South Georgia.

His published books include: *Latin America: History, Art, Literature* (with software), 1993. *The Central American Peace Process, 1983-1991: Sheathing Swords, Building Confidence*, 1992. *Introduction to Spanish Translation,* 1992. *Geopolitics of the Southern Cone and Antarctica*, coedited, 1988. *Antarctica and South American Geopolitics: Frozen Lebensraum*, 1988. *Regional Cooperation and the Peaceful Settlement of Disputes in Latin America*, ed., 1987. *Conflict in Central America: Approaches to Peace and Security*, ed., 1986. *Quarrels Among Neighbors: Geopolitics and Conflict in South America*, 1985. *Latin America: International Relations*, coauthored, 1981. *Unequal Alliance: The Inter-American Military System, 1938-1978*, 1980.

Computer software authored (Macintosh Hypercard): "Latin America: History, Art, Literature", "Introduction to the Geography of Latin America", and "Introduction to Latin American Literature".

ZOROASTER

ZOROASTER

LIFE AND WORK OF THE FORERUNNER
IN PERSIA

Received in the proximity of Abd-ru-shin
through the special gift of
one Called for the purpose

GRAIL·FOUNDATION·PRESS

GAMBIER, OHIO

Library Systems and Services Cataloging-in-Publication Data

Zoroaster : life and work of the forerunner in Persia :
received in the proximity of Abd-ru-shin through
the special gift of one Called for the purpose. -
2nd ed. Gambier, Oh. : Grail Foundation Press, © 1996.

264 p. ; 23 cm.   (Forerunners)

Summary: Relates how the young boy Saadi matured through divine guidance
and eventually realized his true identity as the long-awaited prophet Zoroaster,
and highlights the effect of his prophetic works in Persia.

ISBN 1-57461-012-0
1. Zoroaster 2. Zoroastrianism—Persia—Biography.
I. Abd-ru-shin, 1875-1941.
299'.51463 Bdc20
BL1930.B357 1995

Printed on recycled paper.

The complete titles in the *Forerunner Book Series*:

LAO-TSE
The Life and Work of the Forerunner in China

BUDDHA
The Life and Work of the Forerunner in India

ZOROASTER
The Life and Work of the Forerunner in Persia

Forthcoming editions:

EPHESUS
The Life and Work of the Forerunner Hjalfdar in Prehistoric Times

MOHAMMED
The Life and Work of the Forerunner in Arabia

FROM PAST MILLENNIA
Moses
Abd-ru-shin
Mary
Jesus

PAST ERAS AWAKEN
Volume I
Krishna
Nahome
Cassandra
Mary of Magdala

Volume II
Atlantis
The Realm of the Incas
Abd-ru-shin
Cassandra
Jesus of Nazareth

Volume III
Egypt
Nemare
The Pharaohs
Unknown Events from the Life of Jesus
The Apostles

THE SEER OPENS WIDE HIS EYES AND SEES.

BEFORE HIS GAZE ARISES LIFE,

WHICH HAS BEEN INDELIBLY ENGRAVED

IN THE BOOK OF THIS GREAT CREATION:

BEFORE IT BEGAN ITS raging downward rush over the rocks, the wild Karun issued from innumerable bubbling springs high in the mountains. There, between menacing cliffs, lay a vast plain.

Thick bushes of thorny tragacanth surrounded it, so that paths had to be hewn through this prickly mass before human beings could set foot there.

Only at the time when the Sun and Moon gods held equal sway over the days of men was this wide expanse covered with green. But then it was indeed ineffably fair.

The grasses and mosses sparkled like gemstones, enjoying their brief two-month existence, drinking in the light. Fragrant, golden blossoms adorned the thornbushes, resembling the delicate sun-birds fluttering round them on gaily coloured wings.

Then people would flock to this wonderful region, setting up camps wherever they found a place among the wild rocks to pass the night. A prolonged stay on the plain was not permitted them by the Atravan, the priest.

It was sacred to the Sun god, Mithra, the luminous, benevolent god who dispensed blessing and loved human beings.

Therefore sublime, wonderful festivals were held in his honour. The rocks resounded to the jubilation of human voices singing hymns in his praise.

Sometimes from afar the roar of a lion answered them, but not a single heart beat fearfully on that account. As long as they were on Mithra's plain, no beasts of prey could approach them.

With his assistants, the Mobeds, the Atravan was eagerly preparing the stone-piles on which the sacred fires were to be lit at nightfall. Only the two oldest Mobeds were permitted to help him with this work. They had to lead an unblemished life, for only completely pure hands must touch the sacred stones.

The remaining five Mobeds, the youngest of whom had scarcely out-grown boyhood, ran about killing snakes and mice, or simply driving them away.

The camping places for hundreds of worshippers were being prepared. But not until the song of the Atravan had signalled the beginning of the festival would anyone have dared to approach Mithra's garden.

It was the Atravan too, who established precisely the cardinal points for the placement of the tall, carefully layered heaps of stone.

One stood where the golden rays of dawn dispelled the twilight of Maonha's realm. It was the largest stack of all. The next stood directly opposite it; the remaining two to the right and left, all equidistant from each other. In the centre of the site three stone-piles had been erected in a triangle.

Reciting prayers to Mithra, the Atravan placed a deep iron bowl filled with small dry twigs on each of these offering places.

All the seven Mobeds then had to prepare bundles of thorny tragacanth branches with which it was their duty to ward off insects throughout the festival.

So that no one would be injured, these had to be held aloft until needed. That was sometimes a strain, but being permitted to be a Mobed was a high honour not only for the youth himself, but for his entire family, so that the task was gladly undertaken.

In the meantime the Atravan had stepped behind a protruding rock and attired himself for the festival.

He wore a white woollen garment devoid of any ornament. Encircling his brow was a coronet inlaid with dull, blue-green stones so closely set that nothing could be seen of the gold from which it was fashioned.

Stepping into the centre of the open square, he clapped his hands.

From behind another boulder there appeared four maidens dressed in white. Silver embroidery adorned the loosely flowing garments that en-veloped their lovely forms.

Wound several times round their necks and entwined in the bluish black hair of their braids they wore chains of blue-green stones.

In their hands they held golden vessels containing precious oil with which they replenished the bowls while the Atravan prayed.

He invoked the grace of Atar, the god of the flames, upon the festival.

As a younger brother of Mithra, from whom he received all the fire he needed, it was to be hoped that he would not disturb a Mithra-festival. Thraetvana, the god of lightning, was the youngest of the fire brothers, the most restless and unrestrained of them all.

Now all was in readiness for the festival.

The youngest of the priestesses approached the Atravan and placed a splendidly-embroidered, white silken cloth over his face so that it covered his mouth and nose, lest the man's breath touch the sacred fire.

The priestesses required no such protection, for their breath was considered to be pure. Solemnly, while the Atravan continued to pray, the four maidens stepped behind the rock and brought forth a bowl of fire, from which they placed firebrands in each of the seven bowls.

When the last offertory bowl was alight, the priest fell silent, while the eldest of the maidens took his place at the three central flames, raised her arms and hands and prayed to the gods for their blessing.

"Pure as the flames that consume all evil may our hearts be, you Sublime Ones!" she implored in the prescribed manner. "Send us the spirit of sacred fire that it may cleanse and purify us!"

Then she moved to the eastern bowl while her companions tended the three other flames, and the Atravan remained standing in the centre.

In a sonorous voice, he then began a hymn glorifying both Atar and Mithra.

Now those celebrating the festival gathered. From all sides they streamed forth, some clambering over rocky ridges, others slipping along the paths in the bushes, but nonetheless with innate seemliness and dignity.

On one side of the square the women, in their multi-coloured garments, and adorned with beautiful chains and headbands, presented a colourful picture.

Opposite them stood the men, splendid of figure, tall and slender of build, with suntanned faces. Their garments were black, richly decorated with silver; over this most wore a wolf's skin held together by a silver chain. On their heads they wore tall fur hats. Their hair was cut at the nape of the neck.

11

Those standing joined at once in the song of the Atravan, so that a full chorus of male and female voices surged aloft.

When the sacred songs were over, the oldest priestess brought a silver goblet and a silver pitcher with the juice of the haoma-plant to the Atravan who, while uttering prayers, filled the goblet, drank from it and then passed it on.

Every adult man was permitted a sip of the drink. From time to time one of the people returned the emptied goblet to the priestess, who refilled it.

All this proceeded with great solemnity, in dignified silence.

When all the men had been given a sip of haoma, the priestess poured the remaining juice over the offertory bowl where she stood. Bluish smoke assumed peculiar forms as it rose upwards.

The few moments in which this occurred sufficed to show the maiden all manner of things which she now proclaimed in a gentle singing tone.

The crowd listened spellbound, for from the words of the sacred proclamation they drew something special for their own lives in the twelve months to come.

When she had finished, the people burst forth into shouts of jubilation.

These were meant to bespeak gratitude, gratitude to the Sun- and Light-god, Mithra, who again had granted promises for the immediate future.

A call from the Atravan brought the proclamations to an end. The four priestesses went to the central flames and began to sing a hymn in praise of Diyanitra, the pure, gracious woman.

Thereupon the Atravan said a long prayer, and in solemn procession the priestesses departed with the women.

The latter kindled a prepared bundle of dry twigs on the offertory flame nearest to them, as though wishing to feed the fire of the domestic hearth from the sacred flame.

But the men seated themselves in a circle. Fermented haoma juice was brought in stone jugs, from which they drank in long draughts at will. Over-indulgence in the intoxicating drink was unknown. In Mithra's garden respect was taken for granted.

The Atravan sent for a bundle of animal-skins upon which he seated himself along with the Mobeds.

Night had fallen. Maonha sent down shimmering rays from the dark blue sky. There was no longer any need to be afraid of snakes, and other animals were kept away by the flames.

"Tell us a story, tell us a story!" the men shouted eagerly.

For a little while the Atravan let them plead, as was seemly. Then he looked up at the sky and began:

"You men of Persia, you know how this world was once created.

"The wise, Holy Spirit, Ahuramazda* lived all by Himself in the seven heavens. Solitude was all about Him; immeasurably vast were His realms, but He was alone, utterly alone.

"So He resolved to create something that could give Him joy.

"He conceived of beings, and as He conceived of them, they appeared! First He devised Mithra, the radiant sun, for Ahuramazda loved everything bright. Thus He loves Mithra most of all the gods He created.

"Beside Mithra He set Maonha, the god of the pale, still moon. He was to share the days with Mithra. His light is less powerful than Mithra's, therefore he was to take over the day's beginning which we human beings call night, so that the radiant one might follow him.

"But his light is too weak, sometimes it goes out altogether. See how his rays quiver!

"Ahuramazda saw this and gave him help: Beside him He placed Tishtrya with the luminous mantle. Countless to the human eye are the sparkling stars that adorn the mantle of the Star-god.

"Then Mithra implored: 'Lord, You have given Maonha a brother, give me one too, so that I need not be alone!'

"Ahuramazda consented; but the brothers who were granted him at his request were not to help him. He was to keep watch over the wild ones: Atar, the fire-spirit, and Thraetvana, the god of lightning. But Mithra rejoiced that they were radiant like himself.

"'Flame-brothers are we!'" he called out across all the world.

"And Ahuramazda created the air-god, Vayn, who comes rushing along in his wide mantle, in whose folds the winds are concealed, warm and cold, gentle and strong, a whole race of nimble fellows. They play with flames and teach them to dance. But Maonha's rays are too pale for them.

* also: Ormuzd

13

"Then Ahuramazda thought of clear, bubbling water, how it dances along in ripples, how it babbles and laughs, sings and roars. And as He mused, a lovely woman was formed. Singing and laughing, with strings of pearls in her long hair, she stood before the wise God Who had conceived of her: Ardvisura Anahita, abounding in delights.

"Suddenly there was life in the seven heavens, joyous life, but Ahuramazda thought of His solitude and knew that He had loved it more than the scintillating life around Him now. And He conceived of a world in which the gods should rule. From above He would look down, summoning them one at a time whenever He longed for company.

"Behold, you men of Persia, thus arose the Earth, our Earth, on which we live. Rocks, waters and plants were created by the thoughts of Ahuramazda; and the gods played with the earth for a long, long time. A human being cannot begin to imagine the remoteness of that time.

"Ahuramazda was content, the gods were occupied and did not disturb Him. But no sooner had He entertained this thought, than they came with another request:

"'Lord, place beings on the earth who will be subject to us.'

"'What are they to look like?' the wise God asked benevolently.

"'They should resemble us,' pleaded Ardvisura Anahita, the lovely one.

"'Let them be quite different, plump and misshapen, but strong and courageous so that we may enjoy them,' cried Atar.

"And Ahuramazda conceived of two beings, man according to Anahita's request, the bull according to Atar's wish. And the gods were happy and contented.

"Again aeons of time passed. They brought abundant change on earth; for ever again the gods directed events down here in different ways.

"Man had multiplied; many kinds of people had come into existence. It was likewise with the bull, from which came all the animals known to you. The gods had all wished to have specific kinds of animals under their dominion. That you know.

"The birds belong to Vayn, the fish, snakes and frogs to the lovely Anahita."

The Atravan fell silent. The jugs had been emptied.

"Go on," begged many of the listeners.

But the flames were dying down, it was time to go and rest.

The following day the mountains resounded with joyful shouts. The women went in search of fruit-bearing shrubs for refreshment; the men roamed about, peering into the eyries of large birds, destroying poisonous snakes, and speaking of what they had heard the day before.

When Mithra began to conceal his rays, a metallic sound rang out: one of the Mobeds was using a heavy stick to beat rhythmically on an iron disc, suspended from one of the taller bushes.

The sound was not beautiful, but it could be heard far and wide; it was the signal granting the men permission to assemble and hear the words of the priest.

Eagerly they came. Although they had heard most of it before, the Atravan always presented the story differently, always added something new.

It was the only time during the year when all were instructed. It was their food for thought.

Most of the men were solitary herdsmen whose lives gave them time and leisure for reflection. Their thoughts dwelt with the gods, of whom they were now again permitted to hear.

Under Maonha's pale rays the one learned secrets about the co-operation of natural forces; from Mithra's fire another drew manly courage and fearlessness.

When the square was filled, and no further stragglers were to be expected, the Atravan lit the three central bowls, no longer filled with the sweet-smelling offertory oil.

The flames served only for illumination, and were fed by the Mobeds with the dry branches they had brought.

The Atravan seated himself. Today he wore a dark brown robe of soft wool held together by a white cord. He was without the coronet.

"Yesterday I told you, you men of Persia, how wondrously the earth and all that lives upon it was created.

"But Ahuramazda, the wise God, perceived how men clung to the gods whom they saw, and who held sway over them, forgetting that He was above the gods, and that a single thought of His could bring about the destruction of all things, just as He had caused their creation.

15

"Then He conceived of beings who, at His behest, could be sent to men to influence, help or reward them.

"But these beings were to serve Him, to remain near Him, to stand between Him and the gods.

"And He conceived of Truth, a wonderful female figure clad in blue, with clear, blue eyes. Wherever He sends her all shadows are dispelled.

"As a sister He gave her Purity, in silvery white raiment, with a luminous veil covering her lovely countenance. Cool is she like the snow on the highest peaks of our mountains, unapproachable, and yet accessible to all who strive towards her.

"Having sent these two to human beings, Ahuramazda saw that those who followed them would consider themselves to be better than the others.

"'That must not be, or else men will destroy the very thing that was meant to bring them salvation.'

"Considering this, Ahuramazda, the wise, benevolent God, brought forth in His solicitude a simple, plain female figure garbed in silvery grey. She attends Truth and Purity, extending gentle, kind hands to those who are about to be carried away with themselves.

"Humility is the name of this winsome child, who bears deep within the treasure bestowed by Ahuramazda, the God, Himself. He who recognises and is loved by Humility will receive bliss.

"These female attendants rendered faithful service to the Supreme God. They became dear and indispensable to Him.

"To demonstrate His pleasure He permitted them to conceive of whatever might arise from their activity on behalf of men as a blessing for them. He would then animate their thoughts, granting his faithful servants the resultant beings as their reward.

"Truth conceived of Wisdom which could always abide with those souls striving for Truth; it became her companion."Purity smiled, and the loving God knew what His dearest child desired, and granted her the blossoming of human souls who let themselves be guided by her.

"You do know, you men, that those who strive for purity here on earth become a joy to us all. Think of your women! Think of the fairest earthwoman we know of, Princess Diyanitra.

"Then Humility asked: 'Lord, let the desire to pass on what they receive arise in the souls. Let them move out of themselves and find their way to others.'

"Then the God conceived of Love, which forgets self.

"'Six pure women surround me,' He reflected, 'they arose from my thoughts. From my Will, however, I will place a man beside them: the Hero! He shall bear within him all virtues of true manhood.'"

With these words of the Atravan, the listening men began to stir. They straightened, their features shone. The hero's virtues were known to them; from their earliest years they strove to become true heroes.

The Atravan continued:

"Aeons of time went by. Generation upon generation of men came into being and passed away. Faithfully the servants of Ahuramazda exerted themselves on behalf of the earth-inhabitants. With joy the God looked upon His creatures.

"Then something terrible came to pass. To grasp what happened, you must know that any wrong we humans perpetrate falls below the earth. There is a place where all this refuse is gathered.

"There, too, go all wicked words and evil thoughts. In the long, long period of time that had elapsed since the creation of the earth, inconceivably much had accumulated there.

"But in some of it there was yet life. And this life clustered together, and was strengthened and became Anramainyu, the spirit of evil. Born of the refuse from all that is earthly, he could produce only frightful things. He knew of Ahuramazda and wanted to equal Him.

"'As You live in the seven heavens above the earth,' he cried, 'I shall live in the seven caves under the earth! You have conceived of gods, well then I shall do likewise!'"

The men shuddered. In some their hearts shrank, others clenched their fists and smote the air.

But the Atravan continued:

"However much Anramainyu attempted to create gods, he did not succeed; for he himself was not God, but only an evil spirit. There is a great difference. Thus he could actually produce only spirits.

"He looked up to the sky. With what should he rival Mithra, Maonha and Tishtrya? His desire grew excessive. And Azhi, the great sinister cloud-serpent arose. You have all often beheld it when it rolls past ominously."

The men nodded.

"Thereafter his evil volition created Apaosha, the drought-demon, which ever again causes the gods anxiety and trouble. Then Anramainyu laughs and deems himself the highest of all gods.

"But when he compared his creatures to the gods, he saw that they were dull and ugly. None could compare with the radiant figures. Tremendous rage seized Anramainyu and brought forth Aeshma – Anger. In strength he is like unto none, in fervour he might well belong to the flame-brothers, but he has one great defect – he is blind."

The men laughed. They were pleased that Anger must be inferior to the gods. That he could not see whom he struck was fitting, often causing harm to himself and those he led.

"Gradually," the Atravan went on, "Anramainyu discovered that Ahuramazda had brought forth yet other special servants, whose activity was beneficial.

"So he too must create beings which in turn could destroy what the others built up. Carefully he investigated, insidiously he watched. Then he knew.

"In place of Truth he created Falsehood which, at first glance, appeared scintillatingly beautiful. A closer look, however, revealed that everything about her was false. But so affable was this spirit, so much more amiable than the retiring Truth that men flocked to her, letting themselves be deceived. And so they came to know falsehood.

"Lovely Purity appeared too unassailable to him, he did not know how he could oppose her. Then he created three beings: the Passions. They pulled and tugged at man until he had defiled himself. Then he soon went down altogether. The blustering, shrieking Passions were zealous servants of the evil spirit.

"Humility he confronted with Arrogance – an easy task; this danger man had virtually created for himself. What the other servants of Anramainyu failed to accomplish, Arrogance, along with Egotism – for these servants too required companions – easily brought about.

"Falsehood selected Cunning, but the Passions created Disease.

"With all these servants Anramainyu now emerged to wrest the kingdom from Ahuramazda. It was his goal to bring humanity under his dominion. The more that had to be thrown on to the rubbish-heap, the stronger was the evil spirit's following.

"You cannot imagine how terrible the battles were, nor how many fell victim to them."

As the Atravan paused, one of the listeners asked:

"Why did Ahuramazda, the highest of all the gods, not put an end to the adversary? Surely it would have been easy for Him."

"Certainly," the priest affirmed, "He could have done so had He wanted to. But He wanted His creatures to decide for themselves for good or evil. Let him who desired nothing else simply fall prey to Anramainyu and thus to destruction. That was better than to have a realm of helpless human beings.

"You too take special delight in those animals of your flocks that seek their own pastures. The mass of cattle that follow one another blindly wearies you. Thus the wise God left men to their free will, permitting the gods and His servants to help only those of good volition.

"In the process, however, the evil one gained victory upon victory. The flowering garden which the earth once presented became a mass of stone, a wasteland such as is now familiar to you. You can no longer conceive of a land in beauty, though you sense it vaguely during the two months when Mithra causes our fields to blossom."

"But surely things cannot continue in this manner for ever," sighed one of the younger men. "Otherwise there will be nothing left of our earth in the end to delight the gods and Ahuramazda."

"No, things will not continue like this for ever," the Atravan confirmed. "We have a prophecy that the earth will not endure eternally. Its time will be immeasurably long, and has been divided by Ahuramazda into three parts of equal length. The first lasted from the creation of the earth to the time when the God conceived of primeval man and the primeval bull. "The second part will end when the Forerunner, the Zoroaster, is born. Then the third epoch will begin in which the Saoshyant, the Helper, proclaimed by the Zoroaster, will be given to mankind.

19

"Who the Saoshyant will be, and how He will liberate men from the evil one we do not yet know. But He will come and we will be happy."

With a deep sigh, the speaker concluded his lengthy account, but he did not rise as usual. It was noticeable that he still had something, perhaps the most important thing, to say.

Meanwhile one of the men asked:

"Will it be a long time before the Forerunner comes?"

The Priest rose to his feet. Solemnly he stood before them.

"Men of Persia," he said, emphasising each word, "all these things I have told you in such detail, in order to proclaim to you something new.

"Our observation of the stars has revealed that the Zoroaster has been born." He could not continue speaking, thunderous jubilation broke forth. For a long time he tried vainly to restrain them; finally he was able to resume.

"With this the second earth-period has come to a close. The earth will be helped so that it may again become that for which Ahuramazda created it long ago. Let us give thanks to Him!"

Deeply moved, he prayed spontaneously from the heart. Then he sent the men away. Night had fallen.

Now came the third day of the festival. Once again the women participated. They came, full of excitement, for the men had passed on to them the great news of the Forerunner's birth.

This last festival-day began when Mithra was at his zenith. No fires had been lit, but there was a lovely scent in the air from the vessels which had been filled with fragrant oil.

The Atravan had taken his seat among the men; the Mobeds discharged their duty of driving away annoying and harmful animals.

The seated listeners made a pleasing picture, men and women strictly separated.

One of the priestesses went up to the central stones and chanted the tale of the cloud-serpent, Azhi, which had resolved to darken the entire sky. Ominously it winds its way upwards, covering section upon section of the radiant blue sky, spreading out more and ever more, swallowing up stars from Tishtrya's mantle and snapping at Maonha, who is too delicate to defend himself.

Then Thraetvana leaps forth threatening the monster with his ringing sword! The strike finds its mark; it severs the head from its loathsome body which hurtles noisily downwards. Long afterwards, the rumbling continues in the mountains.

"Praise be to thee, Thraetvana!"

The narrator stepped back; another priestess took her place.

Likewise half-chanting, but with different tones and a different rhythm she recounted how Anramainyu had given the cloud-serpent another, more vicious head. This time however it had tried to be more careful, by leaving the stars and the moon in peace, but placing its huge heavy form before all the lights of heaven, so that even Mithra's rays could no longer penetrate to men.

Then another of the flame-sons had leaped forth in great ire: Atar, the fire-spirit, drew his sword! He struck not the head, but the large loathsome body on all sides, so that the blood poured down toward earth. Azhi had grown faint, ever fainter, and finally she herself had followed the streams of her blood.

"Praise be to thee also, Atar!"

The third priestess came forward. Her words were accompanied by soft notes from the small stringed instrument she carried.

She told of Apaosha, the drought-demon, who long ago had seized power at the behest of the evil one. Not a drop of rain had fallen for weeks. Man and beast had been parched with thirst.

All had prayed to Ahuramazda for water. But the wise God knew that only because of men's wickedness had Apaosha been able to gain control. It lay with them to bring about change.

Finally they realised this and began to improve. Then the Supreme God permitted His gods to intervene. They begged Ardvisura Anahita for water, and she promised to give as much as would ever be wanted, if only they would convey it to the skies. How was this to be done without Apaosha's drinking it all up? Finally the decision was reached.

Tishtrya sent out fiery stars with long rays designed to pierce the demon in many places at once. Howling, he retreated to the seven caves.

Now all the stars had to draw up water; Maonha, too, assisted them. Soon there was enough water above for the gods to let it rain.

In single, heavy drops the rain began to fall, then it increased until a beneficent flood poured over the thirsting earth.

"Thanks be to thee, kindly stars!"

The high priestess came last. She related how the evil one had created a new servant: Deceit. Everywhere it placed itself before Truth, obstructing its work with men. They should be cautious lest they fall prey to it.

A prayer spoken by the priestess ended the festival. The people set out on the homeward journey at once, since it was more pleasant to travel under Maonha's rays than under Mithra's burning heat.

The plain at the source of the Karun lay still and deserted after the Mobeds had carried off the heaps of stone, and used them to raise walls before the entrances.

Deep in thought, the Atravan was the last to leave the place.

Now he had been permitted to proclaim to the people that the Forerunner had been born. Would they understand? Would they grasp the significance? The Forerunner was to be thirty-one years old before entering upon his task. They would still have to wait that long. He would no longer experience it.

The Atravan travelled about teaching, as was his task, visiting the herdsmen with their flocks, the nobles in their rock-hewn palaces. Meanwhile on the edge of the salt-desert, an infant son had been born to a young couple at the exact time proclaimed by the stars.

The old women who assisted the mother were most surprised that the little one was born with a smile on his face instead of uttering the expected cry.

"Will you be something special, child?" they asked. "Do you expect something beautiful from life?"

The child's face remained sunny as if reflecting a different kind of light. And yet life began in such a difficult way for the little Saadi: his mother died after three days.

The delicate, beautiful Zharat could no longer enjoy her little child. Gradually she faded away, leaving the boy to the care of the old women.

Dshami, the father, who had loved his wife ardently, did not understand why she had gone, leaving him with the child, whose care was quite beyond him.

Little horses he reared with great skill and understanding. This was his vocation, and he devoted himself to it with all his powers. But the little human being was in his way. If only Zharat had taken him with her!

When the little one cried at night, his father got up and went to his horses in the corral. He would rather sleep with them than be with the sobbing child. Yet Saadi never cried aloud as other children do.

The old women took turns in looking after him; but they were already becoming disgruntled. Other duties awaited them, they had their own households to think of.

Let Dshami get himself another wife, there were women enough. They made all sorts of suggestions, but he would not hear of it. At last he became so annoyed that he threatened to take the child with him into the mountains if they continued to harass him. So they stopped trying to persuade him, but they also stopped coming.

Dshami had been all alone with Saadi for only a few days when he realised that things could not go on this way. He let the child be suckled · by a mare so that it would not go hungry, but surely that was not enough to sustain the young life.

Crestfallen, Dshami stood one morning at the little one's bedside. He could not neglect his horses for the sake of the child. Should he wrap Saadi up and take him along? He looked at the little boy who gazed into the world, unconcerned and happy. Then across the threshold of the simple dwelling came a beautiful, stately woman, clad in a long garment of dark blue. Without a word of greeting, she stepped to the man's side, at the same time gazing into the eyes of the little one.

"You no longer have a mother, poor child," she said tenderly. "Dshami, give me the boy, I will bring him up."

The man regarded the speaker with alarm. She was noble in appearance and fine-featured. Her braids were snow-white and unadorned. She appealed to him, but to be separated from the boy?

True he had toyed earlier with the idea of giving the child away, because it was a burden to him, but now that someone had come to take the little one from him, it seemed impossible for him to part from his son.

23

At first, both of them remained silent for a long time. It was quite understandable to the woman that the man was unable to decide at once. Then suddenly he said quite firmly:

"If you have come to me out of neighbourly love, you will understand that it will do the child no good to remove him from his accustomed surroundings. If you have the child's well-being at heart, then stay with him. I will honour you and not let anything happen to you. You will be the mistress of my home; I will be your servant."

"I will stay," the woman replied simply, removing the large silk shawl that enveloped her figure and taking the child into her arms with maternal solicitude.

With a cry of joy the little one acknowledged that he perceived her love.

"He is very intelligent for a child barely two weeks old," said the woman admiringly, busying herself with him as though she had always been there.

Dshami stood by embarrassed. He would so much have liked to go out with his horses in search of better pastures, but did not know whether he should.

The woman glanced back over her shoulder.

"You can set your mind at rest, Dshami, and go about your work. I will not take the little one from you. You will find him well cared for whenever you return. Just tell your neighbours that I am here with your consent; leave everything else to me."

"What shall I call you when I speak of you?" enquired the man.

"Madana is my name," was the answer.

"And where do you come from, will you not tell me? Did you know that Saadi had lost his mother? Who told you?"

Madana gave the enquirer a friendly smile.

"The time will come when I may answer your questions. Trust me, Dshami."

Her look and her words won the man's heart. Expressing his thanks, he left.

The child was indeed well cared for. He wanted for nothing. When the most urgent housework, quickly accomplished at her hands, was done, the woman seated herself beside the little one's bed, singing.

Soft, sweet melodies she sang, bringing a smile to the child's face. At the same time, she made exquisite embroideries, such as the women, who sometimes called in, had never seen before.

At first the neighbours had treated her with suspicion, but her clear eyes, her words, which were full of love, overcame all prejudices. When the women fully realised that Madana knew all sorts of things which were of help to them, they praised and commended her behind her back, and came to her in their every need.

For every hurt she had a remedy, balm for their wounds, comfort for their troubles.

"Madana is like a priestess," said the women.

Thus it came about that they asked the stranger to tell them of gods and eternal things. She did this in the evenings when they had usually sat together laughing and chatting.

Wonderful things she related, such as they had never been told before. Without shyness they could ask about anything, and were given a friendly answer. Saadi lay there with big, knowing eyes.

"One would think he understands what you are saying, Madana," the women often commented. Invariably the reply came:

"He knows and understands."

Then the neighbours would laugh. Yet they had to admit that from birth onwards Saadi had been a special child. He grew and thrived under the excellent care, but he remained finely proportioned, as though he were not the child of a horse-breeder, but rather of noble parentage. –

One day, in Dshami's garden a flower blossomed, whose like had never been seen here. It was deep red, with a strong, sweet fragrance. Its slender stem came from a stalk completely covered with shiny green leaves.

Madana had planted the little stalk, the women knew that. They enquired eagerly about the flower and asked for seeds of the rare plant.

That evening Madana told them a new story:

"In the Celestial Gardens above there is the most exquisite garden which is filled with these flowers. Roses they are called, and they are the symbol of Divine Love.

"Ahuramazda has them tended with special care; He loves the dark red blossoms that tell of so much beauty. He loves the fragrance that wafts

25

through all the heavens. But only where love and purity unite can this rare blossom flourish.

"Purity, fairest of all the goddesses, besought Ahuramazda to send down some of these blossoms to the wretched earth. They are meant to bring fragrance and beauty into the life of women.

"Wherever woman is imbued with purity, wherever love for others is the mainspring of her deeds, the Rose, the dark red Queen of all flowers, is able to thrive.

"There are regions in this vast realm that resemble a rose-garden. There, milder breezes blow than here, there the women are less austere..."

One of the women listeners interrupted:

"Is the rose the blossom of the fabled Princess Diyanitra?"

"Yes, it was Diyanitra's flower," Madana answered. "But why do you call the tidings of Diyanitra a fable? The great, noble Princess actually lived."

But the women did not want to hear about the Princess now, they wanted to have roses. Were they really pure enough for the heavenly blossom to flourish among them also?

Madana promised that when the time came she would plant a small rose in every garden; the neighbours were delighted.

Just where could Madana get the roses? They would have liked to know, but none dared to ask. There was a deep reserve about the otherwise so kind Madana.

From time to time Dshami came to see the boy. He found him developing splendidly, and left well satisfied. Saadi learned to walk and to speak just like any other child.

He liked to play with the neighbourhood children, but here he showed himself to be very strong-willed. He never intended any harm; but whatever he wanted he would carry out. Quarrels he avoided.

He achieved his purpose by emphatic demands or requests, whichever was appropriate. In all the games he devised, he was the leader. Mostly they were about the gods, and depicted battles with the forces of evil.

The children lived completely in Madana's stories. It was natural for them to ask the gods for help in every small or great misfortune.

YEARS passed. Roses bloomed in all the gardens, and the women rejoiced. Good children were growing up everywhere, healthy and cheerful. Everywhere Madana's influence was evident.

Saadi was seven years old when his father once again returned home.

Dshami gazed with joy at the sturdy, though finely-proportioned lad with beautiful features and laughing eyes.

"The time has come, Saadi," said his father, "for you to learn to ride a horse."

"I have been doing that for a long time now, Father," was the boy's proud reply. "Madana let me ride long ago."

Amazed, the man looked at the woman, who said calmly:

"You gave me a boy to look after, Dshami, not a girl. I have brought him up like a boy; he will not shame you when you take him out with you now to the pastures."

"I am to take him with me?" asked Dshami in disbelief.

He had never considered this. But the woman said quite placidly:

"The time has come for him to pass from the hands of a woman and be reared by his father. He can learn a great deal from you, Dshami, if you adjust your life accordingly. The gods have appointed you to be his teacher, otherwise they would have placed him in a different house."

Without wasting another word, Madana turned and packed the boy's clothes into a bundle.

"You must take these things with you when you go to the pastures tomorrow. His body is still too delicate for him to wear the same garments for weeks at a time. He is not accustomed to wearing anything that is soiled."

Then she went over to Saadi, who looked up at her with understanding:

"Farewell, my little one. You have rewarded my love abundantly. I thank Ahuramazda that I have been permitted to look after you. Do not forget what I was able to teach you. Above all do not forget that a great task awaits you!"

With a warm greeting to Dshami she left the dwelling as simply and naturally as she had entered it seven years before.

Dshami gazed after her, uncomprehending, while Saadi quickly wiped away a few tears.

"Why is she leaving? Who is she?" the words burst forth from the father's lips.

Amazed, the boy looked up.

"Does Father not know? She is a stranger from another people whom the gods sent to us so that I might be brought up in the right way."

"A stranger? From another people?" stammered his father. "How do you know?"

"Madana herself told me. Now she can return whence she came."

"Yes, indeed," Dshami could still not work it out. "Who was Madana? Where did she come from?"

"I never asked," replied the seven-year-old with the nobility sometimes characteristic of him.

"She is a very noble woman, and I have loved her."

The man felt that too. And now she had left without his having uttered a single word of gratitude!

He went down on his knees by the side of her bed, and thanked Ahuramazda from the very depths of his soul for the grace He had shown him. And he implored abundant blessings upon Madana.

Next morning, father and son locked up their dwelling, and went out to the vast plains where the horses were led from one grazing place to another.

The boy remained in his father's care for seven years, as was ordained by Ahuramazda. During these seven years he grew strong in body and spirit.

His father taught him what he needed for life. From the horses he learned cheerful courage and a noble bearing. Yet his best teachers were found among the smallest servants of Ahuramazda, whose work was in forest and field, mountain and river. Themselves so very wise, they knew how to teach the lad many things.

Firmly they established the young soul's link with the earthly, where he was to engage in the work of preparation. But he did not yet know this. He had even forgotten that a special task awaited him. The little ones did not tell him. The time would come when he would be permitted to discover it, indeed must discover it.

But when the seven years had come to an end, the father sensed that he

28

would have to be separated from Saadi. How this inner perception had come to him, he would not have been able to say, but he knew it was so.

Yet it seemed to him quite impossible to part from the boy whom he had come to love and treasure deeply. And he implored Ahuramazda:

"Thou great and wise God, Thou Who knowest men; Thou seest that I cannot part from Saadi. I will no longer use him to help me if that is not Thy will. Send him a teacher; I will provide for him. But leave the boy with me."

Though he sensed immediately that it was wrong to ask in this way - for how would any learned man have journeyed with him from one grazing ground to another, spending the nights in the open – yet he begged and pleaded against all reason:

"Thou wilt find some solution, O Sublime One. I cannot give up Saadi!"

And Ahuramazda found a solution, which had not occurred to Dshami.

One morning, when Saadi awoke, his father's lifeless form lay beside him. Imperceptibly the spirit had left it. Where had it gone? The boy could not tell. He still knew too little about things he could not touch with his hands.

For the present it was also far less important to him than the questions assailing him. What should he do with his father's body? How could he tend the large herd of horses all by himself? Just what should he do?

He became aware of his youth, his incompetence. Then he recalled the lessons he had learned from Madana. Often she had said:

"For you there is never an 'I cannot'. Look upwards in every situation of your life. If you are pure, you will never be without help."

He remembered these words at the right time. A great courage filled him, almost like an answer to an unspoken entreaty.

Then the little ones, his friends, came.

"You must dig a hole, Saadi," said they kindly, "and place Dshami's form in it. That will be right."

When this was done, it seemed to Saadi that he heard a powerful voice:

"You have reached the point where your path divides into two roads. You yourself may choose the one on which you will continue.

"You can become a horse breeder like your father. You have learned

29

everything that you need for this task. You will easily find helpers, and you will become a rich, respected man who in due time can take a wife. That is the one road, it is broad and pleasant.

"The other path is narrow. It leads uphill, over boulders and stones, in privation and self-conquest. You may never find the woman who is willing to tread it with you."

The voice fell silent. Again Saadi remembered what Madana had taught him: "Your way will lead uphill. Avoid walking the comfortable, level ground!"

Without hesitation, Saadi cried out:

"I choose the second path which I know is meant for me!"

"And you will not ask what it will bring, to what goal it will lead you?" the voice enquired.

"That I will discover on the way," Saadi replied, laughing with courage and joy.

With this decision, which he took for his earth-life, his childhood came to an end, and he matured into a youth who advanced towards his task. He fell asleep with a prayer of gratitude.

WHEN HE awoke, two men approached him. The one resembled Dshami, the other was lighter and foreign in appearance.

The first addressed him:

"I am looking for Dshami, my brother. I received a message that he needs me."

"Then you are Sadif," replied Saadi, not at all surprised. "Indeed I have need of you; for Dshami, my father, has gone to Garodemana, whence there is no return. I cannot become a horse breeder. Who is to take over the horses unless you do?"

"Why not?" Sadif said reflectively. "All my life I have wished to own horses. Are you giving them all to me?"

Before Saadi could answer, the other man said:

"Choose a steed for your own use, Saadi. And choose a mare which Sadif is to look after for you. He is to guard faithfully for you all the offspring of this mare. You will need them."

30

And Saadi chose.

He was prudent, his father had taught him admirably. He took as his own a small black stallion, and he chose a white mare to be reared for him.

Sadif was satisfied and promised to look after mare and foals faithfully. After all he, who all his life had only been a servant of others, had now quite suddenly become a rich man.

As if it were the most natural thing to do, Saadi turned to the stranger:

"May I go with you?"

Sadif assumed that the man had been an old acquaintance of his brother. It did not strike him as unusual that Saadi entrusted himself to the man.

The parting was brief. Saadi mounted his black steed called "Trotter", while at the man's call a light-coloured horse had come galloping up for him. They rode off together.

Sadif gazed after them for a long while. Then with a jubilant shout of joy, he assumed his responsibility with the horses.

For a long time Saadi rode silently beside his companion. He would very much have liked to know where he came from and who had sent him. But Madana's third teaching arose within him:

"If you are approached by luminous beings whose origin is unknown to you, do not ask. At the right time you will learn what you need to know."

For two days they rode, rarely exchanging a word. At night they rested in the open.

On the third day they came to a large village such as Saadi had not seen before. The huts were similar to those at home, but larger, nicer and more light.

One of the largest belonged to the Atravan, whom they now sought out. He appeared to be already informed of Saadi's arrival, for he greeted the riders like long-awaited friends:

"Behold! My new Mobed! He is a handsome youth!"

While Saadi looked after his steed, the other two entered the Atravan's house. But after a short time Saadi's companion re-emerged and invited the youth to go with him into the garden behind the hut.

There he told him that, at a higher behest, he was to remain with the Atravan and learn all that the priest could impart to him.

No service that would be expected of him was too lowly, no task too onerous. He should submit eagerly to everything. As soon as he could learn no more here, he would receive instructions to move on.

It was hard for Saadi to part from his companion whom he had hardly come to know at all. The latter perceived this and said pleasantly:

"I am leaving you now, but we will see each other again. In every decisive moment of your life I am permitted to be near you."

Saadi looked up at him gratefully; then the stranger left. Had any doubts remained with the youth, it was now clear to him that the stranger, like Madana, came from another people.

While Saadi was still contemplating what he should do he was summoned. The Atravan, a very old, white-haired man, stood in the doorway of his house, gazing at the new Mobed.

"You will live with me, Saadi," he said kindly, "since you have no family here in the village. First of all, tell me about your life hitherto. Who were your teachers?"

And Saadi told him of Madana, to whom he was indebted for the best things, of Dshami, his father, who had trained him physically, and of the little ones who had shown him the link between human beings and the Nature around them.

"I am very ignorant and have yet much to learn, my father," Saadi said modestly after he had related everything.

"I will tell you what I know. It is not much, my son. For a long time now I have been frail and weary. I could not understand why Ahuramazda did not call me away from the earth. Now in you arises for me the most beautiful task of my life. I thank the great, wise God for it!"

From then on Saadi was systematically instructed in all the religious teachings preached by the Atravan.

Soon the training of the new Mobed had progressed so far that the instruction could take place in the company of the future Atravan, who had already had years of preparation for his work. What he mastered with difficulty awoke in Saadi immediately.

It seemed as though he had known everything already and better even than the old man. If there were anything he did not understand right away, he did not ask at once, but carried the question outside into the garden. There, hidden in the dense bushes, he had found a rock on which he liked to sit.

Then he called for the little helpers, and discussed with them what was occupying him inwardly. Clarity would usually come simply by expressing his thoughts. But often they did not know either what to make of the so-called wisdom Saadi put before them. Then he was certain that he had misunderstood something, or that the Atravan had been in error. –

It was a great event in the life of young Saadi when he was permitted to accompany the Atravan to the mountains for the Festival of the Equinox. He was allowed to perform the duties of a Mobed, he, who had never attended a festival before.

With unparalleled zeal he arranged the stones for the offertory flames. His whole thinking was prayer.

He saw the little ones who were eagerly helping everyone, and who busied themselves in the bushes and flowers. But it was also given to him to see in part the luminous entities coming from above, and to become aware of the forces emanating from them.

The festival itself filled him with great joy; his veneration for the aged Atravan grew. For the first time he came in contact with priestesses whose pure service reminded him of Madana.

Then came the evening that brought the stories of the Atravan. Seated among the other Mobeds, Saadi listened as though his life depended on not missing a single word.

"The stars have not deceived us," said the old man, "when, nearly sixteen years ago, they proclaimed the birth of the Forerunner, the Zoroaster. Since then we have had unmistakable proofs that he is living on earth, that he is being prepared for his high position."

"Sixteen years," thought Saadi, "almost as old as I am. How does he feel? Does he know what his task on earth will be, I wonder?"

Suddenly a thought flashed through him:

"For whom then is he to prepare the way?" And he cried without hesitation: "Tell us, my father, of Him for Whom the Zoroaster is permitted to prepare the way!"

A few heads turned towards the Mobed with the childlike voice who dared to ask, but for most this very question came from their hearts.

The Atravan directed a penetrating gaze at Saadi. Why did he ask? Then the old man saw that the question had been asked without any ulterior motive, and he proceeded to answer it.

"The Zoroaster is to proclaim the Saoshyant, the Helper, Who will come to deliver the earth from the fetters of Anramainyu," he said solemnly.

"To him it will then be given to know everything about the Holy One which we can only divine from old prophecies. We have ancient sayings by seers which were transmitted by word of mouth from one Atravan to another.

"One says that the Saoshyant will sweep the earth clean as with a broom made of rods of tragacanth. Another says that He will have eyes to see man's inner being. He will know what men think and feel without their telling him. He will deal with them accordingly, and not according to what they wear outwardly."

The Atravan fell silent. Soon after, the fires went out, and the men dispersed.

That night Saadi had his first vision.

He seemed to be standing at the summit of a very tall mountain, looking down into the lowlands where people were bustling about. Suddenly, however, they were no longer human beings, but snakelike creatures with forked tongues and a slimy excretion, to which adhered anything that crossed their paths. He was overcome with disgust so that he felt nauseated, yet he was as if spellbound and had to look.

Then the skies opened up above him and down came One, Who was at once Power, Light and Truth. He moved swiftly among the snakes and smote off their heads. But the earth was reduced to a bloody, slavering mire. The foul liquid spurted up. But it did not touch the One Who had come from the Heavens.

A voice spoke:

"Behold the Helper as He will purify the Earth!"

Saadi spent the rest of the night in prayer. He was shaken to his inmost core, though he was unclear as to what had happened to him. Had he been dreaming or had he actually been permitted to see?

When he called on the Atravan in the morning to bring him fruits, the latter saw that something special must have happened, but he asked no questions.

On the last day the high priestess announced that Anramainyu had again been able to create a new helper, because of all the evil supplied to him by men. This new evil spirit was called Avarice.

It was unclothed, for it wanted to save every rag, or turn it into money. It begrudged itself neither food nor drink. With greedy fingers it rummaged in its treasures or in what it counted as such. And human beings had to emulate it.

Then voices were heard here and there, confirming that such people were already known to them. They were wretched, pitiable creatures no longer able to enjoy anything. Even their treasures became a source of torment, since they lived in fear of losing them.

When the festival was over, Saadi went down to the valley at the side of the aged Atravan. Below, the priest was awaited by Mobeds who carried him on a litter to his house.

Saadi was allowed to ride Trotter. What a joy! He shot along like an arrow, turned and came back swiftly alongside the old man, who was watching him with pleasure. With cheeks flushed and eyes shining, Saadi rode for a while beside the litter until high spirits and the zest for life again seized hold of him and made him gallop away.

"Is that worthy of a Mobed?" asked one of the older Mobeds with a sour face. "He has only just attended the holy festival on the Mountain, and now he romps about like a frolicsome colt."

But the Atravan rebuked him.

"Let him be," he said with understanding. "Everything about him is genuine. All that he senses intuitively fills him completely."

And after a moment of deep reflection he added: "His life will be very hard and demanding. Do not begrudge him this youthful joy."

As they approached the village where the priest had his abode, a procession of riders came towards them. They rode fine horses so lavishly bridled as is seen only on the steeds of princes.

By the dwelling where the bearers had just set down the Atravan, the riders also dismounted, and one of the men approached the priest with a deferential greeting.

35

He wished to speak with the Atravan, who conducted him inside, while the other riders admired Trotter whose small size so sharply differentiated it from their own horses.

Without shyness Saadi answered their questions about the horse's lineage.

"You would be welcome in our cavalcade," said one of the riders, laughing, and his strong white teeth flashed forth out of his black beard.

"Who are you?" Saadi asked.

The answer came freely.

"Our master, who is speaking with the priest just now, is a powerful prince. This whole vast land, extending from shore to shore, belongs to him. He wants to become thoroughly acquainted with his realm; that is why he rides with us from province to province, from place to place.

"Usually he does not disclose his identity. The effects of this are remarkable, for in this way he discovers what the people really think of him. We experience many beautiful things, but also others which are quite alarming."

The rider probably would have continued talking, but at that moment the Atravan called to Saadi.

Inside, the young Mobed found the Prince on the only comfortable seat. The priest was content with a couch made of rugs. This did not appeal to Saadi. The Prince was so much younger than the Atravan!

He was about to give voice to his disapproval when the priest began to speak.

He told Saadi that Prince Hafiz had been pleased with his horsemanship and had come to enquire whether he would join his escort on the long ride through his realm.

"Here you have learned all that I could teach you, my son," said the old man kindly. "Besides, my days are numbered, and the question of whom you should be entrusted to has already weighed heavily on my soul. It will be good for you now, under the Prince's guidance, to get to know human beings, not only the good, but also the bad. Whatever life may demand of you later, this knowledge will help you."

Saadi was not asked whether he was inclined to go with the Prince. Nor would he really have known how to decide. His youthful disposition looked forward to the adventure, while his childlike gratitude bound him to remain with the old man who would now probably end his days in solitude.

He was about to give expression to these feelings, but the Atravan motioned to him to keep silent. Prince Hafiz rose to his feet.

"We will not ride far today and will call here again tomorrow, Saadi. Be ready by then with your horse so that you can accompany us."

Treading heavily he left the room.

For a short while both were silent, the old man and the youth, then the latter began to speak:

"Is it the Will of Ahuramazda that I go with this Prince, my father?" he asked in a childlike way.

"Some weeks ago now I received tidings that riders would call for you as soon as the festival was over, Saadi. Now Prince Hafiz has told me who sent him to this of all places, so that there can be no doubt that the Wise God Who guides your life has ordained this change as well."

"But I will never be a prince, of what use to me then is a life with Prince Hafiz?"

It was the first time that Saadi had questioned what appeared to be a final decision.

The Atravan was not annoyed with him. With patience and kindness, he explained once more that he would now be permitted to gain the knowledge of men which he would need for his future task.

"My task?" asked Saadi. "Will my father tell me what is to become of me some day? I only know that I will not be a horse breeder. That I relinquished voluntarily," he added.

The Atravan smiled.

"Apart from the vocation of horse breeding which you have abandoned, there is a whole range of others which you could practise. Wait and see what will be placed in your way.

"A day will come when your soul will exult in the recognition that just what is demanded of you is your real life. Then do not hesitate a moment. Seize the opportunity and hold on to whatever is offered you. But in the meantime learn as much as you are able to absorb.

"Let me say one more thing to you on this last evening, my son: You will be brought together with many wicked people. You will get to know them in every way. Listen to the voice within you which will warn you against them. Learn to know them aright so that they are not able to deceive you later, but keep your distance from them, even if they court your favour.

"Remain pure so that at any time you could gaze steadfastly into Madana's eyes. More than this I am not able to say to you."

Deeply moved, Saadi bade farewell to his old teacher. It was good that he did so, for the riders came for him quite early the following day. His most recent companions he did not see again.

ONCE MORE a change had taken place in Saadi's life. This time it was a sharp break. He had to wear different clothes, and could no longer do as he pleased. He had to learn to submit to more than one will.

He was the youngest in the troop, therefore also the one to whom all tasks fell – great and small.

Among his playmates he had always been the one to whom everyone adjusted. Now he had become the one who had no say at all. He had to be silent even if he disagreed with the demands of the others.

On the face of it, Prince Hafiz took no notice of him, having decided what clothing should be given to Saadi and beside whom he should ride. In reality, however, the Prince kept a sharp eye on the youngest who had been warmly commended to his care.

At the court of the Prince lived an old sage who had once been his teacher. Prince Hafiz revered him like a father and still sought his advice.

This wise man, Dshayava, had come to him just before his departure and told him that he must take with him and instruct a youth who at present was being taught by the Atravan. This had been revealed to him at the behest of Ahuramazda.

But only the priest was to be told of this mission; apart from this, Hafiz must find a way of enlisting the youth in his retinue quite inconspicuously.

The young man was destined for great things, and for him it was paramount to gain knowledge of human beings and of the country. But he must also learn to serve, for he had never before been required to submit to the will of another that did not conform with his own.

Saadi's open, frank nature pleased the Prince, who rarely had contact with a completely true human being.

He also liked the way in which Saadi was able to assert himself in the face of gibes from the others. He did what they asked of him without flattering them. If it was awkwardly done, he was willing to be shown what was wrong, and did better the next time.

In riding and looking after the horses he excelled; yet he was quite inexperienced in the use of weapons, and when the Prince handed him a sword with orders to have himself taught how to wield it, he stammered in alarm:

"Surely, Master, I will not be required to shed blood?" The others burst out laughing. But the Prince said kindly:

"You are right, Saadi, it is a sin to shed blood. But if others seek to spill yours, then it is good if you know how to use a weapon in defence. Hence learn to wield the sword and only draw it when your inner voice bids you."

And the mockers fell silent and looked in amazement at the Prince, who had never before spoken to them in this way.

Whenever they spent the night in the open, the Prince had tents pitched. This was unfamiliar to Saadi, who preferred to sleep under the starry sky.

"Are you not afraid of snakes?" the others asked him.

"I ask the little ones, who keep them away from me while I am asleep," was Saadi's calm reply.

"Which little ones?" his companions wanted to know.

"Ahuramazda's little servants," Saadi said matter-of-factly.

Again the others laughed. Again the Prince rebuked them. He asked Saadi to tell him of the invisible ones, with whom he associated so intimately. "You are better off than we are, Saadi," said the Prince, almost sadly, "that you can see the little beings and speak with them. I fear we are not pure enough for that. We have forfeited it."

Then the others were annoyed that Hafiz was now favouring the newcomer so openly, and they decided to cause him an injury.

He had nothing that was dear to his heart but his Trotter, with whom his relationship was remarkably close. Often it seemed to the others as though he were talking with the animal. If they were to harm Trotter, he would be upset.

In the middle of the night two of them crept up to the enclosure where the horses grazed. So much smaller than the others, Trotter was soon found. One of the men stooped to grab one of Trotter's forelegs, but received such a violent blow to the head that he fell over.

The other man wanted to rush to the aid of his companion, but felt as though paralysed and rooted to the spot. It seemed as if innumerable little hands held his legs down. Horrified, he remembered Saadi's invisible friends.

"Release me, you little ones," he pleaded quite humbly, "I will do no more evil."

Instantly he was free. With a sigh of relief he sensed how what had surrounded him withdrew. He picked up his stunned companion and carried him into the tent where, hours later, he regained consciousness.

Both decided to say nothing about their experience. The one simply resolved henceforth to leave Saadi in peace, but the other took with him from that night a firm belief in the little ones. He sought out Saadi's company and asked him more and more about the little beings.

Soon he was able to see a few of them. Now he understood Saadi's happiness in the association with these friends, for he too felt happy in the awareness of being everywhere surrounded by the kind helpers. –

Prince Hafiz and his retinue rode onward through the realm.

Saadi came to know diverse regions and even more diverse kinds of people. There were vast areas, he observed, in which the people would not hear of the gods. They considered these to be stories for children. When Saadi, horrified, asked them who directed their destinies, they answered:

"We ourselves."

Yet the fear of demons and devas was rampant. Above all they feared Druj, the phantom of death. Saadi could not understand this. If they denied the wise God, then surely they must also reject the evil spirit.

Often at night Saadi called the little beings who were also present in those regions, and asked them about it. And the little ones had this to say:

"Men have become so wicked that they must always be afraid. Their souls find no further escape. In Anramainyu they fear retribution for their deeds. They will hear nothing more of a good God for they fear their punishment must be worse the moment they acknowledge Him."

"But it is the very opposite," rejoined Saadi eagerly. "Were men to seek refuge in Ahuramazda and be repentant of their sin, all the gods would be permitted to help them. What could Anramainyu do to them?"

The little ones listened earnestly and nodded.

"Men would need to be told!" exclaimed Saadi. "Won't you do it, you little ones?"

No, they would not. They knew that men would not listen to them at all.

"They no longer see us, they only laugh when we are spoken of."

The little ones imparted this indignantly.

"*You* must tell them. That will be your task, you luminous human being!"

"My task?" Saadi said in surprise. "Oh no! I am nothing at all really. I still have no occupation, although I will soon be seventeen. I myself do not know what is to become of me one day. But the Forerunner has already been born. He will tell the people."

The little ones rejoiced at his words.

The Prince's retinue came to another part of the country. There the people had gods, but basically it was Anramainyu whom they worshipped. They called him Ahriman and said that he was a great, knowing spirit who helped men on earth to attain to power, wealth and happiness.

Saadi ventured to ask one of the men: "And what will become of you later?"

"When later?" retorted the other, who knew quite well what Saadi meant.

Undeterred, Saadi asked:

"One day you must die and leave your earthly treasures behind. You cannot take them with you. What will become of you then? Do you want to cross over to Garodemana in such a wretched state – naked and bare?"

"Of what concern to us is the 'later'! We do not believe in a life after death, therefore we make things as pleasant as possible for ourselves down here. Ahriman also says that everything is over for us once we are dead. That is enough for us."

"Indeed all that is good will then be over for you, I know that too," the young man confirmed earnestly.

Most of them did not listen to him, they were glad to have silenced the troublesome questioner. Only one looked up, struck by the sound of the young voice.

When Saadi went to the corral to look after Trotter, the man followed him.

He asked Saadi what he had meant. And Saadi had to explain and enlighten him all night. The man, so much older than the youth, listened with a sincere desire to know. In the morning he thanked Saadi and gave him a stone mounted in gold.

"Take it in memory of this night. Wear it under your clothing. Perhaps in this way I can repay you for the service you have rendered me today. I thank you!"

Taken aback, Saadi hung the gemstone around his neck. It felt strangely warm and alive so that from then on he wore it gladly. -

But Prince Hafiz also came to regions where the people believed firmly in Ahuramazda, endeavoured to have good morals and led happy, industrious lives.

That everything here prospered was quite evident. The vast land resembled rose gardens, bright with colour and sweet-smelling. Lightly-veiled women walked to and fro in these gardens, tending the flowers and singing quiet tunes as they went. Children played round them.

"That is how it must be in Garodemana," Saadi said.

The Prince, who had heard him, agreed.

"But," he added, "why is it not like this everywhere in the great realm?"

"Because elsewhere people have forgotten Ahuramazda," Saadi explained promptly. "It will be better when the Zoroaster comes. He will guide the souls of men back on to the right path."

"If he can," the Prince interrupted him, wistfully. "Believe me, Saadi, the Forerunner will have an extremely difficult task."

"It seems to me a glorious one!" cried Saadi enthusiastically. "I could envy him. He is now exactly my age. I would like to be his servant!"

ONE EVENING they had come to a very mountainous area. High up among the rugged rocks a castle had once stood; it was clearly discernible. Prince Hafiz pointed it out.

"Look, those are the ruins of the castle where the noblest of all princes, Ara-Masdah, once dwelt with the lovely Diyanitra. You know the story, of course?"

They said they did and looked up with excited interest at the jumbled rock.

"Does nobody live up there any more?" the Prince asked one of the villagers who had rushed out to meet them.

The answer was no. After the death of Prince Ara-Masdah's son, most of the castle had been reduced to ruins in an earthquake. It was dangerous to climb up there.

Though it was said that vast treasures lay hidden under the rocks, so far no one who had wanted to dig for them had come back alive.

"Our old folk say," whispered the man mysteriously, "that there never was a Prince Ara-Masdah in flesh and blood. Ahuramazda is said to have sojourned here on earth for a lifetime under this name to be close to men and change them for the better."

To this Prince the people ascribed all the crafts they had learned, while to Diyanitra they attributed the rich array of flowers in the valleys and on the mountain slopes. Thus it was evident that these could not have been ordinary mortals. But it was not to be spoken of openly; it was a sacred mystery.

Saadi had listened, deep in thought. While he did not believe this legend, it was quite understandable that a completely pure human being, such as Prince Ara-Masdah must have been, was permitted to bring blessing to his surroundings. He was filled with these thoughts.

He retired early, choosing his resting-place so that he could view the ruins which seemed to look down mysteriously in the moonlight.

That night he had his second vision:

He saw a Child betread the ruins of the castle. He was luminous, clear and radiantly beautiful. Above His head there hovered, with outspread wings, a white bird of a kind Saadi had never seen before. From above, a golden ray fell upon the little Child.

At that He raised His luminous head and spread out His little arms. Thereupon He walked a road marked out for Him by the golden ray. Calm and assured were His steps, and the white Wonder-Bird accompanied Him.

The path of the Child, Who grew as He walked, led far into the distance. A hero without equal, He proceeded on His way. The golden path broadened! For a long time it seemed to lead across the earth, then it rose. The Hero became a Luminous Figure and disappeared in the Light.

Deep sorrow filled Saadi's heart, but a voice comforted him:

"The course of all life is a circle, you know that. This circle too will close. Pray and wait!"

Saadi began to pray. He implored that the Luminous Hero might once more approach the wretched earth. Suddenly he no longer prayed to Ahuramazda, but appealed to the Light-Figure, Whom he had seen disappear:

"O Thou Luminous Hero, Little Child from Heavenly Heights, come back! The earth is in need of Thee. None other can deliver it from the fetters with which Anramainyu's cunning has bound it!"

He prayed fervently for a long time. Then the Heavens seemed to open above him, and the White Bird soared forth. Exultant, Saadi sprang to his feet and bowed down again and again.

Once more the golden path of rays stood out against the night-blue of the firmament and now He, the Radiant Hero, appeared in golden armour, the Sword in His hand.

It was He, it had already once been given Saadi to behold, He Who had cut off the serpent's head! Jubilant, Saadi prayed:

"My Lord and my King!"

And the Hero descended and became a child again. He did so for the sake of men, Saadi was sure of it.

"What a sacrifice," he stammered, deeply moved.

And suddenly the thrill of a blissful certainty filled him:

"That was He, the Helper, the Saoshyant, Whom the world was await-ing!"

It was He Whose coming the Zoroaster would proclaim.

Saadi was stirred to the depths. He could no longer contemplate an ordinary life such as he had been leading until now. At daybreak he was resolved:

"I must hear more about the Saoshyant! I must seek and find the Zoroaster!"

Without a second thought he went to the Prince and asked to be re-leased from his service. Prince Hafiz was shocked. If Saadi left, he could not fulfil his appointed task. If only he could ask Dshayava what he should do.

He saw that Saadi was hardly to be restrained. Should he tell him why they had been brought together? He had promised the Atravan to keep silent. Must he keep the promise even now?

For the moment he was relieved of making a decision, for messengers from the capital came with important news. Thus he turned to Saadi who stood before him, trembling with excitement, and said kindly:

"Let me attend to my business, my friend. Then I will hear why you wish to leave me. If I can honour your reasons, I myself will assist you."

Saadi had to be satisfied with that for the time being. He saddled Trotter and went on a long solitary ride. However, he lost his bearings, and although he called upon the little ones to show him the way, he did not find his way back to the Prince's camp in the evening.

Instead he came to a lone hut built into the loose rocks – a welcome shelter to him, for a violent storm was gathering.

"You are right, you air-beings, that you would cool my hot blood," he shouted into the raging elements. "Thraetvana, you fiery one, spare me. I must seek the Zoroaster. I cannot yet leave this earth."

He had shouted the words aloud, thinking himself alone.

In the flash of lightning he noticed a smaller shelter for Trotter, to which he took the horse immediately, rubbing it down with the saddle-cloth.

Then he walked to the door of the hut. Perhaps he would find a bed inside where he could stretch out. Now he began to feel the effects of the sleepless night and the day spent on Trotter's back.

But before he could find out how to open the door, it was opened from within. A very old man with a burning faggot in his hand stepped across the doorway.

"Are you the one who is seeking the Zoroaster?" he asked, looking intently at the young man standing before him.

"Did you hear me, Father?" asked Saadi, somewhat embarrassed. "I thought I was alone. Yes, I am seeking the Forerunner; for I want to hear of Him, the Sublime, the Only One, the Saoshyant, for Whom my heart burns as though it would consume me."

Never before had Saadi been so unreserved. And now he spoke to a stranger of that which moved him most deeply? He was about to be overcome with shame when a flash of lightning revealed the kind, radiant eyes that were turned upon him. Now all constraint fell away.

"May I stay with you, my father, until the storm has abated? Will you tell me about the Saoshyant and His Forerunner? I sense that you know of Him!"

Breathlessly, the words had poured forth.

The old man smiled knowingly. Instead of answering he moved back so that Saadi could step quickly across the threshold. The door was slammed with a thud. Outside the storm was raging.

Inside the room a small fire burned, spreading some light and making it pleasantly warm. The old man invited Saadi to remove his wet clothing. Gladly he did so and slipped into a dark garment which the hermit gave him.

He was unaware that the eyes of his aged host were riveted on the stone which had become visible while he was changing.

After the guest had been refreshed with food and drink, the hermit enquired as to whether he now wanted to sleep. He must spend the night with him; for after such a storm, which had not even yet abated, the forest would be utterly impassable. Falling stones could easily strike horse and rider dead.

But Saadi had forgotten all about being tired, just as he had only realised while eating that he had not taken any food all day. Trotter had been well looked after, but he himself had not felt hungry.

In reply to the old man's question, he asked first to be permitted to hear more about the Saoshyant. The hermit willingly acceded to the urgent request.

"There are many ancient prophecies which were handed down among the priests and the people. Some have become known to the public and will be familiar to you. But the most beautiful and sacred is a secret; only a few know of it. To only a few may it be revealed. Listen:

"The earth, which Ahuramazda had created to His own delight and that of the gods, had to suffer from the moment when men inhabited it. A sand-grain of sin with the father became a stone with the son, a mountain with the grandson. Sin was piled upon sin, guilt upon guilt.

"The wrongdoing of men created Anramainyu and his evil spirits. They are not ashamed to have become subservient to him whom they themselves called into being! With every generation begotten by man the earth grows a little heavier. Already it has been forced down far out of its course. Its tone is missing in the song of the stars.

"Already it can be calculated when it will have sunk so far that it can never again rise to its appointed place. Already the stars indicate that there must come an end to the human spirits on earth.

"The gods watch the destruction with sadness, Ahuramazda looks down with ire. But He will put a stop to men's riotous activities.

"He summons those that populate the earth to be judged! Not He Himself will bring this Judgment, but a son of Ara-Masdah will come to sit in Judgment over the souls of men. He will be the Saoshyant, the Helper, Who will bear the good ones up with Him to Garodemana for all time."

"A son of Ara-Masdah, of the Prince?" stammered Saadi. "Should it not be: a Son of Ahuramazda, of the God?"

"I can only render the prophecy as I have received it, my son. Do not brood over it nor deprive yourself of the blessing that it contains. The main thing is that a Saoshyant will come. We do not yet know when He will make His appearance, but I believe that the day is no longer far off."

"His Forerunner has already been born," Saadi affirmed. "The Atravan has seen it in the stars. He was announced about eighteen years ago. The Zoroaster is supposed to live in obscurity for thirty years, thereafter he is to step before the world to proclaim the Helper.

"I can hardly wait to hear him. And that is why I will go in search of him, though I must traverse the entire country! I will and must find him!"

"And when you have found him what will you do?" asked the old man kindly.

It was obvious that the question did not spring from curiosity. Therefore Saadi answered him willingly:

"I wish to serve him with all my powers. It must be glorious to be allowed to proclaim the Helper to wretched mankind! I would like to be present when this comes to pass.

"Do not imagine, my son, that it will be simply joy for the Zoroaster," the old man warned earnestly. "He will meet with much disbelief and ingratitude, scorn and persecution on his way. His life will be arduous."

"Prince Hafiz said the same," mused Saadi. "But I cannot conceive of it. And were the last drop of blood required of me, I would give it joyfully if it would permit my paving the way for the Saoshyant."

"Are you a servant of Prince Hafiz?" enquired the hermit.

"I ride with his retinue, but today I have asked him to release me from his service, so that I can go in search of the Zoroaster."

"And what did he say? Has he given his permission? Tell me about your life. Truly, it is not curiosity that prompts me to ask!"

"I sense that, my father. I will gladly tell you what little there is to tell."

Saadi's account was sincere and straightforward. When he had finished, the old man said pensively:

"Childlike faith you learned from Madana,
manly virtues from your father.
The religious teachings of the adults
were imparted to you by the Atravan,
your knowledge of human nature and of our country
was gained through Prince Hafiz.
The elemental beings linked you with the Laws of Nature;
I was allowed to tell you about the Saoshyant.

"Six pearls of wisdom were bestowed upon you; it only remains for you to find the Zoroaster!"

"You see, my father," rejoiced Saadi, "I knew that you would agree with me once I had described everything to you in detail. I wish to go out into the world, not resting until I have found the Zoroaster."

He sprang up from the floor where he had lain partly reclining on an animal skin. With a smile the old man pressed him back.

"You cannot leave tonight. The storm has started up again. Hark how the wind-spirits are raging. Vayn has spread out all the folds of his cloak simultaneously. He and Thraetvana are chasing one another across the firmament. It is not good for anyone to be out in the open at such a time.

"But then I would like to give you this advice: Search for the Forerunner in silence! The more you seek solitude, the sooner you will be able to find him. In the noisy hustle and bustle of men you will look for him in vain."

"I thank you for your advice, my father. In solitude will I seek him. Pray for me that I may find him soon!"

But the old man seemed to be unwilling to go on talking today. He lay down on another animal skin beside his guest, and soon both were fast asleep.

They awoke at the same time early in the morning. On shrubs and rocks still wet with rain the sun was smiling; Nature was refreshed and wonderfully fragrant.

After a warm farewell, Saadi parted from the hermit who asked him to come to him sometime when he had found the Zoroaster.

"It need not be in the first few weeks, Saadi," he said quietly, "but come as soon as it is possible for you. I will then have a message for you."

"For me, my father?" replied Saadi, quite amazed. "Can you not give it to me right now? I am sure to find the Forerunner."

"No, my message is for him who has found. Do not forget to return, my son."

Trotter was pawing the ground impatiently. Saadi departed. Little helpers guided him.

For half a day he had to ride. At last, the camp of the Prince came into view not far from one of the bigger villages.

He asked the little ones why they had abandoned him the day before. They laughed.

"Was what you found instead not worth anything?"

And he had to admit that it might indeed even have great value for his life.

"Remember, Saadi, requests are not always fulfilled as men imagine they should be. If things went their way it would sometimes bring them more harm than benefit."

Saadi understood, and thanked the little ones for having his well-being at heart.

How would Prince Hafiz have taken his absence? Would he have thought that Saadi had left without his permission? Even before he could apologise, the Prince addressed him kindly:

"I was not anxious, because I knew that you would be protected."

The Prince then invited Saadi to accompany him to his tent.

"My old teacher, Dshayava, has also arrived with the troop of riders that came to meet me yesterday. He wishes to see you, Saadi."

With these words the Prince ushered the youth inside the tent which he had never entered before. He was dazzled by the splendour surrounding him. But once his eyes had come to rest on Dshayava, he could no longer take them from the dignified, aged man. Forgotten was all the beauty around him in the radiance of these deep-blue eyes. Blue eyes! They appeared completely unearthly to Saadi!

After the old man had enquired about Saadi's life, he asked him:

"Why do you wish to leave the Prince who is so very good to you?"

"It is not ingratitude, my father," the words burst forth from Saadi. "I must find the Zoroaster to hear from him about the Saoshyant! If I am allowed to serve the Forerunner, then, through him, I will also serve the Helper, the Radiant Hero Who will come to judge and redeem the world."

"How will you find the Zoroaster?" the venerable man enquired.

"I will go into solitude as the hermit advised me to do. O my father, he understood the fervent longing which consumes me. He understood why I can have no more peace until the object of my search has been found! Try to understand me!"

"I understand you, my son, and I approve of your intention. Go into solitude, listen, learn! You alone must find the Zoroaster, no one can show him to you. But when you have found him, come to me. I will then have a message for you."

Saadi gave him a blissful smile.

"Thank you, my father, for your understanding. But the hermit said exactly the same. He too has a message for me once I have found the Zoroaster. Before then he is not allowed to give it to me. I will come to you. If only it could be soon!"

"Sooner or later, my son, as long as you find him," replied Dshayava.

Prince Hafiz explained that he must remain with them one more night, so that a pack-horse with supplies could be made ready for him.

Why did he need provisions, thought the impatient youth. He would manage somehow. But he did not dare to say so; he acquiesced.

His companions were sorry to see him go. He had been a dear friend to them although his presence had aroused many jealous and envious feelings. The Prince told them that Saadi had been called away on a secret mission. This they respected and no longer plied the youth with questions.

Again he positioned himself for the night so that the ruins of the Castle were before him, but this time he was given no vision. He slept quietly the healthy sleep of youth.

NEXT MORNING the farewells were brief. Dshayava hung a golden capsule around his neck, instructing him not to open it. If he, Dshayava, were no longer alive when Saadi had found the Zoroaster, he should take the capsule to his successor. He too would then be able to give him the message.

Prince Hafiz had provided for him as for a departing son. The sturdy pack-horse was richly laden with everything that a person living in solitude would need.

After a few windings of the road the camp had disappeared, and Saadi asked himself where he should head first.

Had he not reached a decisive turning-point of his life, the point where for the first time he was left to his own resources? But his luminous helper had promised that he would be near him at all decisive moments. Surely he could venture to call him.

And while Trotter ambled along at a leisurely pace, Saadi prayed deep within, calling his guide.

Like a luminous cloud he stood before him, and his voice spoke from the cloud:

"You are on the right path, Saadi. Seek the Zoroaster with all your heart. You will find him. Go into solitude, learn from the beings, great and small, from shrub and blossom, from animal and waters, but do not forget your goal. When you have found the Zoroaster he will guide you to the knowledge of the Saoshyant. You will be blessed, as will your mission!"

Before Saadi could give thanks, the cloud had disappeared; fervent gratitude rose upwards to Ahuramazda.

Then he entrusted himself to the guidance of little beings who promised to take him to a hermit's hut which was not in use. They led him in the direction of the ruins.

Saadi's heart beat faster. Since he had been permitted to behold the sublime picture, he loved the ruins. But the little ones warned him never to venture higher than they would lead him.

There were dangers lurking there. At Ahuramazda's command great beings guarded Prince Ara-Masdah's treasures.

"When the rightful heir appears the day will come when they must release them. This they know," said the little guides with an air of importance. "When that will be we do not know; nobody does. But the day will come, that is certain. And then not one precious stone must be missing of what belonged to Ara-Masdah."

"Did the collapsing walls not destroy the treasures?" asked Saadi, concerned.

He envisaged cracked and flattened vessels, shattered stones. But the little ones laughed.

"Do you think that when we are told to keep watch over something it would not be done? The great beings were there even before the palace burst asunder from the quaking of the earth. They had carefully rescued everything. But they had to leave it in place for the heir actually to find it."

"The heir, you say?" asked Saadi pensively. "If the son of Ara-Masdah died childless, there can be no heir surely!"

"Human sagacity! Human cleverness!" the little ones called out and had no wish to continue the dialogue.

In the meantime, they had arrived at the place where Saadi was to stay for the time being. Safe from storm and inclement weather, a spacious hut was so fitted into the rocks that it could scarcely be distinguished from them.

A mountain overhang shielded the roof and had no doubt protected it from rain for a long time, for all the woodwork inside was also dry and solid. A good supply of wood was piled along one wall. The fire-place was carefully built of stone, with a ventilating shaft; wood had been neatly stacked beside it.

The little ones showed him an equally good shelter close by for the two horses.

"Remember that you must not set foot on any path leading from here upwards!" they warned him once more. "There are enough paths for you. But the way to the castle ruins is dangerous."

They were gone before Saadi could ask any further questions. He heard only their carefree laughter from afar.

His first task was to look after the horses and to store the supplies. Every blanket that the Prince had given him, he hailed with gratitude and joy. He felt ashamed.

"How annoyed I was in my independence," he thought, "simply because Hafiz detained me to equip me with things which in his wise experience he deemed necessary!"

Now he had enough warm covers for the animals and for himself, for it was cold up here.

From the distance sounded the thunderous rushing of a mountain-stream which he must now find. He had also unstrapped two water-vessels from the pack-horse. With these he set out. There was no missing the way, the desired water announced itself too loudly for that.

Then he stood almost devoutly before the spraying and foaming that cascaded down to the valley. The sunbeams were refracted in the thousands upon thousands of drops which were flung up and fell again. Colour and sound were interwoven.

But at the point where the water rushed down for a while in two broad streams, side by side, the torrent parted, and out of it a winsome face greeted him.

"Ardvisura Anahita," he rejoiced and bent his knee.

The lovely being laughed, a rippling ringing laughter, that even seemed to awaken a faint echo.

"I am but one of her lowliest servants," she explained, still laughing. "Anahita does not show herself to any mortal. And even I am visible to you only because your radiation is pure. It came to me through the water and called me."

"May I take some of your water?" he asked modestly. Again the rippling laughter was heard.

"Take as much as you like, and if you are hungry, I will give you a fish as well. But you must not ask for more than you actually need.

"You may come, too, if you should be lonely from time to time. I have many beautiful things to show you and much to teach you," she said.

With joy in his heart, Saadi returned to his hut with the filled water vessels.

The following days were spent roaming about in the immediate vicinity. He soon realised that he could let the horses browse freely. When it became too cold for them, they returned to their shelter on their own.

Now he also perceived the wisdom of providing him with a pack-horse. Trotter could not have withstood the solitude alone. Pleased that the good animal had been cared for, he now felt himself to be superfluous.

Suddenly he became thoughtful. Why had he withdrawn into solitude? In order to find the Zoroaster!

Could he find him if he did not seek? But where should he seek? He had been directed to go into solitude. Consequently that was where he must seek.

What did he expect of the Forerunner? That he should tell him of the Saoshyant!

As though it were a magic word, all of Saadi's thoughts now revolved around this one concept: the "Saoshyant", the Helper, the Redeemer, the Radiant Hero! If only he might see Him once more!

Ever again he tried to conjure up the glorious picture in his soul. Given ever fresh sustenance, the glowing spark within blazed and burned, filling him completely.

Imperceptibly his longing for the Zoroaster had changed into yearning for the Saoshyant. He had seen Him as a Child. Was it by chance that the Little Boy had stood on the ruins of Ara-Masdah's Castle?

"There is no such thing as chance!" whispered a quiet voice. "Every event brought into being by Ahuramazda has meaning and purpose. In every experience seek out what it is meant to reveal to you, what you can learn from it. Only in this way will you find the Zoroaster's path."

Saadi listened attentively. If his vision of the Little Child in this place had not come about by chance, it was associated with this Castle. The prophecy recounted by the hermit occurred to him:

A son of Ara-Masdah would be the Saoshyant.

Would that be right after all? How could a son be born to a dead Prince? How could a Helper arise in the Castle ruins? For the Helper could not yet be on earth, since the Forerunner had not even entered upon his mission.

Suddenly the words of the little ones came to mind: "When the Heir comes!"

The Heir? So they too were awaiting a son of Ara-Masdah?

He called on the little ones for information, but they did not come. Only yesterday they had appeared at once when he had just wanted to know if the red berries he had found on the bushes were safe to eat! Did they come solely in answer to earthly questions? Must he find the answer to all others himself?

This seemed to be the case. He prayed, imploring the luminous helper to show him the way to find the answer he sought.

Then the luminous cloud stood before him once more, and the familiar voice was heard:

"Pray and wait patiently, Saadi! Nothing is achieved without effort. It will be given you to see and comprehend everything that you must know. But you cannot insist on an answer.

"You see, these questions settle like seed-grains into your soul, which is still young. Let them grow strong and take root. Then they will strive upwards, and in the light from above their buds will open, one by one. But you must be patient and may not hastily seek to force the delicate blossoms open before their time. Despair would be your reward!"

Patience! Did the Luminous One really know with what consuming intensity the flame was burning within him? He would try to be patient.

So there was a time of sowing in his soul. That was indeed the way of it. When he observed himself, he perceived how question after question arose within him. But he must not seek the answers, unbidden they would come to him.

But what could he do to strengthen the young shoots within him? Pray, and awaken only pure, beautiful thoughts in his inner being!

Lately he had considered how he would recognise the Zoroaster. He knew nothing about him except that he was of the same age as he himself. Well, this too would be resolved; in this also he would pray and wait.

Often he visited the water-sprite, but she did not always come at his bidding. Sometimes she kept him waiting or teased him by letting her song be heard from far below. When he arrived down there in leaps and bounds, her laughter in turn rang out from above.

"You are becoming too lazy," she taunted him. "I must see to it that your limbs are kept supple."

When he drew closer, the foaming water drenched him.

"Run into the sunshine to dry off!" she called out, laughing.

On days like these he could learn nothing from her. But at other times she was communicative. From the bottom of the water she fetched exquisite stones and shells. Once she even brought milk-white lustrous pearls like those he had seen in the Prince's headband.

Another time she showed him fish-eggs and explained how little fish develop from them. It all seemed to him like a beautiful miracle. Miracles lay hidden everywhere in Nature. The more fully he opened himself to the weaving in Nature, the more deeply he revered its Creator.

One day when the sun was almost directly overhead, the water-sprite was already expecting Saadi. She had placed her finger on her lips as a sign not to utter a word. With the other delicate white hand she pointed to a boulder bathed in radiant sunlight and covered with green moss.

Saadi crept quietly closer and caught sight of a small, green-grey snake, on whose little head he saw a golden crown. It coiled in the heat, raised its dainty head, and the little crown shone.

With an effort Saadi suppressed a shout of jubilation.

Now there was a rustling on the ground, and a second snake, somewhat larger than the first, also adorned with a little crown, came wriggling towards the first one and slid gracefully on to the boulder.

The water-sprite had swum close to the spot and with radiant eyes gazed upon the enchanting scene.

The snakes seemed to converse with one another, while their glittering bodies entwined and slid apart again. Suddenly, without any outward cause, they wriggled away in different directions.

Now Saadi's joy burst forth. He thanked the water-sprite over and over again for showing him the delightful spectacle. Then he wished to know why the snakes were allowed to wear crowns.

"Why do men wear crowns?" laughed the water-sprite.

"Because they are princes!" Saadi answered promptly. "Are the two snakes also princes?"

"They are king and queen. Ahuramazda has bestowed more on them than on ordinary snakes. For that reason, however, they must also be an example to the others."

Again Saadi had learned something of importance to him. But the joy in the beauty he had experienced filled him still more.

His little helpers also taught him many things. They let him peer into the caves of the animals. They showed him how exquisite minerals lay embedded in rock, faithfully watched over by specially appointed guardians, who looked quite different from the beings that gambolled about among the trees and bushes.

But all this seemed to occupy his spirit for only a short time. His longing grew ever more ardent, more intense. At times he could no longer bear inactive thinking. Then he would leap up and run into the forest.

THUS IT ALSO CAME ABOUT one sunny day following many weeks of rain. Saadi had walked down the mountain to breathe in the sweet fragrances of the trees and bushes that were steaming in the sunlight.

Then suddenly, he saw before him on the edge of the forest a slender gazelle. The animal gazed at him with intelligent brown eyes, as understandingly as if it could grasp each thought of this human being.

"What a splendid companion you would make for me in my solitude!" Saadi exclaimed, and hastened towards the animal.

The latter let him approach to within a few paces and then at a bound disappeared into the thicket. Saadi hastened after it.

Now every nerve was taut. He must win the friendship of this little animal. A merry chase began. Again and again Saadi was so close to the little creature that he thought surely he would catch it; but then the gazelle would throw its head round, and bound speedily away.

Ever further he pursued it, with no attention to where he was going. Out of breath, he panted as he ran swiftly uphill. Then suddenly a thunderous voice was heard:

"Do you not know, man, that we allow no one here on the mountain?"

It was the voice of a giant. For an instant Saadi saw the gigantic body towering menacingly over him, then he fell headlong down over the rocks.

He lay unconscious at the foot of the mountain, bleeding from a head injury. Gentle hands attempted to succour him.

"We must wait until he wakens," said one of the little helpers. "There will be other injuries besides."

"But we must not let him see that we pity him," reminded the other. "He has more than deserved the punishment; for he had been warned."

"But Holder, the giant, also knew about him and might have been satisfied with a scolding," grumbled the first.

Saadi began to revive. The little ones slipped behind a tree-trunk. First the injured one felt for his head.

Then he wanted to rise to his feet but it did not work. The pain was too much, and he had no control over his limbs. With a cry of pain he fell back. For a long time he lay in this position, then he looked around him as best he could.

The surroundings were quite unfamiliar, he must be rather far from his hut, for he knew everything in that vicinity. Now he recalled his pursuit of the gazelle.

"I forgot your warning, little ones. That is why I must suffer!" cried he mournfully.

Immediately they emerged from behind the tree.

"Since you acknowledge your mistake, we are permitted to help you," they said cheerfully. Without further ado they bent down over the painful leg:

"Oh dear, this is bad! You've broken your leg! You will have to lie here a long time while it heals."

"Can't you fetch Trotter, to carry me to my hut?" Saadi suggested.

"How would you climb on to his back and get down again?" countered the little ones. "What a blessing that the rainy season is over. We know how to protect you from too much sunshine."

Then the band dispersed with assurances that they would see to the horses and also take care of him.

There he lay, motionless. He, to whom the solitude in the mountains had become unbearable, was now totally unable to move. And thoughts came and would not be dispelled. The voice had told him before that he should draw from every experience what could be learned from it. What was he to learn from this mishap?

He must no longer rush blindly into things, as had been his wont, and his nature.

He must listen to well-meant warnings, that was the other lesson.

But the main thing no doubt was that he must learn to reconcile himself to any situation with patience. What if in the meantime the Zoroaster went past his hut? The very thought made him shudder.

Desperately he prayed for the luminous helper. This time he appeared in the most delicate embodiment as a handsome, noble man.

His manner was friendly as he bent over the injured youth, who had expected to be rebuked.

And in a kind voice the luminous one said: "Now you must learn in this painful way what is indeed so important for your whole life: to let things come as they will!

"But as regards the Forerunner you need not fear. He will be shown to you in such a way as to dispel any doubts. For now lie here quietly. Stop reproaching yourself, and strive to learn what is offered to you.

"When you have attained the necessary inner composure, you will surely be helped to new inner experiencing. Do not attempt to force anything artificially. Think of the flowers which of themselves must open to the Light so that the blossom may unfold and bear fruit."

Great peace had entered Saadi's soul after his guide's departure. Now he knew that it would be given him to gain from this test. He wished to do everything in order not to forfeit the opportunity.

The little ones came each day and thus helped him over the difficult time.

Now and then they also told him what was happening in the forest. But there was always time enough left for the soul to become quiet and immersed in sacred things.

Again one night he was shown a picture.

He saw an infinitely vast room. It was full of light, although there seemed to be no window-openings. Light appeared to stream into it from above.

In radiant beams it descended into a red-golden Chalice in which it began to bubble and seethe.

At any moment Saadi expected the Chalice which appeared filled to the brim to overflow. But this did not happen. From all around the sound of beautiful music arose. Then the picture faded.

But it returned, night after night, becoming increasingly clear and radiant, until one time it appeared during the day. A solemn peace prevailed all around, it was as if the whole of Nature were permitted to share in the vision.

High above, the very top of the vast, light-filled room, became visible with ever fresh streams of light flooding into it.

The Chalice shone radiantly as never before. Luminous forms seemed to surround it. Suddenly He, the Sublime One, the Radiant Hero, stood behind the Chalice and raised It. Then Its emanations poured downward.

Tremendous power filled the beholder. He could not avert his eyes, though the radiance dazzled him. He beheld the Blessed One, the Helper!

"My Lord and King," he cried in jubilation and longing.

Slowly the picture faded. The sky closed again to a cloudless blue. But the power which had been bestowed upon him remained with him, and invigorated him. He raised himself.

It worked! He wanted to stand up, but there was nothing for him to hold on to. He must wait until the little ones came. He had learned to wait now; it was no longer difficult for him.

There, they were already tripping along. How rejuvenated they looked!

"What has happened to you?" Saadi called out to them.

"The same as has happened to you," was the quick retort. "We have all been permitted to receive of the Power which pours down upon the whole of Creation once a year. It is the highest Festival Day on earth, which you human beings, however, have long forgotten.

"We all, the animals and plants, know of it and absorb the Power consciously. It is also bestowed upon you human beings. But you hardly perceive it and, if you sense that something has strengthened you, you do not reflect upon where it comes from."

They were pleased that he wanted to try and stand up. It might well be possible today.

"Patience, Saadi," they encouraged him, "we will go and fetch Trotter, then you can ride home."

They brought the animal, which showed great pleasure at seeing its master again, and Saadi succeeded in mounting the horse.

He rode slowly on the path which the little ones indicated to him. How familiar his hut appeared to him, how comfortable the bed! The other horse had also greeted him, neighing cheerfully.

Then a hurried patter on light feet: the little gazelle came to his bedside, which he had reached with difficulty.

"How did you get here, little gazelle?" he asked, stroking the friendly animal.

Then he seemed to hear a voice: "To him who can wait will come everything that is meant for him. If you had not dashed about so ridiculously after the animal, you would already have been permitted to catch it in the forest."

"Permitted?" Saadi asked, astonished. "Who could have forbidden it?"

"The Lord," was the answer. "You were to learn by this. Just as the gazelle has come to you, because the desire for it was so great in your pure heart, so will you recognise the Zoroaster one day when the time has come. Not an hour before."

As he slowly learned to walk again, the nimble forest-creature pranced about him, and he did not tire of gazing in admiration at its dainty movements.

But what he had learned through the gazelle still occupied his thoughts. Was it not right then to exert oneself, should man always wait until the things he desired dropped into his lap?

That seemed almost to be the Will of Ahuramazda; but deep down in his soul Saadi perceived intuitively that it was not so. Who would resolve this inconsistency for him?

That night the Luminous One came to him again.

"Saadi, hear me! There is a great Law which pervades all of Creation: He who does not sow shall not reap either. It means: He who would receive must exert himself.

"But to exert himself does not mean to pursue something impetuously, trying to force the fulfilment of a wish at all costs. When the wish will be fulfilled, when the harvest is ripe, is dependent upon the Will of Ahuramazda.

"Once man has done his part, he must wait. Exactly at the hour ordained by God he may then receive what he has earned by his efforts. This you must learn!

"You were allowed to court the animal's friendship. Your impetuosity frightened it away. When you were quiet, it came of its own accord.

"You may strive to become as you must be so that you may recognise the Zoroaster and with him his sacred mission. But as long as you only sigh impetuously for this point in time, you are not yet sufficiently prepared and only postpone the moment ever more yourself."

Saadi understood all that the Luminous One taught him, and was grateful.

He was to prepare himself quietly in silence in order to mature. That was his wish. He strove for it with all his soul. In fervent prayer he turned to Ahuramazda for strength.

62

Only now did Saadi recognise what riches were available to him in solitude. When he approached a question with prayer and quiet anticipation, what had appeared insurmountable was resolved without effort. Moreover, soft voices imparted words of wisdom to him, which he absorbed so that his understanding constantly expanded.

He had long since been able to walk as before. His head injury was no longer painful and had healed. Meantime, months had passed, or was it years? He had given it no attention, and had lost count of his own years.

ONE evening a violent storm raged like the one which had once driven him to the hermit's hut. One flash of lightning followed another, and the thunder roared so loudly that the knocking at Saadi's door could not be heard. But one of the little ones tugged at his robe and pointed to the door.

Astonished, Saadi opened it. In the long, long period of time no one had ever come to him. But today a traveller stood outside. His clothes were dripping wet, his face could not be recognised.

Nor did Saadi enquire as to his visitor's identity. He sought to provide the guest with dry clothing and a hot drink as quickly as possible.

Not until he had cared for the stranger's needs, and the fire was burning brightly, did Saadi take a close look at his guest. He was a dignified man, middle-aged and apparently of noble rank.

The wet clothes hanging by the fire were of a costly fabric, elaborately embroidered. His features were handsome. Saadi was an ardent admirer of beauty; but there was something in the stranger's face that repelled him.

Instinctively, he looked around for the little ones who had just been playing with the gazelle. They had disappeared, and the little animal lay huddled in the darkest corner, apparently asleep.

The stranger must have noticed the searching look. He turned to Saadi with a striking smile and said:

"What do you think, will you give me a roof over my head tonight, or must I go out again into the storm as soon as I have rested awhile?"

"The gentleman will be accustomed to better things," said Saadi, unintentionally availing himself of the polite form of address which he had never used before. "But if the gentleman will be satisfied with it, my roof bids him welcome."

The stranger laughed abruptly.

"I have no choice but to make do with it, for it is considerably more unpleasant out there. Have you something for me to eat? I will gladly pay for it."

"It is not customary here to pay for hospitality," retorted Saadi, declining the offer.

Silently he brought what food and drink he had.

"Share the meal with me," the stranger demanded.

Saadi was hungry. He sat down to the meal, but first he raised his hands as he was used to doing, and thanked the Gracious God for His gift.

The stranger had risen to his feet, opened the door a little as if to see about the weather, and now returned casually to the bed, on which both had seated themselves.

"Do you always pray, or did you do it then on my account?" he asked pointedly.

Saadi looked at him in surprise.

"Can one pray because of another?" he asked in reply. "I pray because I would not enjoy a single bite otherwise. Does the gentleman never give thanks when he receives something?"

The stranger chose not to answer, and began to eat. But Saadi was unable to share the meal with him.

On the pretext of having to look after the horses, he left the hut, returning only when he was certain that the stranger had finished his meal.

Sure enough, the guest lay staring into the glowing fire, on an animal skin that he had taken from the bed and spread on the floor by the fireplace.

Saadi thought he could go out again without being seen, but the stranger looked up and beckoned him to his side. He seemed accustomed to giving orders, his movements were imperious and overbearing. Saadi complied reluctantly, but doing so made him even less favourably inclined towards the guest.

He sat down by the fireside, huddled up as if to refuse any contact whatsoever with the man. The latter turned on Saadi his handsome face

64

that seemed almost aglow in the rosy light of the fire, and began by asking:

"Are you here of your own free will, my friend, or has Prince Hafiz sent you into exile?"

The nature of the enquiry displeased Saadi.

"I am my own master and can do and not do what I feel to be right," he retorted defiantly.

The other man laughed abruptly.

"Damaged your self-esteem?" he scoffed. "Forgive me for offending you. It was not deliberate. So, after careful consideration you have gone into solitude here. What made you do it?"

"Various reasons," replied Saadi and was about to get up. The guest restrained him.

"No, do stay. You need not answer my questions if they make you feel uncomfortable. It is not curiosity that prompts me to ask you.

"Just put yourself in my place. I journey into the mountains, am caught in a storm and take refuge in a hermit's hut. Instead of the expected uncultured holy man, I find a youth, almost a man already, who is of the upper classes, is educated, is perhaps even the son of a prince. Surely that must arouse my inquisitiveness.

"Moreover, when I now tell you that I am travelling incognito – for you will have noticed that I am no ordinary man – in search of a person for an especially responsible position at the court of a great prince, then you will understand that I *must* question you."

Again the man turned his face towards the fire. Saadi saw it in profile, saw the fine, quivering wing of the nose above the beautifully curved mouth. Perhaps the stranger was not bad as it had seemed to him at first, but simply different from the people in this country.

"Does the gentleman come from far away?" he asked hesitantly.

"Yes, from very far away. The country where I should like to take you is magnificent. It is like a flower-garden. Wherever you look beauty abounds. The people who live there are happy. They pass their days free from care, for they have everything they need."

What a splendid voice! That Saadi had not perceived this melodious sound, which was like music to his ears, before now! Surely he was still a very inexperienced youth, to have allowed himself to be so influenced by the first impression.

Unconsciously his tense limbs relaxed. The stranger noticed it, a subtle smile played about his lips.

"A wise prince rules this blessed land. No one is his equal in cleverness and intellect..."

"Is he also good?" Saadi interrupted him impetuously.

"Is being good not the same as being clever, Saadi?" said the stranger casually, and was about to continue. But in Saadi something had been aroused that would not be silenced.

"Cleverness is usually a gift of Anramainyu," he said informatively. "But then it is not consistent with goodness."

"Are you not being a little narrow-minded, my friend?" the stranger asked, turning his beautiful eyes upon him. The look cut him to the quick. Saadi sensed it keenly.

"I do not understand what you mean by 'narrow-minded', stranger," he said, unconsciously using the familiar form of address for the first time.

This too the guest noticed at once.

"You have probably been taught that everything Anramainyu conveys to men is bad. But if you think about it, you will find it is only human beings who have made bad what in itself is good, indeed excellent..."

"Precisely as with the gifts of Ahuramazda," the words escaped Saadi.

It was as if a sudden radiance brightened the hut as he spoke the Name! Subconsciously he absorbed this intuitive perception.

"When Anramainyu, or Ahriman as he is also called, brought men cleverness, it was surely a wonderful gift. He bestowed it unselfishly to make men happy. Rightly applied, it helps them to better their lives on earth, to use more wisely everything the earth produces, everything that is put in their way.

"Consider a moment, Saadi: What would you be if you did not have the light of the intellect? You would disdain something which you cannot fully comprehend. If only for this reason it would be good for you to experience other circumstances where you would learn to regard things in a different light. Much that is new would be revealed to you; it would make you fit for the battle of life."

66

He had risen to his feet, as had Saadi. The stranger placed his hand on Saadi's shoulder. Something coursed through his body like fire.

But it was not invigorating like the power that sometimes flowed to him through his luminous helper. Heavy, sleep-inducing, it permeated him; he felt relaxed.

For a moment he yielded to this feeling. Then suddenly he straightened; the stranger's hand dropped from his shoulder.

The guest resumed.

"I do not yet know whether you would be qualified for the prospective office. But I have taken a liking to you. I see that vast areas in your soul still lie fallow. I would be minded to sow seed there, which would surely bear glorious fruit.

"I would like to make a suggestion to you:

"Come with me. Give up the solitude for a short time. Learn to know and to judge real life. Only when you can do that will you be able to decide how you wish to arrange your own. Then you will in no way be committed. No one will force you, indeed no one will even attempt to persuade you. You will be free to choose. Believe me, I have only your well-being at heart."

The voice was enticing, the face and figure radiantly beautiful. But Saadi did not hesitate for an instant: "I thank the gentleman for thinking of me so kindly and for seeking to enlighten me. Indeed I realise that my inner being is still empty, but I await the Master who is to help me fill it. I require no alien seed. My path lies clearly before me."

How did he suddenly know?

"I await the Call of Ahuramazda! I belong to Him, I am His servant! No one shall tear me away from Him!"

The stranger flinched. The refusal apparently affected him deeply, for he looked literally debilitated.

"I will not yet take this as a refusal, Saadi," he said more quietly than before. "The night often brings clearer decisions. Let us sleep, you may give me your answer in the morning."

He stretched out on the animal skin, expecting Saadi to do likewise. But Saadi called the gazelle and left the room with it. He wished to spend the night in the shelter with the animals.

Nestling between the warm bodies, he did not feel the cold and he was more at ease outside than in his room which seemed to be filled with a sinister sultriness.

He wasted no further thought on the stranger and his offer. He prayed, as was his wont, and sleep bore his soul to other regions, there to strengthen and refresh it.

He was up early the next morning, to fetch water, and tend his animals. He peered into the room. The stranger seemed to be still sleeping. He lay quietly stretched out beside the extinguished fire.

Saadi regarded him with curiosity. What was it actually that had seemed so beautiful to him yesterday? In reality the man's features were coarse, with sharp lines furrowing them.

Now the guest awakened. Recognition passed across his face, which seemed suddenly transformed.

"Well, Saadi, are you prepared to come with me? You can lend me your pack-horse until we reach the village where my baggage train awaits me. Then poverty will be at an end for you, my dear fellow. Whatever you desire shall be yours."

"I thank the gentleman for his kind intentions. But I cannot go with him. I must remain here and await the Zoroaster."

Peals of scornful laughter answered him:

"You blind fool, the Zoroaster will never cross your path, though you were to wait to the end of all days."

But the laughter had enkindled in Saadi's soul all the flaming ardour in which it abounded. Proudly and with great dignity he answered:

"The gentleman may think and say what he will. He cannot convince me. But it would be more seemly for the guest not to deride things he does not understand."

"Then farewell, you simpleton, you fool!" cried the stranger and left the room without touching the food that Saadi had prepared.

The latter sighed with relief. He went to the door and opened it wide. Air – different air must flow through the room! Then already far away he saw the guest, disappearing with hasty steps as though he were being pursued. How good that he was gone!

Saadi sat down outside the hut and began to eat. His meal was frugal; it consisted of water and grains, nuts and a bread-like fruit. But he relished it and was blissfully happy that he did not require the rich food which the stranger had described to him so enticingly.

Suddenly his little friends were with him again. He scolded them: "Where were you last night? I was so lonely and you did not come!"

"You had company, Saadi," they reminded him. But he would not accept that. "He was an intruder, not a welcome visitor. I would have been grateful if you had helped me."

"We were not permitted to, Saadi," they explained. "You were meant to deal with him on your own. You yourself were to recognise the nature of the spirit from which he spoke."

"It was not a good one!" Saadi affirmed. But then he turned his attention to something else. He wanted to forget the stranger.

AGAIN months had gone by uniformly and in joyful inner learning. Saadi endeavoured to curb his impatience. He would wait until the Zoroaster came. What had the guest said?

"The Zoroaster will never cross your path!"

What did the stranger know of the Forerunner? Saadi did not let it confuse him. One day, He, the Promised One, would come.

There was a gentle rap on the door. Before he could open it, an old, white-haired man crossed the threshold. A hairy garment covered his body, his feet were wrapped in animal skins.

In spite of his simple attire, the man did not look poor. His movements had something youthful and sprightly about them. After a few steps, he stood still, modestly, and asked for food and drink.

Saadi invited him to rest on the bed. Then he brought what food he had available. The old man praised the quality of the fruits, the cool clarity of the water. He ate slowly, looking around the room.

When he had refreshed himself he began to speak. He asked Saadi his name and age and seemed to be delighted with the latter. Then he wished to know why such a young person had withdrawn into solitude.

Something in Saadi warned him against speaking freely and without restraint. So he replied:

"I simply wanted to be able to live completely alone with my thoughts."

"It is not right that you should evade well-intentioned questions, my friend," the old man reproached him. "I know very well that your whole life is one long waiting."

"You may be right," Saadi conceded, "but that is solely my concern."

"And that of him for whom you are waiting," was the quick reply.

Surprised, Saadi stared at the guest in whose eyes a ray of youthful fire flared up. Could this be the Zoroaster? But he was an old man? Saadi was not yet clear as to what he should think when the old man said emphatically: "I have been directed here by supernatural powers to seek one who awaits the Zoroaster. You owe me an answer: are you the one?"

Trembling all over with excitement, Saadi answered:

"Yes, I am awaiting the Forerunner. Where is he?"

"Just look here!" cried the old man, pulling off the white hair and headgear. "I am he for whom you are waiting!"

A young man, about the same age as Saadi, stood before the astonished youth.

Whenever Saadi had pictured this meeting to himself, he had been certain that he must fall down overwhelmed, at the feet of him whom he had at last found. A great and lofty intuitive perceiving must draw him upwards to Luminous Heights, thus he had envisaged it. But the reality was quite different.

Astonishment filled him, boundless disappointment and disenchantment. He reproached himself for not sensing any of the overpowering joy which had always filled him at the mere thought of a meeting. He was close to tears!

Dumbfounded he stood before the Forerunner. Then the latter spoke again. With kindly forbearance he censured Saadi for being so unresponsive.

"Really, Saadi, I had pictured it differently! I looked forward to meeting you at last, having heard how long you have faithfully awaited me. That is also why I came to you in disguise, so that the surprise should be all the greater, and now it has rendered you dumb and motionless. Do you no longer wish to be my servant and helper?"

At last Saadi found words:

"If you are the Zoroaster, I shall go with you wherever you wish. I shall serve you; for only thus am I able to serve the Saoshyant, Who fills my soul."

Impatiently the other demanded:

"Well then, let us hurry. Come with me. You may take your horses. Apart from these, you probably have nothing of value to you. As my servant you must be poor, that is what our vocation calls for. Are you able to comply, Saadi?"

"I can be poor, and I can be rich, whatever is the Will of Ahuramazda, of my God!" retorted Saadi earnestly, but he made no move.

"Come then, Saadi!" urged the other. "As my servant you must be able to obey. You have just said yourself that you wish to be my servant!"

It sounded almost threatening.

Where did Saadi get the courage, from whence did the words flow to him? Calmly he looked up and said simply, but emphatically:

"I said: *if* you are the Zoroaster! Prove to me that you are he!"

"You must feel it, Saadi," replied the other impatiently. "How should I prove it to you here?"

"Tell me about the Saoshyant!"

"There will be more than enough time for that on the way. I am in a hurry to move on. But I will go out of my way to be of help. Listen to me: for now, accompany me; I will tell you everything you ask. If then you are not satisfied, you may leave me!"

Saadi's eyes had opened wide. Horror-stricken he stared at the other:

"Who, who are you? You are not the Zoroaster! If you were the Forerunner I would know, for I was promised that I would be allowed to behold him in such a way as to leave me in no doubt. If you were the Zoroaster you would indignantly refute my doubt at once. The fact that you wish to bargain with me proves that you are a liar. Yes, you are a liar!" he shouted, beside himself.

He leaped to the door and pulled it open:

"Begone with you, you evil spirit, whoever you may be! Be gone!"

The guest complied promptly, but outside he turned and cried scornfully:

71

"You will regret having driven the Zoroaster from your door. Henceforth your life will be of no avail!"

Already the figure had disappeared around a turning in the path. Breathing a sigh of relief, Saadi leaned against the stone wall of his hut.

Without thinking, his lips repeated the words "Driven the Zoroaster away! What if indeed it was he?"

For a long time he stood musing, then he raised his head:

"If this was the Zoroaster, then he is not worthy of being permitted to proclaim Thee, Thou Radiant Hero! No, no, he was not the Zoroaster! His mouth would have had to overflow with Thy praises, Thou Helper of men! If he were the Zoroaster, he would have had to know Thee. And who can know Thee and not worship Thee with every breath?"

"You are right, Saadi," the voice of the Luminous One rang out. "This was an evil spirit, who came to divert you from the right road. You have passed the test. The knowledge of the Saoshyant is firmly engraved in your soul. Soon you will be fully prepared."

"Was this a test?" Saadi stammered. "Perhaps the visit of the stranger some months ago was also a trial?"

"Yes, Saadi, both were tests imposed upon you by the evil spirit, because your purity did not fit into his scheme. He wanted to divert you from your path."

"Thanks be to Ahuramazda, Who gave me the strength to resist!" the youth said simply.

For a moment both were silent, then the Luminous One asked kindly:

"And do you not enquire at all, Saadi, why God permitted you to be so severely tested?"

"It does not behove me to enquire," replied Saadi, simply. "What Ahuramazda ordains or permits is most exalted wisdom, to which I bow in reverence and gratitude."

"Saadi, Saadi!" said the Luminous Helper, with deep emotion resounding in his voice, "you are truly prepared to recognise the Zoroaster and his mission. It will not be long before you are allowed to enter upon your task."

"I thank Ahuramazda that my waiting will come to an end," whispered Saadi, who was forced to his knees in adoration.

Thus he remained for a long time. When he rose to his feet the Luminous One had disappeared. But in Saadi a jubilant life burst forth. His fiery nature came to the fore once again.

Joyously, he rushed through the forest to the waterfall, calling for the water-sprite. He wanted to tell her that he would soon, very soon have completed his time of waiting.

The lovely face smiled out at him:

"I know already, Saadi," she said playfully. "I have already been permitted to see the Zoroaster."

"You, you have seen him!" Saadi exclaimed, almost enviously. "Where is he?"

But she disappeared, smiling:

"Wait and pray!"

If the water-sprite had seen him already, he certainly could no longer be far away, Saadi mused. He became quite excited. "You little ones," he called out, "have you already seen him too?"

A host of little helpers danced round him:

"Of course! We have been permitted to see him! He is not far at all!" Already they had vanished.

If indeed he was so near, Saadi must no longer leave his hut. In haste he returned to it. The gazelle bounded up to him trustingly, rubbing its dainty little head against his arm.

"Have you seen him as well?" he asked.

The gazelle was silent. Its big eyes were fixed on the man who had become its friend. He read in them sadness at the impending separation.

"You are right, little animal," said he, calming down, "then we will have to part. I cannot take you with me."

He sat down quietly outside the hut, the animal close to him, and began to reflect on all that had happened.

He must actually be grateful to the evil spirit who had put him to the test. Through this he had learned that the Zoroaster was near and that he was sufficiently prepared to be allowed to help him.

Who could have come to him this morning in the guise of the old man?

Probably one of Anramainyu's satellites, perhaps Druj, who personifies deceit? Never mind, whoever it may have been, he, Saadi had better things to consider! Now he would soon hear the truth about the Saoshyant.

Ever again he called forth the pictures he had been permitted to behold. He was unaware that the sun was setting, that the sky had assumed the deep blue of night, and that the stars were rising. The little gazelle had long since sought the warmth of its companions in the shelter. He sat and meditated.

His soul had wandered far away. He was not conscious of it. The will to serve and the longing for Truth had grown so overwhelming that they had lifted him into more luminous realms. He sought Him, Whom he was permitted to serve.

And his longing was answered:

Again it was given him to behold a picture, but it was clearer, more beautiful than before.

Again the heavens opened, and a glorious room became visible. White forms soared upwards, seeming to support the ceiling; but this ceiling could not be seen for the splendour and magnificence radiating down from Above.

In the centre of this room stood a golden Throne whereon sat One surrounded by rays of light, so that Saadi could hardly look upon it. But it was just He Whom he wanted to see! For it was He, the Radiant Hero, the Helper, the Saoshyant!

"Thou Who art glorious beyond all measure, Lord and King!" Saadi exulted. Then he cast himself down on the ground where he stood.

But he continued to gaze upward. And he saw that the rays crossed behind the Helper. It almost appeared that He Himself was this Golden Cross, then again It seemed to be floating behind Him.

Above Him was the wonderful Bird, gleaming in purest white. In His Hand the Hero held the Sword.

Saadi gazed and worshipped. Then luminous, female figures appeared beside the Saoshyant. A roseate glow shone to his right. Roses upon roses seemed to intertwine. But in their midst there stood, like a rose incarnate, a gracious Woman whose eyes radiated Love in the purest light.

"O, Thou wondrous Woman, Queen of Love!" he whispered rapturously.

Then a Luminous Figure in white raiment approached. She held wondrous white blossoms in her hand. Light beings floated about her.

She knelt at the feet of the King, behind Whom at that moment there came a third veiled Female Figure, in a mantle of deep blue, with a radiant crown upon her head. The rays of this crown, however, united with those of the King's.

From Saadi's overpowered soul came the fervent entreaty:

"Lord and King, let me serve Thee upon Earth!"

And a Voice rang out, powerful and yet restrained. It thrilled him to his innermost being.

"Thou art chosen to serve Me, Forerunner of the Helper!"

What did the King call him? Forerunner of the Helper! His head was whirling, but he subdued any emotion in order not to miss a single one of the Holy Words.

"Thou hast prepared thyself in purity, now serve in purity! Bring to mankind, bring to thy people tidings of the Son of Ahuramazda, Who will come to judge the World and to lead the Faithful to Garodemana.

"Thou art prepared to bring Blessing; the Blessing of the Most High is with thee, My Servant, My Forerunner!"

Again the Holy Voice had called him by that name. Human spirit, art thou able to contain so much bliss? He felt very small. What was all his volition, all his serving compared to this inexpressible Grace?

"Lord and King, I solemnly promise Thee that I desire nothing but to be Thy Servant, obeying Thee in all things. Lord and King, I thank Thee!" Trembling with happiness he spoke the words, and added with overflowing intuitive perception:

"O, Thou Luminous Ones! Thanks be to Thee that I, a wretched human being, was permitted to behold Thee. I wish to be your servant also. Saadi is nothing now, the Zoroaster will be everything."

Slowly the celestial picture faded. With a slight shudder Saadi awoke from his absorption.

"Enter, Zoroaster!" the voices of the little ones greeted him.

Almost reverently they accompanied him into his hut where the gazelle awaited him. He thanked them; then he sat down and tried to fathom all that he had experienced.

Was it possible that he himself was permitted to be the Zoroaster? He, the poor Saadi, son of a horse-breeder? He, the ignorant Saadi?

But had not the Holiest Mouth Itself said so? Had not the Pure Luminous Women heard it as well? Forerunner He had called him, His Forerunner!

He was not to be servant of the Zoroaster, but servant of the Saoshyant, of the Blessed One, the Holy One! No word was sublime enough for His praise, Whom he had been permitted to behold, for Whom his soul lived.

Soft light from unearthly rays encircled him: the Luminous Helper gave him greeting.

"Blessing rests upon you, Forerunner of the Lord of all Worlds! You have sought faithfully, now you have been permitted to find! You have sown in humility, and you will reap strength!

"Your time in this hut is over. Tomorrow you will be led to another place in accordance with the Will of Ahuramazda, so that you may learn what you still lack in recognition and wisdom.

"Absorb what you are able to grasp. Only that which comes to life within you will survive the storms which you will not be spared either, and will be yours to pass on to mankind.

"But if understanding should ever become too difficult for you, or the path too dark, call for me. You will not call in vain so long as you serve in purity."

That night Saadi did not think of sleep. In him were joy, anticipation, gratitude and the impetuous urge to begin serving. He was blissfully happy.

Early the next morning he loaded his pack-horse and saddled Trotter. Then he hastened to the water to see the water-sprite one last time. But she did not appear.

With his vessels filled he returned to the hut. There stood two of his little helpers, ready to accompany him. First a brief farewell to the gazelle – – then he could go to meet the new life. No longer as Saadi, but now as Zoroaster.

WHEN the sun was at its zenith, they had already left the mountains behind them and sought out shady paths in a vast forest. Zoroaster breathed with difficulty; he had first to become accustomed to the air in the lowlands.

As they were leaving the forest, other little beings stood ready to assume the task of leading him.

"We may accompany you no further, Zoroaster," said his former friends. "Each of our tribes has its own district. But these helpers will serve you as faithfully as we have. We thank you for being our friend."

They were off, as though scattered by the wind. But the others guided him just as safely. In the evening Zoroaster had to spend the night in the open. He was accustomed to it and loved it.

In this way he rode for several days. It was obvious that the little ones sought to avoid all villages.

One day, however, they left the protective cover of the forests and led him along the banks of a river. Zoroaster tried to discover the water-sprite of this river, but he saw only turbid waves sluggishly pursuing their course.

Finally he asked the little ones about it. They laughed.

"This river is trampled underfoot by herds of cattle. Do you think that any water-sprite would want to live in such muddy waters? The lord of this river has withdrawn back to its source in the mountains. Once the water is pure and clear again, he will surely return to the plain. He comes but seldom, for he dislikes the sluggish flow."

Zoroaster had been riding in silence for a long time, when one of the little beings drew his attention to a group of huts clustered at the edge of a small forest.

"That is where you are going, Zoroaster. We were to lead you there, and we shall remain near you also; for we have become your friends. Whenever you need us, simply call. We will come if it is not against the Will of Ahuramazda."

"Thank you, little ones, I shall call you," Zoroaster assured them.

He gazed intently at his newest home. The nearer he came, the bigger the huts appeared to be. They were impressive buildings constructed with care and a distinct sense of beauty.

At the very first building he reined in the horses. Before it was clear to him what to do next, the door opened, and a servant emerged. He was apparently in the service of a distinguished master, for his attire was rich and splendid.

"Enter, Forerunner of the Saoshyant," the servant greeted him, making a deep bow.

This was so new to Zoroaster that he involuntarily looked around for the person who had been thus welcomed. Then he remembered, dismounted from his horse and entered the house with the servant. The building consisted of several rooms.

In the first one they passed through, soft mats were underfoot; it was exquisitely furnished. Beauty was everywhere; but Zoroaster paid no attention to it now.

The servant pushed aside a mat and signalled Zoroaster to enter a second, smaller room. There, on a wide couch covered with furs, sat an aged man with snow-white hair.

"Dshayava," exulted Zoroaster, and made haste to greet the venerable man.

The latter held out his trembling hands to him.

"Forgive me, my son, for not rising from my seat to receive the Forerunner of the Helper as befits him. I am old, and my limbs fail me. But Ahuramazda has increased the number of my years, so that I may serve you, you blessed one."

"May I now stay with you, Dshayava?" asked Zoroaster, deeply happy.

"Yes, you are to stay here for the time being, my son, in order to accustom yourself to human beings and to your task, after the complete solitude."

Servants came and escorted Zoroaster to a sumptuously appointed room. Later they brought him food and drink, after which he was allowed to return to Dshayava.

"Today I should like to have you all to myself, Zoroaster," the aged man explained. "You must tell me of your life. Perhaps I can yet explain many things, which had to be set aside for a time, as incomprehensible to you."

"That cannot all be dealt with today," Zoroaster asserted trustingly.

"Then ask whatever comes to mind."

"May I ask about *everything*, my father?" Zoroaster asked hesitantly.

"You may ask about everything: whether I am able to answer remains to be seen."

"Then let me ask about what occupies me most of all: The Radiant Hero Himself said that He is the Son of Ahuramazda, and the hermit assured me that He is the Son of the Prince Ara-Masdah. Then the little ones spoke of the Prince's Heir!"

Zoroaster sighed, for he became confused whenever he thought about it. But he took heart and continued:

"I know with absolute certainty that the Radiant Hero has told me the truth. He is the Son of the Supreme God. Now I could disregard everything else, but something in me says that it too is true. Do you know about it, my father? Are you allowed to explain it to me?"

Zoroaster's gaze was turned imploringly upon the old man.

"I know of it, my son, and I may tell you that also what the hermit and the little ones told you is the truth. Later you shall learn how the two are connected. It is still a great mystery to men. Give me the capsule which I once hung round your neck, and you will see that one day you shall hear this truth also."

Zoroaster quickly pulled the capsule on the golden chain from under his garment, at the same time revealing the stone which a man had once given him. As he was about to push it back Dshayava asked:

"Tell me about the stone? Who gave it to you?"

Zoroaster gave him a brief account of the man.

Meantime the aged hands had carefully opened the capsule. Inside it, made of gold, was the Radiant Cross as Zoroaster had beheld it in the vision.

"It is the Cross of the Saoshyant," said both men together. But the old man added:

"It is the Cross of Eternal Truth as it was handed down to us from time immemorial. He who bears this Cross is permitted to learn of the Truth. You too will be allowed to hear of It when the time is ripe."

Zoroaster concealed the capsule under his garment with care. After he had seen what it contained, it was even more precious to him. They spoke for yet a little while before they parted.

The next day Zoroaster learned that the various buildings belonged to Prince Hafiz, who liked to come here to recuperate during the hottest time of the year. Thus Zoroaster was actually the Prince's guest.

He looked forward to being allowed to meet the kind Prince again, who was expected that very day.

"He too looks forward to seeing you, my son," Dshayava assured him. "He could hardly wait until the young Saadi had found the Zoroaster."

"So you both knew that I myself was he?" Zoroaster asked, lost in wonder.

"We knew, the Atravan had told Prince Hafiz. But I, like the Atravan, had come to know it through tidings from above."

"So you all knew what was still concealed from me," mused the Forerunner. "How miraculously my path was guided through the Goodness and Grace of Ahuramazda."

The clatter of horses' hooves was heard, merry shouts, commotion, such as attend an arrival.

Then Prince Hafiz crossed the threshold and hurried joyfully to meet his guest. The Prince had aged visibly. His features were more manly, but his eyes had retained the kindly radiance which had always attracted the young Saadi.

Questions and answers followed in quick succession. The Prince's heartfelt joy at the reunion was clearly evident. Zoroaster wanted to thank him for everything he had done for him. Laughing, Hafiz would not hear of it.

"If only you knew how glad I was that just I was allowed to help, to be of use to the Forerunner!" he laughed. "Throughout these ten long years I have yearned for this moment."

"Ten years?" Zoroaster stammered, overwhelmed. "Did I really spend ten years in solitude? To me they seemed like only ten months!"

"They seemed longer to us," Hafiz declared, "and your outward appearance shows that the youth has become a man. You look splendid! But you must dress differently. These animal skins are no longer suitable for the Forerunner."

At a call servants came with magnificent clothes that were already awaiting him. Zoroaster had to put them on, and Hafiz was pleased with his fine appearance.

The Forerunner too was happy, but he almost considered this joy to be unjustified. Then Hafiz explained to him how exalted was the Master he served, and added good-humouredly: "I am glad that there are a few earthly things in which I can still advise and help you."

A COMPLETELY new life began for him who had been accustomed to solitude. Prince Hafiz took him under his care.

As the Prince's guest he had to participate in receptions and banquets. He learned to move with ease, and soon became familiar with the customs, but above all he was a keen observer. It seemed to him that he could see the thoughts of men which so often were not at all in accord with their actions and words.

At such times he felt like reproaching them with their insincerity but something within restrained him. He failed to understand it. One evening he called his Luminous Helper to question him about it.

The latter asked him pleasantly:

"What do you hope to achieve by telling people that they do not speak the truth?"

"They should realise that they are not trusted. Then they will refrain from it the next time."

"Do you really think so, Zoroaster? Well then, at the next opportunity you may fearlessly say what you sense intuitively. You will learn more that way than if I were now to go into lengthy explanations."

"I would like to ask one more question, you Luminous One," requested Zoroaster. "This is, after all, still a time of learning for me. Is it right that I should hold back completely, and say nothing about that which fills my soul?"

"At present you would do more harm than good. At the right time, your lips will be unsealed, to proclaim the Divine Mystery," said the messenger solemnly. Then he left his pupil alone.

Now that he had been given permission to speak, Zoroaster was almost diffident. The next two opportunities that presented themselves did not seem to warrant exposing the deceitful person. He wanted to wait for something more serious. And it came.

One of the princes subordinate to Hafiz sent a message, saying that at this time it was impossible for him to pay the tribute he owed. The emissary gave lengthy explanations as to how a poor harvest and the death of cattle had impoverished the land. As soon as things improved, the taxes would be paid up.

Prince Hafiz was fully aware that the emissary was telling lies, well-considered lies, but he took care not to show it.

The calmer he remained now, the more unabashed the stranger presented himself, the better could Hafiz plan his future course of action. Affably, he sat on the chair which here served as his throne, and let the stranger speak.

Suddenly Zoroaster's clear voice rang out:

"Do not trust him, Prince Hafiz! He is lying. His master has no intention of ever paying his tribute to you. This is only an attempt to see how much you will put up with!"

Hafiz was startled, and asked him to keep quiet. But Zoroaster assumed the start to reflect the Prince's sudden recognition of what he had been permitted to reveal. He wanted to enlighten the poor, deceived Prince still further. He began afresh:

"I see the thoughts of the emissary moving about you like evil vermin, Prince Hafiz. Send him away so that the air here may be clean again!"

The courtiers stood as though paralysed. How dared the youngest speak in this way!

Hafiz, however, rose to his feet. In an unruffled voice he asked Zoroaster not to interfere in the discussion. He went even further: he asked the emissary to pay no heed to the expressions of youthful zeal and concern.

Seething with anger, Zoroaster left the room, saddled Trotter without asking the assistance of the servants, and rode off.

Was this the Prince's gratitude for the well-meant, well-founded warning? He knew that he had not been mistaken in what he saw. Should not Hafiz have made the most of the truth shown to him, and sent the envoy away? Zoroaster understood the world less than ever.

The flames of fury blazed fiercely within him. He had to ride for a long time before he could think clearly again. Finally, he turned Trotter homewards.

He did not wish to stay away from the meal like a scolded boy. With his thoughts calmer, he remembered the words of the Luminous One that he should seek the benefit and the lesson in every experience.

What was he meant to learn today? That he should not interfere? Yes, but then he could not have shown the emissary that he had seen through him. And the Luminous One had expressly permitted him to speak out!

He had done so, and now the Prince had treated him badly! At once he perceived that his anger had been directed at the way in which Hafiz had received the warning. So it had been injured self-love that had caused his flare-up.

Was that worthy of a Zoroaster? Had not the Forerunner wished to lay down his entire ego at the steps of the Heavenly Throne? And now this ego felt offended! That was wrong.

He must neither be angry with Hafiz nor in any way bemoan the fact that his warning had gone unheard. He had voiced it, let Hafiz do with it what he deemed right.

Mollified, even a little shamefaced, he returned, but did not wish to encounter the stranger, in the event that he was just leaving the house. For that reason he chose a rarely-used path leading to the horse stables.

There he heard excited voices talking.

"We will have to be on our guard against the Zoroaster," said the one. "If he is really able to see our thoughts, we will have to conceal them even better than before."

"I still do not believe that he can see everything," the other answered thoughtfully. "After all, in this instance it was obvious to us all that the emissary was lying. You did not have to be very astute to see that. But you are right, it is better not to chance anything. Thoughts can also be forced to lie. Don't you agree?"

The two of them walked off laughing. But an ice-cold shudder seized the Zoroaster. What had he been made to hear?

He thought that by indicating to them his ability to see thoughts he would make them reflect, so that they would no longer permit wrong thoughts to arise in them. Now they also wanted to lie in thought, forcing themselves to think untruths.

This would only make them worse. And he would be to blame!

What could he do to make amends? 'If only I had kept silent,' was all he could think and stammer as he looked after Trotter. On the way to his room he came upon a servant who was looking for him and summoned him to Hafiz.

How was he to face the Prince? Everything within him was still in turmoil. He was almost ready to send a message saying that he would come in a few hours when it flashed through him:

"That would be cowardice!"

He turned and followed the servant. Hafiz received him with his usual warmth. He saw how much Zoroaster had suffered; his lack of experience aroused his pity.

"I have asked you to come to me, Zoroaster," he said kindly, "because I would not like a moment's estrangement to arise between us. Today I have behaved in a way that you could not understand. I would now like to give you the explanation."

Impetuously the other interrupted him.

"It is I who should ask for forgiveness, Hafiz," he spluttered. "I have done everything wrong. I meant well but it was all wrong, much more so than you can suspect," he added when he noticed that the Prince was about to make excuses for him.

"Certainly, you acted wrongly, Zoroaster," the Prince resumed. "The best intention may indeed excuse us, but it cannot undo mistakes. Let me explain the matter to you; try and listen without interrupting. Then you will see more clearly.

"In the entire gathering there was probably not one who had not perceived how grossly the emissary was lying. But I was anxious to let him have his say so that I might perceive the motive behind these lies. They must have a purpose other than the mere refusal to pay the present tribute.

"I remained silent, in order to discover this. And when the Prince to whom the words are addressed remains silent, the courtiers too must keep their peace."

Zoroaster winced, but he controlled himself, and said nothing.

84

"You, being a guest, were allowed to speak. This court etiquette did not apply to you. But by speaking you disrupted my quiet observation, it also put me in an awkward position regarding the emissary, who as an envoy must not be attacked.

"Such people are to be treated with courtesy even though they must be held in contempt. Unfortunately, the sole outcome of your words will be that the emissary will prompt his lord to proceed with even greater cunning in his dealings with me. You will now understand that I had to try and obliterate the unpleasant impression as best I could."

Hafiz's friendly, questioning look was directed at Zoroaster, who could hardly speak for agitation.

"Now I know that I have caused even greater harm," and with trembling lips he recounted the conversation he had overheard. The Prince nodded.

"It confirms my suspicions," he said earnestly. "You have been able to learn a great deal from today's experience, my friend. I too have learned from it. Let us endeavour to have the lesson bear fruit."

"Have I caused you great harm?" Zoroaster ventured to ask.

"I hope I have succeeded in obliterating the embarrassing impression. But in order to do so, I was forced to dissemble and resort to falsehood myself. That distresses me now."

The Prince attempted to change the subject. But Zoroaster had not yet achieved clarity, his inner being was still in utter turmoil. It was best to leave him to himself.

When he reached his room, the troubled one fell on his knees, cried out to the Luminous Helper and relentlessly sought to put into words all he had done wrong. When he had finished, the Luminous One stood before him:

"You see now, Zoroaster, how much this experience has taught you. You would have kept silent out of obedience had I forbidden you to speak, but you would never have grasped why silence was necessary. Now that the reason has become apparent to you in a flash, you will remain silent of your own accord.

"The ability to read the thoughts of men is one of the helps bestowed upon you, that you may approach their souls. You are to be a Forerunner.

To perceive men's thoughts was not given to you as a weapon to cause injury in combat. Consider this well. You are not to fight, but to proclaim, not to injure but to heal!"

It took the Zoroaster a long time to regain his emotional equilibrium. His fiery nature had been somewhat subdued by this experience. He no longer gave voice thoughtlessly to whatever passed through his mind.

But as he distanced himself from the incident, he became more and more occupied with the thought:

"How dreadful that even a man as noble as Hafiz can be forced to lie."

Where to begin if something was to be done about it? Here and there things could be improved somewhat, but genuine help could come only from the One, the Hero Who would strike off the serpent's head.

Now at last, Zoroaster had become clear enough to venture speaking with Dshayava. He had noticed that the aged man never answered him directly so long as he himself had not done his utmost to find a solution.

More fully than intended he put before the venerable man the thoughts that assailed him. He told of what the Luminous One had said to him; he spoke with admiration of the Prince's goodness and trust.

But eventually that which moved him most came out: the supremacy of falsehood in the world.

"I have pondered so much on where falsehood comes from, my father," he lamented. "With most people it arises from fear. They think to escape the unpleasant consequences of their doings by lying. Were fear to be done away with, then falsehood would have no further opportunity."

"Not necessarily, my son," corrected Dshayava. "Think of the many who lie in order to make themselves appear better than they are, who wish to be admired. One moment they exaggerate their achievements, the next, their thoughts.

"Think of those who lie in order to flatter a superior, to gain something from him. No, my son, he who would oppose falsehood must slay Anramainyu, and then all his followers."

"I know it, my father. I know also that the Saoshyant will vanquish the Evil One; but until He comes the flood-tide of evil will grow ever more. And He, the Purest of the Pure, is to set foot in this loathsome mire? Are we worthy of it?"

He had called it out excitedly, and was not at all surprised when Dshayava agreed with him that no man was worthy of this inconceivable sacrifice.

"If only I would succeed in preparing a way for Him, in gathering souls for Him, among whom He can safely tread!" Zoroaster longed for it from the depth of his soul.

THE WEEKS which Hafiz had wanted to spend away from his capital came to an end. The cottages were closed down, a long procession of riders set out, in whose midst rode the carriage bearing Dshayava.

As in the past the Prince delighted in Trotter's gait and Zoroaster's horsemanship.

"There is no sign of ageing in your horse," he said, well pleased. "The animal is as beautiful as it is intelligent."

But after a little reflection he added:

"Nonetheless, I will give you one of my horses as well, so that the little one can be spared, for you will have much riding to do at times."

Delighted at this, Zoroaster thanked him, and then asked:

"Have you ever thought, Prince, on how I shall be allowed to perform the duties of my office? Whenever I think of my future work, I see nothing that could give me an indication."

"I believe, Zoroaster, that it will come about of itself if you do each day whatever work it brings you, what Ahuramazda demands of you. The root does not consider either how leaves and blossoms will one day adorn its branches. It grows. So you too must grow without ceasing. Thus it will be right.

"To begin with, I want to ask you to speak of the gods to those who live at my court, every day at the same hour. There will be ample opportunity to speak of the Saoshyant. So many of the courtiers deem themselves superior to such matters. To awaken in them a longing for higher things would be a task worthy of a Forerunner."

Zoroaster was happy and concentrated his thoughts ever again in silent prayer, that Ahuramazda might grant him the requisite strength, the eloquence that comes from above.

After some days they reached the capital with which Zoroaster was already familiar.

Now he was allowed to see the inside of the Prince's palace, indeed he was to live in it. Two magnificent rooms had been arranged for him, two servants awaited his commands.

When he objected that this was too elegant for him, Hafiz replied:

"You keep forgetting that you are the servant of the Highest of all Kings. For Him nothing is too precious. Remember that many will come to you seeking counsel. Are they to tell others of poverty and want?

"The promised Forerunner must live in splendour and magnificence. Learn to do this. Learn also to avail yourself of the servants. You must do it for the sake of men, but above all, for the sake of your Lord." –

On one of the following days, Hafiz assembled all the members of his royal household, and explained to them that the proclaimed Zoroaster had been found and was living in their midst.

He asked that they listen to his teachings, not only with their ears, but still more with their hearts. It was a Grace of Ahuramazda that the Forerunner should remain here for a short space of time. Perhaps they would never again have the opportunity to listen to his teachings.

Thereafter Zoroaster gave his first address. The words flowed from his lips spontaneously. He knew that strength from above filled him, and he was happy.

A few weeks passed in this manner. Zoroaster began to teach in the circle assigned to him. At the same time he drew wisdom from eternal sources disclosed to him by the Luminous Helper. Whatever he found he could take to Dshayava, where the wisdom was further deepened.

Hand in hand with the inner growth came the outward perfecting. He had acquired the best of etiquette. His manner had become poised, and pleasantly harmonious. The more he forgot himself, the less his fiery nature could break through.

One morning while he was praying, the stone which he wore round his neck fell to the ground. He was greatly alarmed. Had he neglected something? While re-assembling the loose links of the chain he thought hard.

Suddenly he knew: he had not been to see the hermit who was awaiting him!

When he asked Hafiz to let him ride out the Prince acceded gladly, he had long since been expecting the request.

Trotter carried him towards the forest. Only then did Zoroaster realise that he knew neither the way nor the direction. When he had visited the hermit before he had set out from a completely different place.

So he called again for the helpful little ones, and sure enough a host of them appeared.

One of their number undertook to get a message to Dshayava, the others promised to guide him. But he should give them some clue. He told them that from the Prince's camp he had been able to see the ruins of the Castle of Ara-Masdah.

Now they knew exactly. They guided him cheerfully over a broad plain, then slowly upwards towards the mountains.

After three days he had reached his destination, the hut lay before him.

He leapt from his horse, leaving Trotter to seek the shelter. His heart pounded, now he would be allowed to hear the message that the old man had for him.

His knock at the door died away unanswered. No one came to open it for him. Perhaps the old man had gone to fetch water? Zoroaster dared not enter, and sat down outside on the stone where he had sat once before.

Hour after hour passed, no hermit appeared. Had the old man died?

Now he who until a few days before had completely forgotten his promise, was seized with remorse. How had it been possible? He had been so near the hermit when he himself was still living in his hut. Would he now never be allowed to hear the message which the old man had for him?

The day passed, so did the night. Zoroaster had besought his Luminous Helper to tell him what he should do. He received no answer.

Then in the light of the rising sun, he ventured to open the door and enter the hut. There, stretched out on the couch, as though asleep, lay the old man. His countenance was suffused with peace, heavenly peace. The gaunt hands were clasped across his breast. He could have been gone two days at most; his earthly covering was intact.

Zoroaster went down on his knees and prayed. Then he began to lament quietly:

"If only I had come earlier, my father. Now I could not be near you in your last hours, and I shall not receive the message."

"Take heart," it was the voice of the aged man, speaking quietly. "I knew that you would come, and I was permitted to wait for you before setting forth on my upward path."

Beside the couch stood the hermit. It was the same figure as that of the lifeless body on the couch, but it was transparent and luminous, and seemed to be in continuous gentle motion.

The voice Zoroaster heard did not come from it. He seemed to hear it within his own inner being. Now it went on:

"If you would do me a kindness, then bury my body in the soft earth, beside the hut. It will not be hard work. But I will pass on to you the message that I have for you:

"No human being lives but once on earth! You must know that, Forerunner, for it is important. We come again and again until we have learned to be as we must be if Ahuramazda is to suffer us in His Eternal Realms.

"This is the key to the understanding of all earthly life! I entrust it to you, as I once received it from luminous hands.

"Had you come when I was still in my earthly body, I would have told you more about it. But now I see that it is better for you to immerse yourself in this new knowledge, and with help from above to find what you still need to learn.

"But I may tell you one more thing: The Saoshyant too was on earth once before. Reflect on that as well!"

The figure appeared to fade away quietly. Zoroaster, still unable to grasp the abundance of what he had just received, said a fervent prayer of gratitude. He buried the hermit lovingly in the grave which he had adorned with greenery, then he prayed and made his way back to the hut. It still seemed completely filled with the identity of its former occupant.

Suddenly he heard the voice of the Luminous Helper:

"Would you not like to live in his hut for a little while? It will give him joy and be of benefit to you. You will find so many good thoughts here that have emanated from him. They can help you onwards. Stay here!"

The suggestion appealed to Zoroaster. And knowing that Hafiz would be in agreement with it, he did not hesitate to stay.

Not until the following day was he able to grasp what the old man had entrusted to him. Although he did not yet understand its deeper meaning, he could recall the words.

First he remembered the words concerning the Helper. The Saoshyant had been on earth once before? But no one knew of it. The Zoroaster had never heard about it! Had He been here for the Judgment?

Again he called to his Luminous Helper who with understanding words helped to clarify for Zoroaster what he had been permitted to hear.

He began with the hermit's first words. All human beings come to earth repeatedly in order to work their way upwards. As he would to a pupil, the helper gave Zoroaster the task to consider first of all why man is on earth.

Then he asked whether the repeated earth-lives are a punishment or a grace.

"A punishment of course," Zoroaster was about to answer, but he remembered that he never again wished to speak without prior reflection.

And as he reflected his eyes were opened to the Divine Grace which lies in the opportunity bestowed on human beings to improve what they have done wrong in one life and to compensate for what they have formerly neglected.

When Zoroaster had come thus far, wonderful vistas were opened to him of Ahuramasda's adamantine Laws, but also of His infinite Mercy. And out of this Mercy He had sent His Son as the Helper and World Judge.

"How do you picture the coming of the Saoshyant?" the Luminous One asked.

"He will descend as the Radiant Hero," Zoroaster cried out with enthusiasm. "Only in this way can I picture the World Judge."

The Luminous One fell silent. In this silence Zoroaster perceived that his answer had not been right.

He reflected. Had he not been shown a Child Who grew up on earth? Was the Saoshyant, the Son of God, to be born as a child? The Luminous One had disappeared. Zoroaster was left alone with his thoughts.

"Oh, Little Child, what a sacrifice Thou bringest us!" he said, deeply moved. "Holy art Thou, and Thou dost forsake Thy Heavenly Home to become man!"

Yes, the Son of God must become man in order to help humanity.

"O, happy the mother who may fashion Thy body for Thee!"

No sooner had Zoroaster thought this than it came to him in a flash: the mother! That was indeed the key to the great mystery! The Son of God had been on earth once before as the son of Ara-Masdah, of the Prince.

He would come again; thus Prince Ara-Masdah's son would come again, the Son of Ahuramazda, of God!

How wonderful it was beyond all understanding! Again and again Zoroaster had to tell himself. Then all at once he also understood the words of the little ones: the Heir would come to claim the treasures of Ara-Masdah's Palace.

The Heir was none other than the Saoshyant!

This knowledge made Zoroaster so immeasurably happy that he felt urged to speak with someone about it. He called for the Luminous Helper, who came and said:

"Now you have found what seemed like a mystery to you for so long. Believe me, in this way one thing after another will be resolved, if you truly seek and do not drag your paltry human knowledge into it.

"You must absorb in purity from above what you are permitted to receive. And though you must bear it within you for years without understanding, one day the solution will present itself. And it is always quite simple. Take that as unshakeable knowledge from this experience.

"What you have now been permitted to learn about the Saoshyant, keep to yourself for the time being. It is still too early to proclaim it to mankind.

"You may speak of it to Dshayava. It is time for you to return to him. Set out tomorrow to ride home. The little ones will safely guide you."

Zoroaster did as he was bidden and arrived in the capital a few days later.

"Sublime knowledge has been granted you, my son," Dshayava greeted him. "Ahuramazda has imprinted a Luminous Sign on your forehead as proof that you are deemed worthy to proclaim Him."

With joy the Zoroaster recounted what he had experienced, what he had heard and learned. Deeply happy, the venerable man listened.

"You bring me much, my son, I thank you for it."

Hafiz heard only a part of what had enriched Zoroaster inwardly, but he did not ask for more. He knew that there were things which the Forerunner, at best, could discuss only with as lofty a spirit as Dshayava.

Zoroaster resumed his talks, but everyone in the audience perceived that something new had been added. He found new words, he was better able to convey what to human eyes is invisible. His words were profound; they inspired enthusiasm. People forgot his youth and listened with their souls.

There was not a single one at the court who did not absorb with joy what Zoroaster brought.

But the Forerunner had given up asking inwardly when his task might begin. With complete trust he relied upon being shown the right moment. He only prayed that he would recognise the signal when it came.

But when that moment arrived, it was in such a powerful manner as could never have been conceived by human thought.

THAT YEAR the rainy season would not end. In Persia grain and fruit spoiled. At last a blue sky once more smiled upon the earth which had been turned into a swamp. But now the rays of the sun grew so intense that weak plants were scorched, cattle collapsed and human beings were parched with heat.

There had been no such disaster in living memory.

Some bore the affliction with dull submission, others gave agonised voice to their lamentations. Here and there people cursed Mithra who was held to blame for everything.

Then still another calamity occurred in the form of an illness. It seized the quietly despairing and those with curses on their lips, nor did it spare those who submitted indifferently.

Only the capital of the Prince was spared, but this was not yet known in the realm. People were too preoccupied with themselves to ask after others.

The blue sky had turned a leaden grey, it hung heavily over the earth. The tormented people looked up anxiously: what else was to come now?

Then in the night a roaring was heard as of boulders tearing loose in the mountains and rumbling down to the valley. Thunderous crashing and bursting filled the air.

All of a sudden the ground began to sway.

Terror-stricken, the people rushed out into the open. Here it was almost worse. Trees bowed; the next moment they were ripped out, roots and all, and whirled through the air. Vayn had unloosed all the winds so that they should disport themselves amid the general destruction.

In many places across the land buildings collapsed, burying people beneath their ruins. No one thought of searching for them. Each tried to save himself. But where was there safety?

People who had fled into caves were forced to experience the shifting of the mountains from behind, so that the caves were compressed as though they had never existed.

Sand-storms ravaged fertile regions. The sea hurled itself greedily onto the land, dragging off whole sections of it.

Then even the blasphemers fell silent. A wail of woe coursed through the vast realm.

"Woe betide us, the earth is coming to an end! The wrath of Ahuramazda is upon us!"

For three nights and as many days it raged, roared and surged. Terrible news came from the mountains, brought by those fleeing from there to the plains:

"One of the tall mountains is burning! It spurts forth rocks and fire. Its fumes stifle every breath."

And of all the horror the city of Prince Hafiz experienced almost nothing. Two buildings collapsed, a few people lost their lives. That was all.

"Truly," said Hafiz with fervent gratitude, "we feel that the Forerunner dwells among us."

At last, during the fourth night, the thrusting, convulsing earth settled down. People could hardly believe that they were able to walk safely again. The howling of the winds died away. Slowly, very slowly, the raging of the elements subsided.

94

That night the praying Zoroaster heard the mighty Voice, Which he had been permitted to hear once before:

"Forerunner, prepare thyself! The time is come for thee to begin thy work. Ahuramazda's servants have cleared the path to the souls for thee.

"With a gentle hand put fresh heart into the bruised, the battered, the broken, and bring them tidings of the Saoshyant Who will come to show erring mankind the way upwards again.

"Teach them to recognise that they were following wrong paths. Show them that all that came to pass was of their own doing. Let them experience true remorse.

"My servant art thou, Forerunner. My Power will be with thee!"

Zoroaster knelt in joyful humility, happy that he was permitted to hear the Voice that resounded within him day and night, in waking and in sleeping.

In the morning he spoke with Dshayava. He was still unsure as to how he would begin. Then Prince Hafiz entered the room:

"I want to travel over the whole of my realm, to see where help is needed, and to bring relief where I can."

"May I ride with you part of the way?" Zoroaster asked.

Instantly he realised that this was his new path. The Prince gladly consented. Let the wise man travel with him. He could bring more to human beings than simply material things.

All was soon in readiness for the departure. Trotter was to remain behind this time. A strong white steed called "Ray" was to carry the Forerunner, who was given two servants to escort him, together with horses and pack-animals.

With this small troop he joined the retinue of the Prince.

THE PRINCE INTENDED to visit first those who had suffered the greatest damage. Thus they rode past much destruction and sorrow, reserving aid until later.

But the Prince could not go as far as he planned. After two days' journey they had seen too much horror in the realm. No sensitive heart could pass it by.

Untiringly the Zoroaster helped with all that could be done to alleviate the suffering. No word passed his lips so long as the souls were still closed with fear and dread.

Only when Prince Hafiz and his retinue rode on, in order to bestow the same acts of kindness on others, – only then did the Forerunner consider that his time had come.

The wounded had been laid in a hastily erected, tent-like structure. Zoroaster had undertaken to wash their wounds, lay herbs on them, and look after the people.

In this way he gained the confidence of all. They thanked him for his solicitude, and poured out their troubles to him. As yet they could think of nothing else.

He listened patiently to them, only occasionally interjecting a word. And these words, sparingly used, which always carried a definite message, made an impression.

People grew accustomed to hearing his words, and reflecting upon them. Every day some still died, at times not even the most severely wounded. But slowly the condition of the others improved.

Gradually they began to move, to walk and to look for the things that had once belonged to them. And often they found more than they expected. Above all they saw that the Prince's men had erected quite a number of dwelling places; others, less severely damaged, had been repaired. Every convalescent would find a home again.

It gave them cause to praise the wise provisions made by the Prince as well as his great kindness.

Zoroaster, however, guided their thoughts to Him on Whose behalf the Prince had acted. He caused them to consider how gravely they had offended against Ahuramazda, that the great punishment had struck them justly, and that they themselves were to blame for it all.

Relentlessly, he urged this upon their souls; and they were so shaken that they absorbed the words.

Zoroaster had learned a great deal at this first scene of his activity. Above all he had come to realise that silence can often make a deeper impression than a great number of words. For him silence had become a habit during his ten years of solitude.

Moreover, he now knew he must never begin by proclaiming the Helper at once.

First through inner or outer experiencing the souls must be brought to the conviction that they needed a Helper. Only then could he begin to speak to them of the Saoshyant.

This restraint was difficult for Zoroaster. He was so filled with Him Whom he was allowed to proclaim that he would have much preferred to speak only of Him.

After some time he left the people whom he had helped to recover, and rode on in the direction indicated to him by Hafiz.

Wherever he came now, he found the work of clearing up and improvement already done. He found people who were trying, as best they could, to make do with what was left to them.

It was much easier to speak with these people. They were so dejected and despondent, and therefore could be readily convinced that they alone were responsible. Here the gift of seeing thoughts stood him in good stead. He could tell people exactly what they needed according to their thoughts.

It was not long before they began to regard him as a sage, a seer; devoutly they listened to what he proclaimed. Their souls opened wide when he spoke of the coming Helper.

His listeners were ecstatic when they heard him thus bearing witness from the very depths of his soul. Inspired as he himself was, he inspired all the others as well.

Now the tidings of his coming and his work even went before him to the next village. People strained to meet him without delay, so that they could hear about the Eternal One of Whom he spoke.

Of course, there were always those who had misgivings about whether the Helper would come in time for them to benefit. The Forerunner could not indicate *when* the longed-for Helper would descend to the earth.

But of what use to them was a Helper Who would perhaps not appear until after three or four generations? In that case they need not exert themselves to live aright.

Whenever Zoroaster encountered such thinking, he almost despaired. How was it possible not to see that each one must do his utmost to prevent the earth from sliding still deeper into the mire! It depended upon every human being! He spared no pains over those who were so half-hearted.

Others again did not even ask about a Helper.

"We have not much longer to live; we can bear whatever is inflicted upon us for the short time that remains. We do not need a Helper."

Wherever Zoroaster encountered such objections, he found it difficult to restrain the ardour within him. Then he would ask what it was that people expected after their death.

Usually the answer was:

"Nothing. We will perish like the flowers in the gardens."

Only a few spoke of Garodemana, which they hoped to enter, although they could form no idea of it.

Then the Zoroaster realised that he must begin at the beginning. He must speak of Anramainyu and his evil companions.

The manner in which this message was received showed the Forerunner that this was the right way. Patiently and tirelessly he instructed the people before the new message could be proclaimed to them.

He stayed for a long time in some places, for there was much work to be done. His two servants had been trained as his assistants, and had long since been teaching with him, but they only spoke of that which should have been familiar to all. They were not to speak of anything new.

As before, the little helpers were his best friends wherever he stayed. They showed him the way to new villages whenever he wished to move on. The manner in which his supplies and the monies received from Hafiz had dwindled away showed that he had been travelling for years.

He felt like a sower who wishes to scatter seed, but must first prepare the soil.

His journey from village to village was still like a joyful procession. People were sorry to see him depart; with joy and expectation they came from afar to meet him.

He did not tell them that he was the promised Zoroaster. Though he called himself by that name, they took it simply to be his name and gave the matter no more thought.

THEN ONE DAY HE returned to a region which he had visited some years before. It was one of those in which he had worked after the great upheavals of the earth. He found the people in a state of eager anticipation. Their fields were uncultivated, their huts had fallen into disrepair, yet an extraordinary joyfulness animated them all.

When they recognised him, they crowded about him.

"Sire, we have good news for you! The promised Zoroaster has visited us. He has brought us tidings that the Saoshyant will come this very year. He has told us that we must prepare ourselves in joy, for he will take us all with him to Garodemana. We are to refrain from any work that is not absolutely essential. We should become accustomed to a life in joy and happiness even down here, so that we can tolerate the bliss up above!"

Horrified, Zoroaster heard the news. What could he possibly say in reply? Instead of answering he raised his hands and prayed aloud, crying out to Ahuramazda in his need:

"Ahuramazda, Lord of Heaven and of Earth! Behold the misled people! Have mercy upon them; for I can do nothing. Another has sown where I prepared the soil. The evil seed has sprung up. The harvest will bring a curse. Ahuramazda, I beseech Thee for Thy help!"

As though paralysed, the people heard the prayer. It made a deep impression on them.

They reflected. What if indeed a false Forerunner had visited them? But how were they to know? It was easier for them now to continue as they had begun.

If the Saoshyant were not to come this year, they would obviously be in trouble, for they simply had not provided for the future. They had slaughtered their cattle, their fields lay fallow. But they must not think of that. It would be too terrible.

Zoroaster tried to speak with individual people, realising that it would be impossible to obtain a hearing before all of them. But his efforts were in vain.

So for the time being he gave up any attempt to influence them, and tried to pursue the false Zoroaster as quickly as he could on horseback.

Wherever he came on this ride, he found the same joyful intoxication, the same indolence, the same pernicious sensuality, which in some places was degenerating into complete debauchery. The false Zoroaster had allowed them to do anything they lusted after or desired.

In order to catch up with the evil one as swiftly as possible, Zoroaster no longer stopped anywhere. But on his way he prayed that he might find the right words to eliminate him, that he might show himself worthy of his Lord.

Often his Luminous Helper approached him and admonished him to be patient.

"Why has Ahuramazda permitted this?" Zoroaster once cried in despair.

Solemnly the Luminous One rejoined:

"It is not for you to enquire into this. All that God permits has its purpose. You will yet come to recognise it."

Again Zoroaster came to a village where the joyful message was given to him. But he could not contain himself and asked:

"How do you know, you people, that he who has told you this is the true Zoroaster? Behold, I also am a Forerunner!"

But the people laughed, saying:

"You were already here before and spoke with us about the gods, but you never told us that you are the Zoroaster. The other man declared himself openly. That is also why we believe him."

Icy cold coursed through Zoroaster.

Was it again his fault that it had been easy for the impostor? He had been reluctant to declare his name and the nature of his work to the people. If it had been modesty, then it was uncalled-for. He realised that now. He should have introduced himself as the servant of His Lord.

He was so dejected that he rode on in silence. After a time, however, he called for the Luminous One, to tell him everything. To no avail. He must himself breach the wall which his thoughts were about to erect before him.

In the beginning, it was definitely right for him to speak to the people only of the gods. But then he should have said:

"You know that a Forerunner was promised, who is to proclaim the Saoshyant. I am this Zoroaster! God has granted me this grace."

It had not required this declaration to make them believe. But now the other man, who had usurped Zoroaster's office, had made false use of the name to supplant the nameless one. Now he knew all at once what he should have done. But it was too late!

Too late? No, never! And even if he had to fight Anramainyu himself, he would take up the battle and triumph in the Power of the Supreme God.

A new experience, a deep pain and a fresh strengthening for the task!

He had paid no attention to the road, when suddenly Ray reared up. Before him stood a little helper who was eagerly pointing in another direction. Zoroaster understood that the impostor had changed course.

Before long the true Forerunner would be face to face with the false one.

"He has heard of you," the little one said with an air of importance. "He is afraid; for everywhere and always the Darkness fears the Light. He wants to avoid an encounter."

Then Zoroaster laughed again for the first time in a long while. And this laughter freed him from invisible bonds that had fettered and oppressed him. He was almost looking forward to the encounter.

A fervent prayer to Ahuramazda, an urgent entreaty to the Luminous One to stand by him, then he was prepared to rush on with fresh courage. But the little one raised his brown hand:

"And you forget us?" he asked reproachfully. "You will need us in order to protect yourself against attacks by the impostor. Do not ignore us and our help."

Zoroaster sincerely averred that he had never doubted the willingness of the little ones. How often had he called for them, how often had they helped him! Now he was allowed to ride on.

On the way he told the two servants of the event that was awaiting them. For a long time now they had been dissatisfied with their master because he had not taken a stand and resisted the lies.

Now they understood why he had hesitated. He wanted to trample the serpent's head before seeking to heal the damage it had caused.

They approached the village, but no one came to meet them, as had been the case everywhere so far. When they reached the huts, there was not a soul in sight.

"Where are they all?" Zoroaster muttered to himself.

Instantly, a few little helpers stood before him and pointed eagerly to one of the largest structures.

Zoroaster dismounted and bade the servants do likewise.

"The people here do not seem to be well-disposed towards us," he said. "One of you must stay with the animals, the other may come with me."

Then one of the servants reminded him that he had changed direction on the way, so that the people of another village were now expecting him, while those here knew nothing of his coming. This was by no means a sign of hostility.

Loud shouts came from the indicated building; the sound was joyful, but to Zoroaster's ears there was an evil tone intermingled in it. Without a moment's hesitation he opened the door which had been left ajar and entered.

A few heads turned in his direction, but in the semi-darkness he was not recognised. He was probably assumed to be a latecomer; no one paid any attention to him.

In the centre of the crowd, on an elevation, – perhaps a large stone covered with a cloth – stood a man talking persuasively to the people in a loud overbearing manner.

Of the same age as Zoroaster, he also bore a certain resemblance to him. His clothing was exceedingly magnificent. Mithra's emblem was in gold embroidery on front and back. Behind him stood two men holding out an embroidered cloth.

Now the speaker raised his hand and pointed to the emblem that adorned the cloth.

"Behold," he shouted, "proof of my identity. This is the sign of the Saoshyant! I am His Forerunner. I am allowed to proclaim to you that He will come within the next few months to lead those deserving of it to Garodemana."

A sigh of happiness went through the room. They all thought of themselves as having earned the distinction. But they were alarmed when a clear, calm voice asked:

"And who deserves it?"

Instead of answering the speaker called out:

"I speak here! Who dares to interrupt me?"

Without a moment's thought, Zoroaster answered in a voice that resounded like the ring of metal over the gathering:

"The true Zoroaster!"

The words had the effect of lightning striking the gathering. Without knowing why, the people shrieked. It was as if something inexplicable were laying hold of them. This they attributed to the stranger and turned against him.

But he remained standing quietly, and the assailants fell back. A delicate radiance surrounded him like a luminous mist. No one dared to touch him. But the tumult increased. The false Zoroaster incited the men to attack him.

Again Zoroaster raised his voice, drowning the uproar:

"You men, look at me! You know me. I came to you at the behest of Ahuramazda, to help you in your great affliction. Do you no longer know me?"

Yes, they knew him. One after the other admitted it. They were ashamed that they had tried to harm their benefactor.

An old man cried aloud:

"You are he who awakened the longing for the Saoshyant in us. Without your teachings we could never have understood the glad tidings brought to us by the Forerunner today."

"How do you know that *he* is the Forerunner?" Zoroaster asked.

"He says so, Master," they cried out happily.

"And therefore you believe him? Look at me. I, whom you know, I say to you that *I* am the Zoroaster, the Servant of the Saoshyant! Now it is my word against his. Whom do you believe?"

Confused, the men looked at one another. There stood he whom they knew, whom they loved, whom they had learned to trust. He was no liar, that they knew. But the other had the insignia of Ahuramazda! It was a painful conflict into which their happiness had been transformed!

Before any of them could think clearly, the man who was still standing on the elevation began to speak.

In contrast to Zoroaster's calm voice, his words were impetuous; he shouted them too loudly.

103

"Do not let yourselves be deceived by one who only wants to confuse you! What he did for you before would also have been done by any other servant of the Prince. He was in the service of Hafiz, and was paid for his work. Hence you owe him no special gratitude.

"If he were the Zoroaster, he would already have told you so at that time!"

Oh, this ill-fated silence! Zoroaster could no longer even understand himself.

There was now an obvious split among the men. A few believed Zoroaster, the others inclined towards the impostor. What he said sounded so reasonable and convincing.

One of the older men addressed himself to the Forerunner:

"Master, this man here says that the Saoshyant will come in a few months' time. But you told us that you did not know the time of His coming. I see the matter as follows:

"When a lord wishes to convey a message, he first sends one servant to deliver it in general terms. After some time, he then sends the second servant so that he can supplement and complete it. The same will apply here as well. You will both be servants of Ahuramazda, sent to proclaim the Helper."

The wisdom of these words met with unanimous approval. It was a splendid way out of a situation which was not pleasant for anyone. The impostor laughed.

"You have spoken well, old man. It is obvious that he who knows how to make good use of his intellect is always at an advantage."

Zoroaster stood by, deeply shaken. He alone could not prevail against so much cunning. But inwardly he prayed for help. While he was to blame for the calamity, it did not concern him personally, it concerned the Sacred Cause of Ahuramazda. God would send him help.

It came from an unexpected quarter. Zoroaster's otherwise so quiet servant was angered on behalf of the Sacred Cause. And this anger made him eloquent. Involuntarily, as though impelled by an invisible force, he blurted out:

"What then can your Zoroaster tell us about the Helper? Does he know Him, by Whom he says He has been sent?"

"He has only told us that the Saoshyant will come and take everyone with Him to Garodemana."

"All right, let him do so now! I shall be the first to bow to him if what he proclaims is true."

The servant, whom nobody recognised, spoke in a brisk and lively tone. They did not realise that he had come with Zoroaster, and thought curiosity had brought him from some other village. The impostor too was misled. Of course, the servant had not intended this misrepresentation.

"The man who calls himself Forerunner is to leave the room before I speak," the impostor demanded.

That was ill-advised. Now the listeners called out:

"If you are both servants of the same Lord, then he may safely hear what you have to say. It will not be unfamiliar to him."

That being the general view, the man dared not raise any objections. He assumed a defiant attitude and began:

"You men, listen! I am to tell you of the Promised One. He is a great and noble lord who will appear among you like a prince. He is not a stranger to you, for he is of your blood. He is a Son of your Prince Ara-Masdah, as was already prophesied long ago."

The people grew restless. Zoroaster remained silent. He knew that he must await the right moment, and that it would be shown to him from On High. "Is this new to you, you men? I thought the prophecy to be general knowledge. A son of your Prince will come. No one knows the people as well as one who is of the same race. He will lead you to bliss. He will guide you into the eternal gardens.

"And therefore I say to you: prepare yourselves for his coming! He will lead you to joy, even now you should experience joy at the prospect of his coming. Leave behind everything that is disagreeable or wearisome to you. Forget everything that troubles or pains you. Abandon all work. You need no longer complete it.

"Before the harvest which you are now about to sow could ripen the Promised One will be in your midst. Then the tools will drop from your hands. With him you will be allowed to enter into eternal joys."

He fell silent. Nothing more came to his mind that he might still have added without too blatantly compromising himself before Zoroaster.

Then the latter broke his silence:

"You men, now hear me also. What that man has told you is a mixture of prophecy wrongly understood, and falsehood!"

The impostor wished to defend himself, but a man called out to him:

"Be silent! This man let you speak until you were satisfied. And what you said was truly of no value."

This caused a few of the listeners to laugh, and their laughter damaged the impostor's standing considerably.

"Continue, Zoroaster," demanded the servant, who stood there as one of the crowd.

"Yes, continue, Forerunner!" the others too called out now. They wanted to hear what he had to say.

And Zoroaster continued: "The Son of Ahuramazda, of the Supreme God, has been promised to you! Out of Divine Mercy the Helper will descend to the earth. In so doing He will leave the Glory of the Seven Heavens. Whether He will come in human guise as a prince, or as a simple man, means nothing at all in relation to the great, the incomprehensible fact that this Sacrifice is made for mankind.

"To the sinking earth, to Creation which was defiled through men's guilt, He will once more bring Light and Truth. But He will also sit in Judgment!

"Men, did you hear that? He will sit in Judgment! Or would that be a God Who would indiscriminately lead the sinners, together with the few good ones, to Garodemana? He will make a careful selection to determine who is worthy of it. Each will reap what he has sown.

"Consider: perhaps you have a neighbour who has deceived you, who deprived you of something that was yours."

Zoroaster could tell clearly by their thoughts that this was the case. Therefore he continued without wavering:

"What do you think: would you deem it right if this sinner were permitted to enter with you into eternal bliss?"

"You are right, Zoroaster," several called out, convinced. "That would be contrary to all justice!"

"And Ahuramazda *is* Justice, for He is God!" Zoroaster cried jubilantly across the audience.

"But He is also Truth! Before Him no falsehood can endure! Do you still remember, impostor, how you came to me when I was still a seeker, and how you told me you were the Zoroaster? A few words sufficed to rout you. A few words will also suffice now.

"As you dare not utter the Holy Name, so also will you not dare to pray to Ahuramazda. If you attempt it nonetheless, well-deserved punishment will strike you!"

"Let him take up the challenge. Let him pray!" the people shouted in a babel of voices.

Most of them were already convinced that he was an impostor. But they wanted to see what would happen.

The false forerunner had flinched. Now he straightened up and said:

"I do not pray on command; to me prayer is too sacred for that!"

Some of the men began to laugh.

"Then *I* will pray!" Zoroaster's clear voice rang calmly through the room.

Where he stood he raised his hands and began:

"Ahuramazda, Thou Eternal, Omnipresent God! Thou seest us even at this moment."

He paused briefly. The words fell like sparks into the agitated souls.

"I thank Thee with all my heart that Thou hast laid upon my tongue the words which bear the power to prove to these men that they almost believed an impostor!

"Deliver us from this servant of Anramainyu, so that the souls may be freed to serve Thee!"

Deep silence reigned in the room, broken here and there by a sigh. Now there were no longer any doubters.

But as the impostor was about to step down from the stone to leave the room, his eyes became glassy. They stared fixedly at one point, then from his lips broke forth the words:

"Take away the Cross, I cannot look at it! It torments me."

All turned towards the place to which he was pointing. All thought they saw the golden, radiant Cross that seemed to hover above Zoroaster.

He was deeply moved.

107

"O Thou Radiant Hero, Thy Sign!" he called out in jubilation. But the other man groaned:

"Take away the Cross, it is killing me!"

He staggered and clutched his heart, then fell down lifeless at the feet of those standing nearest to him. The excitement was indescribable.

Zoroaster went outside, leaving it to the men to remove the dead body. Let them place it on one of the towers of silence – every fair-sized village had one nearby – to feed the giant black birds.

The fervent gratitude within him ascended like a prayer. It was followed by a slight feeling of disappointment. The impostor had been a man of flesh and blood, while he had thought himself to be facing an evil spirit, perhaps even Anramainyu himself.

But this disappointment passed quickly in the great feeling of gratitude and happiness. How easy the victory had been made for him. How wondrously God had helped!

His servant came to him:

"Zoroaster, the men are asking if you would go out into the open air with them, to tell them about Ahuramazda and the Saoshyant. They would not like to invite you into the room where the awful thing happened. But their wish to hear comes from a great, true longing."

The Forerunner acceded to the request.

He spoke joyfully. He did not deny that he had been guilty of not revealing his lofty task when he first taught them. But he also reproved them severely for so naïvely falling prey to an impostor.

And with that he had won their hearts completely. They felt a current from him to them, even though they were not really conscious of it. It was there, and made for an easy understanding. It seemed as though he knew in advance what they would ask. And his answers always gave rise to fresh questions within them. It was glorious work!

Murza, the servant who had suddenly begun to speak, developed into a useful helper for Zoroaster. In following his inner voice, which drove him to speak at a critical moment, Murza had established a connection upwards which always remained intact.

He was clearly guided, though in a completely different way from Zoroaster. With Murza everything was oriented more towards the earthly, the practical. But for this very reason he was a valuable complement to the Forerunner.

He it was who sought to guide the most unresponsive of the souls, by patiently telling them the same thing every day.

Soon he would observe a glimmer of recognition, would fan it into a small flame and then move on a step further. What they had once grasped was then permanently engrained in the souls so laboriously won.

Thus a rich harvest-time of glorious development blossomed forth from the disaster. But it was suddenly evident to Zoroaster that he must tear himself away from here in order to obliterate the traces of the impostor's activity in the other regions also.

He said so to the men, and they understood. Indeed one of them thought further.

"The impostor is dead," he said. "If you come now to one of the villages that he induced to turn to wickedness, as was intended for us, they will prefer to persist in their wicked ways rather than believe you.

"I think several of us should go a few days ahead of you, and let it be known what happened here. After all, we saw how Ahuramazda, the Eternal God Himself, punished the impostor."

Everyone thought it a good idea. The speaker chose who were to accompany him: poor and rich, old and young, so that there should be one from every station in life to testify.

Zoroaster, however, felt it was time for him to leave. Almost reluctantly he remained for the few days they had agreed upon; then he rode after them with Murza and the other servant.

GREAT joy inspired Zoroaster, for had he not been permitted to experience clearly how Ahuramazda's Goodness turns to best advantage even the failings of human stupidity. And this joy caused him to look forward courageously and confidently to the difficulties that lay ahead of him.

Indeed, he had not imagined that things would be all that difficult!

It had been agreed that the messengers should only declare and testify to their experiences; thereafter they were to ride on. They did not feel mature enough to teach. That they would leave to the Forerunner and

Murza. Thus these two found none of the messengers who had been sent ahead in the next village they visited. The inhabitants were like a flock that has been abandoned. They ran about lamenting and complaining. Everywhere they stood in groups, discussing the terrible calamity.

They were in no doubt that what the messengers had told them was true. The best among them had long since already spoken in searing words against the prevailing spread of immorality, indolence and dishonesty.

It had become ever clearer to them that a forerunner who led humanity on such paths could not be the right one. Now that they heard their view confirmed, they began to protest vigorously. But they could not prevail.

The people were utterly despondent.

"Everything is over. We can no longer change!" some cried, while others said: "Harvest and cattle are lost. We have to face the most dreadful deprivation. Let us enjoy the time still left to us. Afterwards, come what must."

To these the Forerunner came not as the bringer of heavenly joy that he actually was, but as a herald of the greatest horror. When he tried to speak they screamed at him:

"Oh, be quiet! We do not want to hear what you have to say. Your words only increase our torment." Or:

"Be silent! Do not take what little we have left; we don't want to hear anything!"

So Zoroaster began to seek out those whose thoughts he perceived to be good. Those he gathered around him, spoke to them, bore witness, but above all he prayed with them for the many misguided people. And as he prayed his eyes were opened to see that here earthly help must come first.

A voice spoke to him:

"Zoroaster, imagine that you find a man who has had a quarrel with another. He is bleeding from many wounds; his life in his enfeebled condition no longer means anything to him. Will you first tell him how shameful it is to quarrel? Will you promise him that if he never again quarrels, he will no longer suffer injury?"

Zoroaster had understood. He told the men who were always around him to summon the others; he would try to alleviate their need.

And they all came, although they feared he would not be able to help them. But he asked how long their fields had already lain fallow. "Since the last harvest," they replied.

"Then something can still be done about it, men," the Forerunner shouted joyfully. "Send to the village from which I have just come, and ask for able-bodied men to come to your aid without delay. Together with them, if we all work hard, we can prepare the fields and quickly sow the seed. In that way we shall still be in time for the second harvest. That is better than having nothing at all."

They stared at him in disbelief:

"Do you think the strangers will help us? Why should they?"

"Out of gratitude that they were spared from a similar fate," said Zoroaster earnestly.

Then he sent Murza and one of the older men from that village, so that the people would know at once that the message came from him.

The work began immediately. Every man wanted to make for his own field. Zoroaster would not have it. After he had viewed all the land to be tilled, he commanded that the work be done systematically, and in common.

These thoughts came to him from above, to him who had no knowledge of agriculture. He felt as though someone were continually walking beside him, not only telling him what had to be done, but showing him the best way to proceed, so that the people could be shown how to make the most rapid headway.

They complied, at first so as not to drive off this last rescuer by their opposition, although they grumbled inwardly. Gradually however they understood what he meant, and perceived the rightness of his instructions.

Now the requested helpers also appeared! Many men had arrived. With the joy that inspired them they accomplished more than the usual amount of work. Their example spurred on the weary, the indolent, who had already forgotten how to work.

Over the fields the joyful singing which the new arrivals had brought with them rang out. It was a measured sounding of high and low notes which made the work swing rhythmically. The others soon learned it, and noticed how happy it made them. Weariness fell away from them.

And in the evenings the helpers told again and again of the great happening in their village. Thus it was that in those other souls too Zoroaster now found soil prepared for the seed from above which he was permitted to sow.

When under the starry sky of evening he lifted up his heart to Ahuramazda, his prayer was totally praise and gratitude.

"O Thou Great, Almighty, All-Merciful God! How glorious is all this! How Thou clearest paths where human eyes no longer find a way. How Thou helpest beyond all comprehension!"

And from these words, coming spontaneously to his lips always in the same way, a song was formed, which he taught the men.

It was a glorification of Ahuramazda; and they were the first verses which people in that region sang. They loved their "song" and often sang it at work.

But Zoroaster had not only taken care of the fields. He had also sent forth men for whom the work in the fields was too arduous, to buy young cattle in the neighbourhood.

For this purpose everyone had to contribute money. Accordingly the cattle were common property. Thus it was assured that even the poorer people would not be without milk, nor later without meat and hides.

Their possessions could then gradually increase, if the people continued to act sensibly.

When the fields had been cultivated and allotted to their former owners, the sowing could begin.

Then Zoroaster felt impelled to go to others in distress. He knew that his messengers had already been at work. But the most difficult task was yet to come.

He told the men that he would probably find still greater misery there, for naturally the fields had been lying fallow even longer. Then he fell silent and looked around him expectantly.

And the people understood his silent question. From both villages a number of men, who considered themselves dispensable at home for the time being, volunteered to go with him and do for others what had been done for them.

"I am glad that you have understood me without my asking," said the

112

Forerunner. "Only now do I see that the heavenly seed has sprung up in your hearts."

He set out with an imposing troop of helpers. The men went on foot, he rode ahead with his companions. It was better that way, so that the fearful people would not reject those who were coming to their aid as extra mouths to feed.

The next village, which was more than a day's journey from the last one, presented a picture of desolation. Huts had caved in, filth was everywhere. Even the dead had no longer been carried into the mountains. The starving people felt too weak to undertake the task.

They stared apathetically into space. It was as though the light of understanding had been extinguished in all of them. How could that be!

Zoroaster tried to calculate how much time had passed since he last came this way. About two years had gone by! And in two years such devastation!

If nothing else showed that the teachings of the impostor came of evil, this must convince the people. But they had sunk too low; even for this they lacked understanding.

What was Zoroaster to do? To give effective help here would require precious months, during which time he would deprive others. Should he leave these degenerate people to their own devices?

In the evening he brought his distress before Ahuramazda, with child-like faith and trust:

"O Lord, I no longer know what I should do. But Thou knowest. Show me Thy Will, and I will follow It."

In the morning he knew what had to be done. The helpers were approaching. He bade them set up a kind of camp on the outskirts of the village, so that at least they would not have to be in contact with the inhabitants during the night. Then he spoke with them.

He pointed out that only through work of the coarsest kind, carried out with untiring patience, was anything still to be saved here. He asked them to undertake this task, while he himself would continue his journey with Murza.

They indicated their willingness at once, only asking for instructions on what they were to do.

Some of them, he advised, should begin to put the fields into usable condition. If there was not time enough for the whole, at least the part with the most fertile soil should be tilled, so that a small harvest might after all be expected this year.

"Ahuramazda, Whom you serve with this work, will bless the labour of your hands, so that the fields will yield richly as never before," he promised them.

The others, however, should attend to the people and the huts. They should see to the removal of the dead bodies and the filth, repair and erect the huts, and urge the people to catch game and gather berries and fruits.

"No one need starve in this fertile region," he said, "unless indolence has debased him."

Thus everything here was arranged in the best possible way, and Zoroaster was about to ride on, when one of the helpers stayed him:

"Master, have you considered that if you leave us all behind, you will have no one for the other regions?"

"Indeed I have thought of that, but here I need every one of you. There is too much work to be done. Ahuramazda will send me helpers, of that I am certain."

Wistfully the men, who were accustomed to his companionship, gazed after him. It would be much more difficult to work here without his presence among them. But they had the song, they had the knowledge of the Saoshyant! Gratitude and joy were the mainspring of their work. Thus they consoled one another.

Zoroaster, however, still in thought with those whom he had just left, was riding towards new suffering.

THE NEXT village, which he remembered as particularly prosperous, lay bleak and deserted. Decay and ruin wherever he looked. But not a soul was to be seen. Had they all abandoned their home? Where had they gone? Had they died?

So he rode on, and now directed his thoughts ahead in intercession. They had to ride round a mountain; three days' journey had to be covered before huts again came into view. Here and there the people who lived in them were also to be found.

The approaching riders were received by a hail of stones. Hard and fast they came, but not a single one found its mark. Hostile shouts were heard:

"Ride on, we do not want to see you. We do not want to hear you! You will tell us only of guilt and failure, of the impostor who misled us all. Where is the saviour whom he promised? Who is to say whether you too are not lying to our faces? There are no gods; there are only evil spirits that plunge men into despair! Help? There is none for us."

At last silence fell. Then Zoroaster began to speak, slowly, emphatically, and so loudly that everyone could understand his words:

"I come to you not with words, you wretched ones, but with deeds. I wish to help you, but first of all your bodies, then your souls!"

They were taken aback, then a few called out:

"How can you help us? What are three people in the face of so much misery? You promise more than you can fulfil. You are liars like the Zoroaster who came before you."

"We do not ask you to believe us simply on the strength of our words, you poor dupes; but give us a chance to prove to you with deeds how serious our intentions are," said Zoroaster, his kindness unchanged.

The warmth and radiance emanating from him made people stop short.

"How do you intend to help us?" they asked, yielding.

"By finding out what your needs are. We have with us provisions which we wish to share with you. That will have to be the first thing."

With these words, life came into the dim eyes. They pressed close around the helper, who reached a quick understanding with his companions.

Then Zoroaster summoned all the inhabitants of the village to an open square where he had proclaimed truths of the faith to them years ago. Only about half of the population remained. He did not ask what had become of the others. It was not difficult to guess their fate.

As his eyes roved over the people, a thought flashed through his mind:

"How many are still lying in the huts?" he asked in a tone which permitted of no evasion.

Then they confessed that, in order to get more for themselves, they had

115

closed up many of their relatives in the huts. They had blocked the doors from outside with heavy boulders. They had helped each other in this.

Although Zoroaster was deeply shocked, he did not reproach them. Their souls had suffered injury in the neglect of their bodies. There was much work to be done here.

He now went from one hut to another, asking for the entrances to be unblocked and those shut up within allowed out. Then he himself entered each of these dwellings, which were choked with dirt, so that he could satisfy himself that now all the inhabitants were actually assembled.

After the people had been counted, Murza and the servant brought food which had been prepared in advance, and Zoroaster distributed it, after first raising his hands in prayer over it, thanking Ahuramazda for His Grace.

Because he himself offered the gifts, none dared look at another to see whether he might have received more. Nor was there any reason for it: the Forerunner had distributed the food with strict fairness.

Some were not able to eat all that had been given them. These were directed by Zoroaster to save the food carefully. Then, however, he summoned all the men once more.

"You have now had enough to eat, through the goodness of the God in Whom you no longer believe. Sleep now in His peace. But soon you must look after yourselves again. We will show you how to do it."

Obediently, like contented animals, they all went to their huts. It was as Zoroaster had intended. He must be alone when he called for his helpers.

He stood in the midst of the fallow fields, overgrown with weeds, and asked:

"You little ones who have promised to help me, and so often have done so, come hither. I need many of you."

Then they emerged from cracks in the fields, from caves and hollows, from forest and meadow. They gathered round him like expectant children who have been promised a new game.

"Behold the fields, you little helpers," Zoroaster indicated. "They have gone to rack and ruin through the fault of men. But it is also my fault that it could come to this. Therefore I must seek to make amends. I must bring help to the best of my ability. Will you help with preparing the fields?"

116

Then life came into the little band. They tumbled head over heels in joyful enthusiasm, scattering in all directions more swiftly than they had come.

Next morning his companions again brought him some of the food, which he distributed among the people after he had prayed.

While they ate he told them that his helpers, the servants of God, wanted to help in preparing the fields for sowing; with their assistance the work should succeed.

The people could not grasp it; a babel of voices arose, talking of miracles, of God's Omnipotence and Goodness.

He seized the moment when their souls were open.

"But now God can in turn expect deeds from you!" Zoroaster admonished earnestly. "Go to your huts and look for tools and seeds. Every grain is precious. After I have prayed you shall scatter the seed in the soil that has been prepared."

They set to work eagerly, and sensed the help of the little ones; one morning the cultivated brown earth lay there awaiting the seed.

Enough grain was found to plant the fields. They worked until far into the night. None was too tired; for with every step they took, they knew that they were going into a better future.

The meal which they shared that evening became a feast. Zoroaster, who had a very beautiful voice, sang with his companions the hymn of Ahuramazda, and the men made an effort to learn it, so that soon a full chorus resounded upwards to the star-studded sky.

Now they felt their weariness; one after the other went to his hut.

Finally the Forerunner and Murza stood alone in the empty square. Then the former servant burst out:

"Master, how inconceivable is the Mercy of Ahuramazda! Remember how we were received here! How these people have changed!"

"Had I not already known how great is the Wise Supreme God, I should have had to learn it here. But now I should like once more to thank the little helpers whose loyalty contributed to making this great happening possible!"

They came, beaming with joy.

"Tell me, you little ones," asked Zoroaster, after thanking them yet again and telling them what they already knew, namely how their activities had affected the lost people, "tell me whether I can do you a loving kindness as well!"

They looked at one another, they seemed to whisper among themselves, then an old elemental being with a long hoary beard stepped forward, and said thoughtfully:

"Certainly you can do us a kindness, which we ask of none other. Pray with us and bless us as you bless human beings."

Joyfully Zoroaster complied.

On the following day the Forerunner again gave out a morning meal. He did not pray immediately, for he wanted to see who would begin to eat without a prayer. Although they stared greedily at the food, none of them took any of it. But some reminded him:

"Will you not pray, Zoroaster?"

After the meal, he suggested that they should go and look for fruits. They should take weapons with them, in case they could bring down some game or other on the way. He himself never killed, but he knew that the meat of an animal was necessary now for these people.

They returned home towards evening richly laden. Everything was distributed, and the preparation left to the women.

Brisk activity began. Forgotten were fatigue and faint-heartedness. Community fires were lit outside the huts for the roasting of the meat.

Then all sat down to the meal, and Zoroaster observed how they tried to pray beforehand, as he had done. Truly, the people were after all not yet as depraved as they had seemed. Here and there he was invited to try a little. He did so to please them. But after the meal he invited all who wished to come to the open square, where he spoke to them of Ahuramazda, of the gods, and of man's ingratitude.

He found willing listeners. It was indeed nothing other than what he had told them in the past, but it went deeper now, after self-incurred misery had loosed their souls.

Behind the men stood the women, who had ventured to join the group. No one turned them away, but no one took any notice of them either. A pair of radiant eyes, hanging as though spellbound on the speaker, attracted his attention.

When the people dispersed to return to their huts, Zoroaster saw this very young woman disappearing into the hut of the tribe's chieftain. She must be his daughter.

For a moment the thought of asking about her occupied him; she seemed to have a seeking soul. But then he discarded the idea. What had he do with women!

Then he seemed to see Madana's eyes turned reproachfully upon him. Madana! She had been a woman. She had guided him, to her he owed the best that his childhood had brought!

But ought he to concern himself with other women on that account? It had always been the custom for women to receive their knowledge, even in matters of belief, from the men, unless they came under the influence of the priestesses in the larger towns. For him there was so much to change and to improve upon, to teach and to proclaim, that he did not wish to initiate anything new in this respect.

But the seeking eyes which had affected him today pursued him into his sleep. They did not desist from asking and enquiring.

In the morning he shook off these thoughts. He wanted to induce the people to renovate their huts.

Now it might have been a good thing if he could have relied on the co-operation of the women, but he avoided that, wishing no further contact with those eyes.

So he directed that those women and children who were able should gather fruits this time. The others were to settle down in the open square. Then he showed the men how to air the huts, remove refuse and clean them.

He himself set to work vigorously with Murza, while the servant saw to the horses and looked after the provisions. The men became very lively in the work of clearing up. They called to each other, comparing notes on who had removed the greatest amount of refuse from his dwelling.

The hut of the tribal chieftain was kept so clean that it aroused general amazement.

"Yadasa was always different from the other girls," the men explained, and then, without being asked, they told Zoroaster what he so much wished to know:

119

Yadasa was the only child of the chieftain, who had wanted an heir and was disappointed with the daughter. Since his wife had died at the birth of the little one, he had entrusted her to the care of a priestess with whom she had stayed until recently.

She had wanted to become a priestess, but her father would not allow it. She was to marry, to bring forth heirs for the old man's extensive possessions. But Yadasa had apparently become proud. She was not so with the women, she helped wherever she could; but the men did not interest her in the least.

Now Zoroaster understood the seeking gaze: she had studied with the priestesses, now she yearned to learn more. He would certainly not exclude her when he spoke next.

But in the evening, when by the light of a fire in the open square he spoke of Anramainyu's attendants, she did not come. And this did not suit him either! Now he had accepted that the woman should listen to him, and she stayed away.

Again the seeking eyes pursued him until he fell asleep. Then it seemed to him that Madana came to his bedside and complained.

"If my sisters have hitherto been passed over by the men, it is no excuse for continuing this injustice, Zoroaster. But to encourage only Yadasa to listen would be wrong.

"You must let all the women and girls come. They will grasp many things more readily than the slow-witted men. Bear in mind that they are the mothers of the rising generation. They can instil a great deal of your present teaching in the young souls. Do not forget the women!"

Whether a promise to Madana had followed her words he no longer remembered. But that made no difference. She had demanded of him something with which he must absolutely comply, although it was not easy for him. He was consoled by the thought that he would await the right moment. Surely he could not suddenly invite the women to come. What would the men think of it?

The day still brought plenty of work in the huts. Many a day would yet pass before all was set to rights again. But there was no need for him to extend his stay on that account. What kept him was the proclamation of the Saoshyant, with which he had not yet begun.

That evening the longed-for rain began to fall, so that they could not assemble in the square. But the wet weather refreshed them all, and helped the seed to germinate. Never before had the fields sprung up so rapidly. It was as though a green haze were spread over them when the sun sparkled in the raindrops after this warm, rainy night. But that night had also awakened something in Zoroaster's soul. He had stretched out on his bed with some relief, for the rain had prevented him from making a decision about the women. Perhaps tomorrow he would know how to proceed.

He could not have been resting for long when he heard sounds of unearthly beauty; at the same time a wondrous fragrance pervaded the room. He sprang from his bed and dropped to his knees.

Then the hut opened above him, so that he could see the starry sky, in which little pink clouds drifted. After that even the starry firmament slid apart, golden rays burst forth, followed by and showered with the most glorious scintillating colours.

Zoroaster's heart pounded. What would he be permitted to behold?

Now the rays parted; he gazed into a vast, luminous hall above him, like the one he had seen before. Three female figures stood there. The one in the middle with the lightly-veiled countenance wore a crown; she had laid her blue mantle around the two standing before her.

For a long time Zoroaster gazed rapturously at this picture, then a clear voice rang out:

"Forerunner, thou seest us! We would remind thee: forget not the women on earth! They stand in our protection. Teach them, proclaim the Helper to them!

"What Ahuramazda bestowed on them they have kept more pure than men have. They will be able to absorb thy teachings more readily. This will be of help to the men."

As if making a vow, Zoroaster raised his hands:

"I will, Ye celestial women! Thanks be to Thee that I am permitted to behold Thee."

Then it seemed to him that the sublime woman in the blue mantle was speaking:

"Accord to women once more that place where, in conformity with the Will of the Supreme God, they are meant to stand: before the men!"

And the lovely woman who appeared to be completely enveloped in rose-coloured clouds said:

"Their love must again become selfless, as it was from the beginning; then they will be able to fulfil their duties in the Realm of Ahuramazda!"

But the lovely white figure seemed to say, as she inclined towards the Forerunner:

"Teach them purity in thought and deed, then the blessing of Purity will surround them!"

After that Zoroaster saw and heard no more, but the vision and the words were forever engraved upon his soul.

THE FOLLOWING DAY as he worked with the men, he instructed them to let the women come in the evening. They stared at him in disbelief.

"But the things you tell us are for men, surely!"

He became as eloquent now as he had been reticent before. So convincingly did he speak that in the end the men had no further objections. That evening a goodly number of women came, among them Yadasa.

Today he spoke of the coming Judgment.

"You must know that the Saoshyant will not indiscriminately take all human beings to Garodemana. That blessed time will be preceded by the Judgment which we all deserve!

"All human beings will have to leave this earth, but as they do so they will come to the great Bridge Tshinvat, which they can only cross one at a time. It is useless wishing to cling to another for strength and succour.

"Each must go this way entirely by himself. And as he moves forward he will see two great, luminous figures, servants of Ahuramazda, at the end of the bridge. Behind them, however, on a golden throne is seated the Saoshyant with the shining sword. His eyes see through every human being."

Zoroaster spoke like a seer. Never before had he given expression to these things. They had come to him out of the silence. He had never yet spoken of them to human beings. Spellbound, the people listened to his words.

"One luminous servant of the Eternal One holds a pair of scales. Now, as a person approaches with slow or rapid steps, depending on whether he has crossed the bridge willingly or unwillingly, a host of little luminous servants rushes up, bringing all his deeds. The good are placed into one, the bad into the other pan of the scales. Nothing counts in this Judgment save that which man has earned for himself. Inexorable justice determines everything.

"And the radiant eyes of the Saoshyant look at the scales. If the pan of the good deeds, words and thoughts sinks down, the human soul may cross the whole length of the bridge and take his place behind the Seat of the World-Judge. But if this is not the case, the soul falls from the bridge into unfathomable depths, never to rise again!"

With a sigh, the speaker ended. Then Yadasa, in a voice trembling with excitement, asked:

"What happens to those standing behind the Seat of the Judge? Are they permitted to enter Garodemana?"

"Not yet, Yadasa," Zoroaster answered kindly. He had not even noticed that it was a woman who asked for an answer.

"The Saoshyant will take them with Him again down to the earth; for now He will establish Ahuramazda's Kingdom, in which the earth is to become a paradise, and human beings are to grow into true servants of God. Thereafter, when they die, their souls will go entirely of their own accord into the Gardens of Eternity, to Garodemana."

Quietly they dispersed. Each was filled with the uneasy certainty that if such was the case, then indeed not a single one among them all would be able to stand in the Judgment.

Only to think of the dreadful things that had transpired among them after the appearance of the false Zoroaster was enough to make them despair. Their life simply was not long enough for them to accumulate sufficient good to counterbalance the bad.

The following day they went about their work quietly. They had become accustomed to working diligently from morning till night, for they saw that Zoroaster did just that. Today each pursued his own thoughts, nothing was spoken in jest, no song rang out.

But in the evening they assailed the Forerunner with questions.

"Is there any point in living on, Zoroaster?" they asked urgently.

Everyone wanted to know the same thing; only the manner in which they expressed the question varied. One of the women said thoughtfully:

"For us women life must still be of some value, for even if we can no longer work our way upward, at least we can teach our children to become better. For the sake of our children we must remain."

"Don't say that, Salane!" called out her husband. "For if you women must remain for the sake of the children, then so must we to provide you with food! But if the downfall is inevitable in any case we would prefer to go immediately. That is what we have discussed among ourselves."

There was an uproar among the women until Yadasa raised her hand and asked them not to forget their dignity altogether. They were not by themselves here. Then the excitement subsided, outwardly at least.

Now they all turned again enquiringly to Zoroaster, who until then had looked on silently.

"It would be very wrong of you to throw away deliberately a life that was granted you by Ahuramazda," he began slowly. "Man's life is not without purpose! Perhaps I shall be able to explain this to you some day. Now you feel that you have not made the right use of this gift. You realise that your actions have been abhorrent, and must lead to your downfall at the Bridge of Tshinvat – unless you have something better to place in the opposite pan of the scale."

"That we have not! Where is it to come from?" came the chorus of men's voices.

Zoroaster was silent until calm was restored.

"Today you have hardly anything to offer; in any case, what little good you have would not suffice. But now I will proclaim to you something wonderful: after your death you will be allowed to return to earth once more, in order to improve on the damage you have done!"

Their initial great astonishment changed to rejoicing, as the people began to comprehend what was offered them.

They were to be allowed to live once more before having to set foot on the Bridge of Judgment! Now that they realised what was at stake, they would surely take care not to commit wrong again. They were almost delirious with joy.

Over all the commotion Yadasa's clear voice rang out:

"Forerunner, no Atravan has ever proclaimed such a thing. The priestesses know nothing of it either. Are you saying this to reassure the souls, or have you received special tidings?"

"I say it, Yadasa, because I know it. It is the truth! I am a servant of Ahuramazda, a herald of the Saoshyant."

"Forgive me," she begged, blushing. "The tidings sound too wonderful. I had to have certainty." "Yes, you people cannot yet fully grasp what it means to be allowed to return repeatedly. I have thought it over a great deal since I received the sublime tidings. In this lies a boundless mercy of the Eternal, Wise God. If you want to carve an implement and the wood is gnarled, so that here something breaks off, there something turns out crooked, what do you do?"

"We take another piece of wood," cried the men, who did not understand why he began to speak of implements at this vital moment.

"And you women: if a piece of raffia keeps on breaking, what do you do?"

"We throw it away and take another one," was the answer here too.

"You see, you would consider the work futile if you had to labour over the gnarled piece of wood or the breaking raffia. Yet God does not discard us miserable, sinful human beings! He permits us to try again and again to overcome our faults and weaknesses.

"Can you understand this forbearing Goodness? It is Divine, you people! Be still before it, worship it, and transform your fervent gratitude into joyful deed. Then it will bear fruit for you."

This time they were quiet when he ceased speaking. They reflected. Then there were questions again:

"Zoroaster, what of the guilt with which we have now burdened ourselves? Will it be left until the Day of Judgment?"

"I too have asked this question countless times, you men," admitted Zoroaster. "Finally the Luminous Messenger of the Most High brought me an answer which I will pass on to you.

"Each of our deeds, be it good or bad, pursues us like a shadow, or as Tungo the other day pursued Tufis who had taken his axe from him. Just as Tungo left Tufis no peace until he gave back the axe, so every bad deed threatens and pleads: make amends for me! Do you understand?"

125

While some nodded agreement, Zoroaster saw that he had still not spoken clearly enough. But he liked his example, so he now presented it somewhat differently.

"You see, first Tufis did something wicked by taking the axe from Tungo. Then he had no peace until he had returned the axe. With that the wrong was wiped out by the good."

Now they understood.

"Can we also wipe out our bad deeds? Must we count: I have done as many bad things as there are fingers on four hands? Now I must do just as many good things."

"No, I do not mean that," Zoroaster indicated. "You must make good *the very* evil which you have committed. Only then are you freed from it, and later it will no longer tip the scales."

"That cannot always be done," one man objected.

"Certainly it can!" Zoroaster asserted, but was interrupted:

"How can we make good for letting our fields go to rack and ruin?"

"By henceforth seeing to them twice as carefully," was the opinion of another man. But the Forerunner said:

"Yes, that would be one way, but I know of yet another." And he told them of the people from the other villages who had gone out to help their neighbours. This they all liked.

"Let us do likewise!" they cried enthusiastically. "When you have to leave us again, Forerunner, we will go with you and redeem our guilt."

"The others did so in gratitude to Ahuramazda," warned Zoroaster, who was afraid that people would now seek to make amends only out of fear of Tshinvat.

"Can it not be done at one and the same time?" asked one of them in quite a childlike manner.

The others agreed, and Zoroaster left it at that for the time being. He must be content with what had been achieved so far.

The next evening brought new questions. An old man recounted the following:

"When I was young I slew my neighbour in a fit of anger. I have often regretted it, and it oppresses me even now. But I can no longer atone for it. He is dead."

The old man sighed. Zoroaster looked around searchingly.

"Who can give an answer?"

The men were silent. But Yadasa raised her head.

"Speak, Yadasa," the Forerunner urged her. Then she began falteringly:

"If Ahuramazda gives us the opportunity to atone for and make good our mistakes through a new life, it would be inconceivable if it were only a half-measure."

"You are right, but explain further. The others do not yet understand you."

"If we are permitted to make amends, then he against whom we have transgressed must surely be on earth also. Hence your neighbour will be your neighbour again in your next life, I think. Then you must serve him as much as you can."

"Is this our first life?" asked another.

"Surely not," said Zoroaster, who had also repeatedly occupied himself with this question.

"Then we must indeed be kind to everyone," one of the younger men burst forth, "since in former times they may have been offended or killed by us."

"We would be bound to know that, I should think," said another.

But Zoroaster explained that life would be unbearable if human beings were fully conscious of their past failings. It was therefore a question of living very circumspectly in order to avoid hurting anyone, and to be kind to all to atone for as much as possible.

That again seemed difficult to them; for it meant that one must constantly be on one's guard against evil. This consideration prompted a man to ask:

"You must have been leading a good life for a long time now, Zoroaster. Is it very difficult?"

In spite of himself, Zoroaster had to laugh.

"To begin with it is difficult, but with a good volition it can be done. The majority of mistakes can be avoided by adjusting our thoughts to Ahuramazda's Will."

Question followed upon question. Zoroaster was able to lead the people ever deeper into the knowledge granted to him.

But after a few days he found that it was time to move on, so that others might also share in the help. He was joined by about thirty men who wished to help others until the time of harvest. And in addition Yadasa came with another girl, and asked to be allowed to go with them.

"Just as it is here, there will be many women in need of help. Let us help them. Let us show them how to put their huts in order, how to bring up their children in the right way. As we work we can also tell them many of the things which you have proclaimed to us."

After thinking it over briefly, Zoroaster was willing to take the maidens with him, especially since Yadasa's father also wished to join him. He was the natural protection for the two girls. But at first the old man would not hear of it.

"If I go, Yadasa must stay at home. Who will look after our property?"

"I have asked the neighbours, Father," Yadasa explained. "They would like to do it, and will do it well because they ruined one of our fields years ago. Now they would like to make amends."

There could be no objection. But the old man was still not satisfied.

"If you wander about the land with us, you will never marry, my child. And you know that is my wish and desire."

"If it is also Ahuramazda's Will, He will send me a husband," declared Yadasa earnestly. "Then I will no longer refuse."

Thus the objections were turned aside, and the girls prepared for the journey. Like the men they had to go on foot, but they were accustomed to that.

THIS TIME the little helpers indicated a different route. If Zoroaster had continued in the same direction as before, he would have come to the desert. Now he had to turn north and soon noticed that the road led into familiar regions.

In the next village he found people whose appearance still betrayed their moral decline, but who quietly went about their daily work. The fields were cultivated, the women wove mats and baskets, the men formed vessels from the rich clay that was to be found everywhere here.

Surprised, Zoroaster asked whether the impostor had not been here, and was told that indeed he had, but that messengers had come one day from the true Forerunner.

Having found the miserable plight they were in, which was truly desperate, they had sent men from the surrounding areas to help them. The strangers had worked very hard.

In return they had asked for mats, baskets and vessels, which were now being made. Much of it had already been delivered. Now they would soon have paid off their debt.

No further assistance was needed here. And now the willing helpers were on their way! What was to be done next?

The luminous messenger with whom he discussed the question advised him to await the arrival of the helpers, then to leave Murza behind and continue the journey with the others. This he did.

Until the arrival of those who came on foot, Zoroaster talked with the men and women while they sat at their work. He laid a foundation upon which Murza, who was listening, could continue to build. Then he moved on with the somewhat disappointed helpers, once they had rested.

The little beings directed him to the west. When he asked whether the helpers would not be required there either, he was assured that they were urgently needed.

This was certainly the case. Of all the villages that the Forerunner had seen so far, the sizeable one which they now entered was the most corrupt. The worst thing was the wide-spread immorality which made Zoroaster regret having taken the girls with him.

He was even considering whether he should not have them escorted home by his servant when Yadasa came to him.

"Do not be angry with me, Zoroaster, if I interrupt your thoughts and contradict them. I know that nowhere do the women need as much help as they do here. They have lost their purity. A man cannot show them what purity is, at least not what it signifies to a woman, and how she can recover what has been lost. I must help these women and girls. Do not be anxious about me, Zoroaster. I am protected..."

Seething with inner emotion, Zoroaster interrupted her:

"Your father cannot be about you all the time, Yadasa!"

"The outward protection of my father is not what I mean. When I was commanded to help these wretched women, I was also assured of protection. On our long journey I have been allowed to perceive it repeatedly. I am not afraid. You must permit me to carry out my charge."

"Who gave you the charge?" enquired Zoroaster.

"A gracious woman garbed in white. She said to me: 'Go to the most wretched of all women, Yadasa, and help them. The protection of Purity will surround you always!'"

"Then fulfil your task, Yadasa, in the blessing of Purity! I will no longer stand in your way."

And Yadasa went her way joyfully, impelled by love for the poorest of the poor. Her kind words, her cheerful look, the motherly way with which she picked up crying children, all these won for her the trust of the women.

Filled with admiration, the men gazed upon her as she passed, looking like a queen; but none dared to address her. The nobility that surrounded her afforded perfect protection.

She soon noticed that a serious disease was rampant in the huts. With untiring patience she nursed and tended the sick. No work was too much for her.

Zoroaster ordered the sick men to be moved to a large tent, erected outside the village, to be looked after by men. But these obtained their instructions from Yadasa. She specified the herbs to be sought and crushed so that they could heal.

Meanwhile the rest of the men attended to the utterly neglected fields and began to make provisional arrangements for sowing.

At night Zoroaster went out and asked the elemental beings for help. But they did not seem particularly inclined to fulfil his request.

"If you wish it, Zoroaster, we will help, but the people have not deserved it. They torment their cattle, they contaminate the water, they destroy the plants. We have long since withdrawn from them. Of our own accord we do not help a single one of them. They are too wicked."

But Zoroaster pleaded:

"Help them this time, and I will let them know to whom they owe the help. I hope they will improve when I rouse their souls. But I can do nothing with their souls as long as their bodies suffer want."

Then the little ones promised their co-operation. And the men who had personally experienced how the little ones had helped them, opened themselves to this help in the realisation that it would enable them to redeem their debt; after some days the rays of the sun fell on fields turned up and steaming in the dawn.

Hastily Zoroaster's men scattered the seed in great joy, while the Forerunner besought Ahuramazda's blessing upon it. Then they called out their gratitude to the invisible helpers.

This pleased the little ones, who had become totally unaccustomed to upright-thinking human beings. They indicated to Zoroaster that they would gladly give still more help to these friendly men.

In response he told them that these people had voluntarily undertaken the work for the others, who were total strangers to them. He told them about Yadasa, who was devotedly tending the sick, some of whom did not even thank her for it.

And from this the little elemental beings realised that not all men had become bad.

In the evening he sat with the men from the village, and told them of the two experiences he had had with the little helpers.

But the men living here were either too ill or too apathetic to attend to a serious conversation. This annoyed his helpers.

"If they do not want to change their souls, then they require no other help either. Perhaps there are people awaiting us elsewhere who would gladly receive your words, Zoroaster."

"But surely there are none who need the help more urgently. There can be none more depraved than the human beings here. I shudder when I look at these miserable creatures. But that must not prevent us from giving them all the help of which we are capable. Always bear in mind how much patience God must have with us."

Yadasa and the girls accompanying her had quietly joined the men.

"After all the terrible things which my eyes have had to witness throughout the day, I long to hear something good. Will you not tell us something, Zoroaster?"

He reflected for a moment. Had they been alone he would have told her about the three Luminous Women whom he had been permitted to see.

But he did not want to speak of it in front of the others. Then something else occurred to him, and he began:

"The other day it seemed to me that I was on an infinitely vast plain. Grass, wonderfully green, grew in lush abundance, studded with glorious flowers. As I looked upon it, several luminous figures came through the grass towards the place where I stood. They did not seem to notice me.

"But I saw that these were a few of the gods who wished to sit in judgment there. Hardly had they seated themselves on some rocks than hordes of animals appeared – cattle, dogs, cats, fowl, nothing but animals of the kind that men use for food or for their convenience.

"And one after the other raised accusations against human beings who tormented them, forgot to feed them and overburdened them with work. Then came the wild animals, and accused the men who hunt them, but often only half kill them, who bring down more than they require, who destroy them in a cruel way. And with each accusation, the highest of these gods seemed to grow more pallid.

"When no more animals came, he rose and proclaimed: 'I will bring an accusation against humanity before Ahuramazda! Men do not deserve the companionship of animals. They deserve nothing better than that many of the animals which were once tame should become wild, dangerous, indeed even poisonous.'

"But you see, my friends, I do not know whether I really beheld this, or whether it was simply a picture given to warn us. Whatever it may have been, it should teach us a great truth: Treat every being created by Ahuramazda as well as possible!"

"We must tell this story to the people here, at work or while tending the sick," said one of the younger men. "They who have treated their cattle so badly that the little helpers were angered can make good use of this lesson."

"Why do you always see only what others need, instead of thinking above all of yourselves when there are wrongs to be put right," Zoroaster censured them. "Who was it who yesterday clung to the tail of the pack-horse, letting himself be dragged along even though the patient animal was carrying a heavy load?"

Zoroaster's gaze rested fully and enquiringly on the young man who had just spoken, who turned his face aside in shame.

On the days that followed there was work enough to be done. Many of the sick men and some women died. Zoroaster ordered the deceased to be buried – contrary to custom – so that the infection from them should be relegated to the earth.

Far from the village, graves were dug, into which the ever-growing number of dead were laid together. The great black birds came for their food.

Gradually the sick recovered. Loyal, devoted nursing had saved them. They found no words of gratitude, but they smiled at their nurses whenever they saw them.

Now Zoroaster began to call the inhabitants together. Whoever did not come willingly was brought. If he nonetheless ran away, as some did, he was not given a meal. That helped.

With such stiff-necked people as he had encountered here, Zoroaster thought the use of force permissible in order to gain influence over the souls. In the beginning they listened reluctantly, but when he told the old legends about the cloud-serpent, they found it entertaining to listen.

Gradually, then, he went on to more serious things. He spoke of Mithra and his helpers, and of Ahuramazda, Who is enthroned above them all.

Long ago they had all known it, but it was buried, probably even before the false forerunner came to them. He had met with no resistance; they had followed him only too willingly.

On the ensuing evenings, Zoroaster spoke of the evil one and his helpers. Then one of the men said:

"When two people on earth quarrel, surely the families do not decide who is to be the victor. The two must fight it out with one another. It must be exactly the same with the gods. What is it to us whether the lord of the bad or of the good triumphs? They should decide that between them; we will follow the victor."

Triumphant at his cleverness, he looked around the circle, but saw only sombre faces.

He was one of those who had been most seriously ill! How could one who had just been saved from death dare to speak in this way? Before

Zoroaster could answer him, the man cried out, flinging one of the small, poisonous vipers into the fire.

It had bitten him, there was no escape. The man howled in terror, pain and fear of death. The others stared at him: within a few moments he would have to walk across the bridge. What would be his fate? They all shuddered.

Zoroaster went up to the screaming man.

"Do you see how you have transgressed against Ahuramazda?" he asked earnestly.

The man stared at him with glazed eyes. He appeared not to comprehend the question.

"You have blasphemed against the wise, kind God Who gave you one more chance. You will regret it. Do you not want to implore Ahuramazda's forgiveness?"

Urgently Zoroaster admonished the man, whose hand was already a bluish-black colour. But he dismissed the Forerunner with a blasphemous curse.

Thereupon Zoroaster left the square, and the others followed him. The offender died alone and forsaken.

The incident made a lasting impression on all. Those who had witnessed it told the few who for some reason had stayed away. Among these was also Yadasa, who had been assisting a woman at the birth of her child.

When she learned of the shocking event she was deeply moved by it. But she could not understand why Zoroaster had not attempted to save the man. In the straightforward manner that was natural to her she questioned him about it.

"Why should I have saved him, Yadasa?" asked Zoroaster in turn. "Indeed I could have tried to cauterise the wound, but with this kind of snake venom, rescue would hardly have been possible in any case. And why, I ask again, should I have made the attempt at all?"

"Had the man been saved from death, he would surely have recognised Ahuramazda's mercy and mended his ways," submitted Yadasa. But Zoroaster retorted:

"Ahuramazda's mercy had only just snatched him from the disease that made him mortally ill! He did not recognise it. When I reminded him of it he even cursed. He would not have allowed his soul to be helped this time either. To the others, however, he was a danger. He would have been able to talk those who were not completely sure into his bad habits and unbelief."

Then Yadasa understood that not all that may appear so is kindness, and that one must also think when giving help. Modestly she said:

"I thank you, Zoroaster; I have learned a great deal."

The days passed in work and teaching. They turned into weeks without the men's noticing it. Only the growing corn showed them how long they had already been here.

Gradually the souls opened. The people came voluntarily to the instruction, they prayed with sincerity, and understood how much grace had been shown to them.

ZOROASTER was already considering departure when one midday strangers rode into the village. That caused great excitement! They rode in orderly procession, their bodies apparently as well controlled as their horses.

Suddenly they uttered a cry of joy: they had caught sight of and recognised Zoroaster! These were the messengers who had ridden ahead of him and were on their way home. Great was their joy at finding the Forerunner.

They recounted that this had been the last village in urgent need of help. In the others they had been able to work effectively on their own. Now all the wrongs caused by the appearance of the false Zoroaster had been redressed.

In addition the people with whom the Forerunner was now occupying himself had been stirred to the very depths of their being, and were transformed.

"Here too blessing has been born of suffering!" exulted Murza, who had arrived a few days earlier.

The men also brought the news that in a few weeks' time the festival on the Mountain would take place. Zoroaster was asked to participate. The Atravan and Prince Hafiz had messengers looking for him everywhere.

Then Zoroaster resolved to ride home with his two companions, promising, however, to return in a year's time at the latest to see how the people had assimilated his teaching, how much fruit it had borne.

The parting was especially hard for the helpers from the other villages. They could no longer imagine a life without the "Master". Yadasa said nothing at all; her unchanging, peaceful countenance did not betray whether she was happy or sad to be going home.

But Zoroaster suddenly perceived that his physical strength had begun to wane. It had been far too overtaxed in recent years, when he had worked unceasingly beyond ordinary human capacity.

He had but one deeply-felt wish: to reach seclusion as soon as possible. Murza understood him, and faithfully made arrangements for a swift departure.

Sooner than anyone expected, the parting was accomplished. But Zoroaster did not get far. Already at the end of the first day he broke down with a raging fever. Murza did not know where to take the sick man.

So he besought Ahuramazda to open his eyes to see the little helpers and speak with them. It was for the sake of the suffering Forerunner.

And the entreaty was answered. Small, kindly beings appeared, whispering to Murza that they knew of an empty hut close by, where he and the servant could take Zoroaster.

Happily they showed him the way to a dwelling-place well protected from the rain, in which there was a good bed.

But Murza was overjoyed at being able to see the little ones. He grew very fond of them. They sensed it, and helped him ever more willingly.

For ten days the Forerunner lay gravely ill. Murza nursed him with great devotion. Finally he was able to look about him again, wondering where he was. Murza told him, with the little beings completing the account and praising Murza's thoughtfulness.

When Zoroaster was sufficiently recovered to mount Ray, he insisted on setting forth for home. So they started out with the little ones showing them the best routes. When they reached the boundary of their domain, other helpers continued to lead them. Then Murza, who had been riding in silence, all at once exclaimed jubilantly:

136

"I can see the new helpers too! Is it possible that I may keep the sight granted me for good?"

He was unspeakably happy, peering behind every tree, into every flower, and exultantly announcing the appearance of a little fairy or a tree-spirit.

As Zoroaster was still weak, they had to ride slowly; but with Murza's joy at the little beings the days passed quickly.

In the evenings Zoroaster, as was his wont, spoke with his companions of serious things. It saddened him to notice that the servant had not progressed inwardly, although he had always been allowed to participate in everything. It was as though he lacked the inclination for anything that was not of the earth.

"Have you no longing at all to hear of Ahuramazda, my friend?" Zoroaster asked him kindly.

He shook his head. "I understand so little of it. I fail to comprehend why Murza is happy when he sees the little vermin. I fail to comprehend why you, the noble master, trouble yourself with depraved human beings and do work which is too lowly for me."

"In that case," said Zoroaster sorrowfully, making one last attempt, "I will not be able to take you with me next time."

He had expected protestations and pleas for another chance, but instead the servant, very happy, said:

"I was actually about to ask you for that! It will be hard for me to part from Ray, but in the long run I will also get used to other horses."

With all the great success of the Forerunner, this failure in his immediate vicinity! What was he to learn from it? –

After a few more days, the capital finally appeared, and before sunset they were able to dismount from their horses outside the Palace of Hafiz.

Zoroaster was welcomed with great joy. The Prince was alarmed to see the pale, haggard face of his friend, but the latter reassured him.

He was feeling quite well again, Murza had looked after him splendidly. Then he asked anxiously if Dshayava was still alive. The answer made him happy: The aged man could hardly wait to welcome the Forerunner!

Now Zoroaster could not wait any longer himself. He hastened to meet his old friend, whom he found more frail, but spiritually very alert.

Here he was able to tell all that he had encountered, what he had thought and experienced. He found understanding which greatly deepened his own insights.

He could have continued his accounts for days. It felt so good to rest in this inner absorption after all the unrest of the recent years. But Hafiz urged him to seek out the Atravan, who had matters of importance to discuss with him.

Zoroaster went to the priest, who received him with deference even though he was considerably older than the Forerunner.

The Atravan told him that he had been directed to present Zoroaster as the Forerunner to all the people at the next festival. He himself would speak of his mission and ask him to do likewise. The best plan would be for Zoroaster to speak to the men on the second day of the festival.

Zoroaster willingly agreed to everything, but he asked that the women also should be allowed to attend his address. He considered it his duty not to leave them in the background any longer.

"They have souls as we have, Atravan," he said, "and these souls are starving. They should be permitted to take the food where their men receive it, and not be dependent on these men to fulfil their spirit's need."

The Atravan did not understand this attitude. As long as he could remember, indeed much longer still, self-effacement had been seemly for women. They had to be inferior to men. He felt that it should continue in this way. Otherwise the women would demand changes elsewhere, which could become troublesome.

"You are not married, Zoroaster," he concluded smiling, "otherwise you would readily understand that women cannot be kept sufficiently submissive."

"My mother was also a woman, the same as yours, Atravan," Zoroaster replied promptly. "If the women were to infer that they are entitled to thrust themselves forward simply because they are permitted to hear the Eternal Truths together with the men, they would not be true women. Then they should no longer be allowed to come to the Hours of Worship. But we must make every effort to accord its due place to the soul of woman."

The Atravan yielded, for he knew very well that behind Zoroaster's statement lay the Will of God. However, he declined to hear in advance what the Forerunner intended to proclaim.

"I shall hear it soon enough with the others," he said indifferently. "I know that you bring the Truth, so there is no need to examine your words beforehand." –

They were to set out in two days' time. The Atravan left it to Zoroaster to choose whether he wished to ride with him or in the retinue of Prince Hafiz.

Zoroaster perceived that the latter choice would suit the Atravan, yet he would make no decision until he had spoken with the Luminous Helper.

Somewhat depressed by the talk, Zoroaster returned to the Palace, and went immediately to the Prince, who invited the Forerunner to ride with him. He would have more time than usual on the journey to seek answers to many a question that occupied him.

"The Atravan, on the other hand, will be happy if he need not have you with him now," said the Prince, and then asked: "How did you like the Priest? Were you on good terms with each other?"

"I like him, but he seems to me somewhat constrained. He is trying to hide something. Every sentence is well-considered. I fail to understand why. After all, he has nothing to fear from me!"

"O Zoroaster, you child!" Hafiz laughed good-humouredly. "That is just it! He is afraid of you."

Zoroaster's look of astonishment made the Prince repeat with greater emphasis:

"Yes, he is afraid of you! If you are the Forerunner, then by virtue of the office vested in you by Ahuramazda, you occupy the foremost position among the priesthood of our land. That must be self-evident."

Zoroaster's incredulous look elicited renewed laughter from the Prince.

"That you yourself have not already realised this shows me how in truth you see nothing apart from your high task. That is as it should be, of course," said Hafiz, growing serious. "But the Atravan, who does not know you, has no idea of the extent to which you plan to make use of this power. To show him how unassuming you are, I asked you to call on him. Strictly speaking, he should have come to see you."

"Then I shall go to him again, and tell him that he is to continue as the highest priest in the land," concluded Zoroaster. But the Prince restrained him:

"That would be very foolish. The fact that he fears you must make you recognise his lust for power, which may become troublesome or embarrassing to you, if even now you allow it free rein. Besides, Ahuramazda has called you, not him, to the highest spiritual rank in this realm.

"That cannot be simply discarded like a useless garment. Go your way steadfastly. Let others fear or love you. A day will come when you will be glad that *one* word from your lips can command obedience even from the Atravan."

"I thank you, Hafiz. I understand it now. You are right, in such things I am, alas, still as foolish as a child," the Forerunner sighed. "What should I do without your wise counsel?"

"That is indeed why I was commanded from above to be your protector on earth. This I was told by the late Atravan. That is why I took you with me even then when you were still in quest of the Zoroaster."

"But one thing I do not understand," Zoroaster resumed, after a prolonged period of silence, "is why the Atravan so resolutely refused to hear anything of what I have to tell human beings. I should have thought that he could not hear enough of it."

"If you knew the priest better, it would no longer puzzle you. All that he knows and passes on he wants to hear from God Himself. For him it is agony that another should receive more sacred knowledge than he. If you now tell him things, he enters into a pupil-master relationship with you, which he does not want. On the other hand, if he hears your truths for the first time only on the Mountain at the festival, no one can tell whether he did not already know everything you say."

"What a pity for the man," Zoroaster lamented. But Hafiz countered:

"He will change under your influence, blessed one, just as we all do. It will take a long time for him, though." –

Zoroaster left the preparations for the journey to Murza, whom he summoned. The loyal follower was looking forward to the festival, and this joy shone through him.

"Have you heard, Master, what has happened to our former servant?" he asked as soon as he had entered the Forerunner's apartment. "I should be sad about it, but I cannot be. All too clearly I see the Will of Ahuramazda in the experience."

When Zoroaster said that he did not know, Murza related:

"The man was not so indifferent as he pretended. He could not close himself to the truths, much as he would have liked to. Above all he dreaded the invisible helpers who he knew surrounded him. He thought that at a distance from you they would no longer be able to approach him. That is what made him so eager to leave you.

"Here he was restored to his old position in the retinue of the Prince, and given several pack-horses to look after. But he longed for Trotter and Ray, who stand together peaceably and are well looked after.

"So he decided – he told me so himself – to visit them one night. But before he came to them, it seemed as though he heard voices:

"'We will have no dealings with a coward whose courage fails him before the servants of the Most High. Still less, however, may one guilty of disloyalty, who out of his cowardice leaves his master and forgoes the Eternal Truths, approach us.'

"That was roughly the meaning of the words he heard. He was alarmed, but his fear prompted him to utter the outrageous words:

"'Have the devilish spooks followed me even here? Are you creatures of Anramainyu? If I do not see the little beings at once, I will curse everything associated with the Zoroaster.'

"Suddenly three gnomes stood before him, clearly recognisable. They looked very angry. One of them spoke:

"'Not to forestall this curse, which cannot harm the Zoroaster, does Ahuramazda open your inner eyes, but perhaps still to save your soul, which was chosen to serve the Forerunner. It is the last attempt, Sadi. Tear yourself away from spiritual indolence and craven fear.'

"You can well imagine, Master, how terrified Sadi was. Throwing off all caution, he tripped, and fell so badly that he broke a leg. Now he has time to think it all over. He sent for me to share his experience, and asked me to tell you about it and to beg your forgiveness."

"I will go and see him later," said Zoroaster, who was as happy as Murza about the incident. "But for this journey we shall need another servant. Choose whoever you wish. Prince Hafiz leaves it to us."

"Indeed I have made the choice already, Master," said Murza modestly. "Among the grooms is a young lad called Marzar, whom I like very much. He seems to come from a good home, is intelligent and inquiring. He cannot hear enough of whatever he can learn from me. It would make him very happy if you were to take him as your servant."

"Then tell him that he should make ready to accompany us," agreed Zoroaster.

Later that day he called on Sadi, who was resting on his bed in much pain. He found him receptive to every kind word, a completely changed person.

After assuring him of his forgiveness, and promising that he would accept him as his servant again as soon as his leg had healed, Zoroaster examined the fracture. Nothing had been done for it, the splintered bones were piercing the skin. Did the doctor not attend to such patients?

The Forerunner was told that the doctor only came if a patient was rich and could pay generously; others had to recover without him, or die.

Zoroaster promised to pay the doctor his due. But if the servant remained a cripple, the doctor would be punished.

That helped. Even before his departure, Zoroaster found Sadi resting comfortably and free from pain. The doctor, however, bowed to the ground and promised that he would do his utmost to restore the use of the leg. –

Dshayava, who had planned to travel with the party, had overestimated his strength and was obliged to abandon his intention. With trembling hands he gave Zoroaster the blessing for the journey.

But Hafiz, filled with joy, galloped out of the city, Zoroaster at his side. Both had much to talk about, questions to ask and things to see. Hafiz was especially interested in the condition of the various villages, and his companion spoke untiringly of all that had taken place there. When he told of the help given them by the elemental beings, Hafiz said:

"I feel almost like your Sadi: I am uneasy at the thought that we are constantly surrounded by invisible beings who can benefit or harm us."

"I cannot understand that anyone could fear them," Zoroaster replied. "To me it is such a pleasant thought to know that the little beings are around me, even when I do not happen to see them."

142

"Do you not see them always then?" the Prince wanted to know, and Zoroaster explained that he usually only saw them when he called for them to come to him.

"But if they bring me a message, or want to warn me, then I see them also," he ended his account.

But he saw that he still had not dispelled the Prince's uneasiness, and considered how this could be remedied. Nothing occurred to him, and he decided to ask his Luminous Helper for advice and help.

As he spoke, Zoroaster could not help mentioning Yadasa. He described her as he had perceived her, and Hafiz showed a lively interest in the beautiful maiden. Zoroaster was struck by that, and suddenly he said:

"Prince, this would be a wife for you; you could not wish for a better one. The purest of earthly women beside you; it would be glorious for your people!"

The Forerunner was quite excited as he spoke. But the Prince said:

"Since the death of my wife I have felt little inclination to re-marry. But after the Festival we can certainly take the route through that region, so that I may become acquainted with the maiden."

Zoroaster was satisfed.

THE TENT-CITY of the Prince was erected at the foot of the mountain where the Festival was to be held. It was the scene of much colourful activity, for everyone thronged to take part in the Festival.

For Zoroaster a special tent had been erected. Outwardly it was clearly distinguishable from the others with their dazzling colours. It was covered with white mats both inside and out.

Very early on the morning of the Festival, the crowds rode up to the mountain. They dismounted just before reaching the place where the Festival was to be held. Servants took the horses from them, and the last stretch of the way was covered on foot at a slow and measured pace.

The first day of the Festival proceeded according to strict rules. Zoroaster stood near the Prince, experiencing in his soul all the prayers and customs. Then the Atravan turned to all those in attendance. He spoke of how men had become increasingly entangled in guilt through their evil doings, how they brought wickedness into the world everywhere. Then he spoke of the promise concerning the Saoshyant, and of the Forerunner.

"When I was still a young Mobed," he said excitedly, "the Atravan was permitted to state: 'The prophecy will be fulfilled. We have entered the last phase of the earth. The stars have announced that the Zoroaster has been born.' The tidings filled the listeners with great joy. They all rejoiced that the Forerunner had come to earth.

"Today I am likewise permitted to proclaim to you something which signals great joy: the Zoroaster stands in our midst!"

He could not continue for the sound of jubilation surging across the square. Even those who already knew let themselves be swept up in the great, overwhelming joy. The Zoroaster in their midst! Now better times were sure to come! Now every evil thing would have to end!

With difficulty the Atravan succeeded in restoring calm. Ever again voices were raised in thanksgiving and rejoicing, until suddenly one of those present, then several, shouted the question:

"Where is he?"

And the Priest indicated him who stood there perfectly calm, his countenance suffused with an unearthly radiance.

"Behold, this is the Forerunner of the Saoshyant, who will proclaim Him and speak of Him to us all!"

They all looked towards him and thought they no longer beheld a human being. At that moment he seemed like a being from another world.

But the Atravan promised that Zoroaster would address them all on the following day, and that at his request the women would also be permitted to attend.

There was renewed jubilation that would hardly cease. No festival had ever been so lively, but neither had anything so glorious ever been proclaimed.

Hafiz had feared that while descending the Mountain, people would crowd round Zoroaster. He had therefore commanded his servants to gather closely about him.

But the precaution had been unnecessary. Everyone fell back in reverence and made way for those walking through. Here and there Zoroaster saw a familiar face, blushing with joy when recognised. From all the villages that the Forerunner had liberated from the traces of the impostor, they had come to join in the celebration.

In the evening, when the Atravan offered the drink to the men and told legends, Zoroaster sat quietly among the listeners. In this way he wanted to reassure the Priest that nowhere did he wish to crowd him out of his office.

Of course the people would have preferred Zoroaster to present the stories to them; but they loved their legends and were content at the thought of the day to come.

This became the climax of the Festival. Zoroaster had spent the night praying for the right words and for strength. He knew how much depended on every soul seeing in him the Forerunner of the Divine Helper. Joyfully he stepped before the people, whose eyes were fixed intently on his lips.

He began by saying that probably no one was in any doubt about man's depravity. And surely everyone would pray for the coming of the Saoshyant as the last and only salvation from perdition.

What their forefathers had longed for, what everyone had wanted, was now allowed to become reality! He was sent by Ahuramazda to the earth as Forerunner, and was permitted to say to them out of his inmost knowledge:

"Rejoice, you despairing ones! Rejoice, you faint-hearted ones! The Radiant Hero will come to redeem the earth from the curse of Anramainyu. He will strike off the serpent's head with the Sword, whose gleaming metal is pure Truth.

"He is Ahuramazda's Son, a Part of the Supreme God! Can you imagine that? Can you comprehend such immeasurable Grace?

"He will set foot on our earth, which through transgression has become a morass! His holy eyes will behold us human beings who are fettered to evil! If you but knew how glorious He is, you would no longer think of anything other than how you might serve Him."

Zoroaster's ringing voice grew ever more resonant, ever fuller. The words flowed to him as he now described the Helper in His Glory, sitting upon His Throne to judge mankind.

He spoke of Divine Justice, which cannot be influenced. He impressed on them that every human being will receive whatever reward or punishment he has earned for himself.

"You must change, you human beings!" he called. "So that in the Judgment some of you may, after all, be permitted to walk across the Bridge Tshinvat in order to serve the Saoshyant."

At that moment it seemed to them so easy to change. They must simply refrain from doing whatever they had hitherto done wrongly, and strive to do good instead. It was easy, as easy as child's play. So it seemed to them. This Zoroaster sensed from their thoughts. Therefore he resumed:

"Do not think that change can be attained without great effort. If you were not so fond of your vices and faults, not so utterly bound up with them, you would surely have discarded them already. You have been warned often enough. Now is the time to make a great effort. You know what is at issue. If you should find it difficult, consider that every victory removes one little stone from the path of the Saoshyant."

For a long time he spoke to them; they descended the mountain in a state of exalted fulfilment never known before.

"Had we doubted that this is a Messenger of Ahuramazda," said an old man to the bystanders, "his flaming words must have convinced us. No man can speak like that out of himself."

This was the general impression.

On the last day of the Festival many of the men wanted to know if and when the Zoroaster would come to their villages. He promised to ride out again soon and to visit one tribe after another. They had to be satisfied with that.

Moreover he mingled again with the audience and listened to the pronouncements of the priestesses. It sounded dull and flat after what the crowd had been permitted to hear the day before. The priestesses themselves sensed it. And suddenly the highest of them turned to the Forerunner:

"Zoroaster, a new era has begun. Therefore the customs may be changed if it seems necessary for the good of all. We shall be silent; you speak to us! You still have much to tell us. So many of us are gathered here. Let us absorb as much as possible of what you have to proclaim to us."

Surprised, Zoroaster looked at the Atravan. The latter turned away. It was clear that he was not pleased, but he acquiesced.

And so Zoroaster began once more to bear witness, but he encouraged the listeners to ask questions as soon as any arose in them.

They did so gladly. During the night so many had reflected and come upon one question after another. With unfailing vigour the Zoroaster answered the questions that were called out to him.

And there was not a single idle, inquisitive or even inappropriate question. Whatever was asked demonstrated that people had given truly earnest consideration to the new that had entered their lives.

Zoroaster extended the gathering up to the last moment. When he was about to end it, he was besieged with requests to be allowed to stay one more day; and Zoroaster granted it.

When the Atravan objected that the duration of the Festival had never exceeded three days, Zoroaster retorted:

"The Festival is over, Atravan. But we will stay together for a while to speak of the Saoshyant. There is no compulsion. Let him who must go home because his duty calls, or who wishes to go home for other reasons, calmly depart. No one will hold it against him. But he who wishes to remain may do so unhindered."

Then the Priest yielded, and he too stayed on.

One day became seven days. Then the Forerunner had fulfilled a part of his task. All the people who now journeyed homewards were filled with the knowledge of Ahuramazda and His Holy Son, the Divine Helper.

On this seventh day, however, something extraordinary happened.

Zoroaster prayed for all who wanted to hear about the Helper. His words bore him aloft; he forgot that people were thronging about him. His soul laid itself at the foot of the Divine Throne.

They all noticed that from his forehead shone a radiance which grew brighter the longer he prayed. Suddenly, just as Zoroaster ended his prayer, the high priestess cried out:

"Behold the Golden Ray descending upon him from above! Behold the wondrous White Bird within this Ray, spreading its wings over him!

"Behold the wonderful Golden Sign floating above his head!"

All eyes turned to Zoroaster, who still stood completely absorbed with upturned face. Many of the people were permitted to behold the Sacred Sign, the Cross of the Saoshyant. Among the seeing ones was also Hafiz.

147

Later he commanded that this Sign be embroidered in gold on the robes of the Forerunner and on the white tent. –

Now the many who had stayed until the last moment really departed. They left the Mountain of the Festival to herald and admonish. Zoroaster, however, returned with Hafiz to the city by the shortest route.

There was no further talk of the ride to Yadasa. They were too full of all they had experienced. Dshayava awaited them impatiently.

While an inner voice had told him that nothing untoward had happened, he could hardly wait for them to recount the events. There was much to tell him, and it took them days to finish.

Sadi was better, but he still could not make use of his leg. Hence he could not possibly ride with Zoroaster yet. It pained him greatly to yield to this, he who but a short while ago had so willingly left Zoroaster's service.

But the Forerunner wished to journey through the lands accompanied only by Murza and Marzar. Prince Hafiz tried to persuade him to take a retinue with him, but Zoroaster would not hear of it.

"I suspect that my retinue would become too large," he said, and left it at that.

Before his departure he called on the Atravan once more and asked him to continue with his duties as before, and not to be deterred by Zoroaster's present tour of the realm.

"You are to teach of the gods, Atravan, whereas I am to proclaim the Helper," he said kindly. "The better you teach, the more perfectly I shall be able to proclaim."

"Will you proceed in the same way at future festivals, Zoroaster?" the priest asked, ignoring Zoroaster's words. "Will you add seven days each time, in order to speak to the people? Then I tell you this very day that I will not tolerate it in future!"

How right Hafiz had been with his warning. Zoroaster had not yet compromised his dignity, thanks to the circumspection of the Prince. Calmly he answered:

"This cannot yet be determined, priest. If it is necessary to convey more than can be said to them all in one day, then more days will simply have to be added. We shall see."

148

"But I will not tolerate it!" the Atravan retorted angrily. "The festival is a celebration in honour of Mithra. If you wish to proclaim the Saoshyant, hold a festival in his honour!"

"We shall see what Ahuramazda decrees," Zoroaster replied with forced calm.

He then took his leave and returned to the Palace. He had intended to speak of this experience with Hafiz, but there was no opportunity to do so, so he left it.

Now Zoroaster had been on the road again for days. Although there had actually been very little time for him to rest, his strength had returned. He was looking forward to proclaiming the Saoshyant, to meeting souls imbued with longing.

He enjoyed the ride through the fertile countryside. This time he had ridden northwards, where he had been only once before. The country was hilly and rose into high mountain ranges.

"Do people live here also?" he asked the little ones who had come at his call. They nodded eagerly.

"People live here, but their huts lie far apart because of the mountains in between. The road will become more and more difficult. You will find no villages at all. May we give you some advice?"

Now it was Zoroaster who nodded.

"Then listen: Remain down here where you are now. This place is not too hard to reach from any of the huts. We will ask the people to come here; then you can speak to them all at the same time, as you did recently on the Mountain of the Festival."

To Murza and Zoroaster this seemed an excellent suggestion. Nevertheless the Forerunner asked:

"How will you let the people know, little ones?"

"The human beings here are still good, because they have always lived in accord with us," they informed him. "Therefore they can also see us. We often help them, when cattle have strayed in the mountains, or when they themselves lose their way. Then they call to us as you have done, and we come. When we tell them of you, they will come joyfully!"

149

So Zoroaster agreed that the little ones should hasten to the huts in the mountains. His white tent was pitched, with the golden Cross embroidered upon it, shining far and wide in the sunlight.

Now he awaited the people. They appeared two and three at a time. All were grateful that the Zoroaster had come to see them.

Trustingly they spoke of their arduous life amidst the mountains and rocks.

"Our goats and sheep are used to climbing," they declared. "But we cannot raise any other cattle up here."

When all were assembled, Zoroaster began to speak, and they absorbed his words with the greatest ease.

The elemental beings had really been right: life in the midst of Nature, and surrounded by the little servants of the Most High, had kept the human beings pure. They looked forward confidently to the coming of the Helper.

It was a great experience for the Forerunner, who had hitherto been accustomed to quite different reactions. With a heavy heart he took leave of the good people.

Now he journeyed south. If at all possible he wanted to visit such districts as he had never been to before.

After a few days' journey he arrived, guided by the little ones, at a village which lay amid flowering gardens. It was beautiful here, amazingly beautiful. He was reminded of the countryside around Ara-Masdah's Palace. There too the roses blossomed in such lavish profusion. The people must be good here!

He had his tent pitched on the outskirts of the village. For this there were two reasons: He would not burden anyone with giving him hospitality; above all, however, he wanted to arouse their curiosity. The people should come, marvel, and ask questions. The golden Cross, the like of which no one had ever seen, should attract their attention.

But things turned out differently.

Many from this region had been to the Mountain Festival; to some of them it had been given to see. When they now saw the Cross, they recognised it immediately. They did not ask questions. Exultant, they rushed to the huts with the news:

"The Zoroaster has come! Come out all of you, to his white tent! He will speak to us, as he did on the Mountain. Now you yourselves may hear what we could only relate to you imperfectly!"

They came running in crowds, and hailed Zoroaster.

They had question upon question! They wanted to know everything, from the very beginning, exactly. He talked with them, gave answers, taught and proclaimed for days on end.

Then he observed that they were preoccupied with something which they could not yet put into words. Kindly he encouraged them to express their thoughts, in whatever way they could.

It seemed as though each expected the other to speak, for among themselves they apparently agreed. Finally one of the younger men came forward and said:

"We no longer wish to serve the gods!"

Now that it was out, they all breathed a sigh of relief. But Zoroaster was taken aback. It had never occurred to him that his teaching could have such an effect.

When they perceived from his silence that he had not understood them, they all started shouting at once. But he understood nothing at all and now began to ask:

"Why do you want to remove the gods?"

"Because they are only servants of Ahuramazda," was the determined reply.

"And will you no longer acknowledge Ahuramazda either?"

Unrestrained laughter answered him, as though he had asked something very silly. That reassured him, as they appeared to stand on very firm ground.

"So you would continue to worship the Wise, Eternal, Kind God?"

"That goes without saying!" came the reply. "He alone is truly God, the others have only been made into gods by human beings. That is now quite clear to us. Do you not think so too, Zoroaster?"

Yes, that was also his opinion. He was delighted. But he was reluctant to ignore those who had hitherto been revered as gods.

"Do not forget that those whom until now you have worshipped as gods are the highest servants of God. They are far superior to you human beings. They help you and contribute much to your development here on earth. Honour and respect them, even though you no longer worship them in the future. Give thanks to them also for everything they do for you."

Emboldened the men asked, "Have you prayed to them in the past, Zoroaster?"

"No, since I actually found Ahuramazda, the others have been no longer gods to me. They are sublime, glorious beings, but they are as far below the Throne of the Most High as we are below them."

"Then it is not right either that the Mountain Festival should in future be held in honour of Mithra," the people reflected, but instantly added: "We have certainly observed that you have given it a different character. That set us thinking."

"If you have observed that, you will also understand me when I tell you that we must not alter the Festival until the majority of all Persians think as you do. Otherwise we should deprive the people of something for which we have no substitute yet to offer them.

"I have spoken with the Luminous Messenger of God. It is also the Will of the Most High that the souls be permitted to grow slowly into the new knowledge."

Openly, as with friends, Zoroaster had laid his innermost opinion before them. They were happy about it, and sought to understand him. But there also arose in them a pride that they were perhaps the first to think in this way.

Zoroaster felt this at once, and endeavoured to let nothing grow here that might become a weed.

"I rejoice with you, dear friends, that you have discovered this, that it has become an experience for you. You will not be the only ones so affected by the Festival on this occasion. You must not forget either that it was God's Grace which awakened these thoughts in you."

Now they stood aright again.

During the night, Zoroaster brought this experience in prayer before the Throne of the All-Highest. It became certainty to him that he could now begin to proclaim Ahuramazda as the only God.

He must proceed slowly, must deal with the souls gently; but again it became clear to him that nothing new can be built without pulling down the old.

Soon afterwards he continued his journey. He had a premonition that trouble would succeed the joy that had been granted him with these human beings. But the thought merely increased the strength that filled him.

He found the next village set on the shores of a beautiful lake. The huts were constructed with a greater sense of beauty than he had found elsewhere. Paintings and mats adorned them even on the outside. Beside each hut was a small garden with an abundance of flowers, although roses were absent.

Now they met the first men, who were busy fishing. Water-sprites sat on rocks in the lake, watching the fishermen. Zoroaster and even Murza could see them clearly.

The men were strikingly dressed. Their garments were colourful, lavishly hung with chains made of shells and other ornaments. This did not appeal to Zoroaster, who could not reconcile it with his concept of manliness.

He could not bring himself to address the fishermen, and walked towards the huts. There he found women and children who, in contrast to the men, made a somewhat impoverished impression. They were shy, for as soon as they caught sight of the strangers they hid.

Zoroaster had left Marzar with the horses at a greater distance than usual. He and Murza must give the impression of being ordinary travellers. Why were the women afraid?

He beckoned them to him in friendly fashion. It took some time before one of them decided to come.

"Don't be afraid, girl," he smiled, "nothing will happen to you. Do you see strangers so seldom, that you are so shy?"

"Sir, almost never," whispered the maiden, greatly embarrassed.

"Do you think I may pitch my tent near here?"

"I do not know," was the uneasy reply.

"Would you sell me some food?" Zoroaster enquired further, at pains not to let the conversation break off.

"I do not know."

Obviously the girl was anxious for the conversation to end, for she fled like a gazelle.

Zoroaster turned and saw the men coming from the lake. Relieved, he turned towards them, walking a few steps in their direction and repeating his request for food.

The men looked at one another, and the oldest of them asked what the two travellers wanted here.

Why should Zoroaster make a secret of it? Calmly he said that he was undertaking a long ride through the whole realm of the Persians, as teacher and herald.

"And what is it you teach and herald?" the chieftain wanted to know.

"I am the Forerunner of the Saoshyant," Zoroaster informed him, believing that he thus conveyed a great deal.

But they stared at him as though they did not understand.

"Do you know nothing of the Divine Helper Who will be sent to men?" Zoroaster asked. They shook their heads.

"Were you not present then at the holy Festival on the Mountain?" was Zoroaster's next question.

Again they shook their heads; but then the old man said:

"No, we do not go to the festivals. We do not believe in the things that the priests and priestesses recount there. Our forefathers no longer went there either."

"But how are you to get through life, if you believe nothing, you wretched ones?" asked the guest.

"Save your pity, stranger," was the proud reply. "Who says that we believe in nothing? We do not believe in the things that the priests say; we have something better."

With that the old man turned to go. But Zoroaster called out quickly:

"Would you not like to tell me what it is? One always likes to hear something better."

The old man gave him a penetrating look.

"But you have Mithra and the others, you do not need our god."

"Now I can say in your words: who says so? But let me request once more: tell me of your god, for I believe that he is the same as mine. You should know that I do not worship Mithra or the others either."

154

"Is that the truth?" enquired the old man. Zoroaster, however, replied almost vehemently:

"He who recognises the true God does not lie!"

"Well then, stay with us tonight. Food you shall have. Later at the fireside we will tell you as much of our treasure as we wish to give to strangers."

Zoroaster went with the men, while Murza, at a signal, returned to Marzar to inform him. Then Murza too came to the meal, which was taken in an open square among the huts.

Only men were gathered there, as was altogether in keeping with the customs prevalent elsewhere. But it was strange that a few beautiful girls had to serve them as they ate. Usually this was done by men-servants.

Already Zoroaster was about to voice his amazement, but he thought better of it. Untimely comment would only make the men uncommunicative. The dishes were tasty, and served with care.

The guests ate with pleasure, and that won the hearts of the men, who seemed to attach great importance to the meal. Afterwards they all settled down in the wide square. The guests were invited to sit near the chieftain, who now began a kind of cross-examination:

"How many gods are there?"

"One," Zoroaster answered, just as tersely as the question had been put.

"Already that is wrong," declared the old man. "There are two gods – a good one whom we call Ormuzd, and an evil one whose name is Ahriman."

Zoroaster knew at once that they were merely the garbled names of those already known to them. "We also worship Him Whom you call Ormuzd. We call Him Ahuramazda, and know that He is the Only One, the Eternal, the Wise One."

Delighted, the old man moved a little closer to his guest.

"The name is not what matters. We both really seem to be referring to the same God. But if you know Ormuzd, you must know Ahriman as well. The one cannot exist without the other."

"We also know Ahriman," acknowledged Zoroaster, "but we see no god in him."

155

"No god?"

The old man was alarmed, and moved away again from the guest.

"No god? I tell you, stranger, he is a god, and moreover he is the stronger of the two!"

Before Zoroaster could stop to think, the words escaped him:

"Then you are under his dominion! You wretched people! Of course he seeks to gain ascendancy everywhere. But wherever men believe him they fall into ruin and darkness."

Alarmed, the old man countered: "Stranger, guard your tongue! You, and we with you, could be struck by the wrath of Ahriman."

"I will defy him," Zoroaster cried firmly. "What can Ahriman do to me when Ormuzd is my Lord? I am a servant of the Supreme God! He will know how to protect His servant."

Thoughtfully the men gazed at him who dared to speak in this way. Then the old man resumed:

"You are still young, stranger. I have experienced more than you. Believe me, Ahriman has gained control over the world. Men obey him. Even if they do not want to, they must. Relentlessly he forces them into his bonds.

"I too, like yourself, once believed that Ormuzd, the Exalted, the Wise One, was the God to Whom all men must adhere! It was a delusion, from which I awakened with pain.

"If Ormuzd were He Whom you consider him to be: why then does he permit his servants to run to the enemy?"

Rage mounted in Zoroaster. All the flames that had been slumbering for so long awakened. The colour rushed to his face, rash words were about to pass his lips.

Suddenly he felt a cool breeze wafting round him. In his ardent indignation it was infinitely soothing. And a gentle voice spoke:

"Here as everywhere, rash anger can only do harm. Consider what you wish to say! You will be helped. Take the poor people into your care. That is why you were sent here. Only kind attention to their thoughts, slow, sure guidance, can still be of help here."

Infinite calm descended upon the heart which only a moment ago had been pounding so vehemently.

"Ahuramazda, Thou great, benign God, Thy Glory is at stake. Help me!"

"There was a time," he began, almost as though he were musing, "when men were pure, just as they had come from the creative Hand of the wise God Whom you call Ormuzd. That was long ago. But in those days human beings were happy, for they lived according to the Will of God.

"He had countless servants, who were revered by the people as subsidiary gods; for they perceived clearly that those luminous beings were superior to themselves.

"Have you ever seen a fruit that has been eaten into by a worm?" he pretended to interrupt himself.

The men, finding no connection between this question and the narrative, looked at one another in surprise, but then said that they had.

So he continued:

"There is no telling from the outside that the creature is spreading itself within. For initially the worm is still very tiny, so that it can hardly be seen. The fruit looks fine. But the worm grows, and as it increases in size it eats the fruit from within. The fruit goes bad. After a time it is no longer what it should be, but a thing that arouses disgust, and is thrown away. Do you understand me?

"Into the human souls entered a worm, a tiny insignificant worm: the first act of disobedience to the great, kind God. He had said: 'I am the Most High. There is nothing beside Me!' And human beings considered each man for himself as the most important and highest. With that he placed himself not *alongside* God, but *above* Him!

"Is that not so, my friends? Just think about it!"

Zoroaster was silent, to give them time to reflect. He could see clearly how it was working within them. But he also knew that the words had flowed to him from above. How otherwise would he have known of Ahuramazda's Commandment, which he had just proclaimed to them?

Deep gratitude, joined with worship, filled him. When they asked him to continue he agreed. He had to speak.

"When Ahriman saw in the human souls this worm which had issued from his hand, he was pleased. He saw to it that ever more human souls were seduced into such disobedience. He rejoices over every human soul that Ormuzd has to reject as useless, for it is then his. And he wants to make himself lord over the souls.

"Do you now see what price you must pay for serving Ahriman?"

Taken aback, they looked at him. No one had ever spoken to them like this. Before he could continue, one of them found the courage to speak:

"Stranger, we have been happy until now! We do not feel ourselves as rotten fruit. We see nothing of the worm; we happily enjoy our lives.

"You may be right as regards other people, but all that is not true of us."

"Nor does the fruit at first notice that the worm is feeding on it," replied Zoroaster. "Nor is it visible from the outside. But just wait: the day will come when it can no longer remain hidden. And the day will come when death approaches each one of you, when the fruit is plucked, when it will be rejected. What then? What then of your happiness?"

Once more they were deeply affected, but again they did not want to admit it. Another man straightened and spoke:

"We have been taught that there is no beyond, that with this life all is over and done. Why should we fear death? It certainly puts an end to our happiness, our enjoyment, but with that everything is really finished."

"No, that is not true," shouted another. "We all know that our women become Peris. So there must be something that transcends death!"

Now differences of opinion arose. Increasing uproar filled the square, until finally the old man banged together two pieces of metal that lay beside him.

When silence had been restored, Zoroaster asked:

"Will you tell me what Peris are? I have never heard this word."

"When a woman dies, she would have to go into a dark realm, for women are deceitful, vain, unfaithful, and have many other faults besides. If her husband or a child pleads for her, she becomes a Peri, that is a spirit-being which must fulfil all kinds of duties in order to redeem itself from guilt."

Although Zoroaster could hardly remain silent any longer, he let the man finish speaking.

"If the Peri has served faithfully, it may live in a garden of the God Ormuzd, otherwise it becomes a Druj, which torments human beings. It creeps into houses as a ghost and commits evil deeds."

As the man lapsed into silence, Zoroaster broke out:

"He was quite right who just said that your disbelief in a life after death is refuted in your belief in Peris. Or do you imagine that only your women go on living, while you men are eaten by the great black birds, and then you are finished?

"Make no mistake! You too must answer for your deeds. You too must atone for all your wrongdoing. You must be glad that you are permitted to atone!

"O you wretched, misguided men, what wrong paths you are taking! Now I know why the servants of God have led me here. I will help you if you will let me speak. Dear friends, let yourselves be helped!"

There was a compelling ring in Zoroaster's voice. They all felt that it was a matter of great concern to him to bring them what he considered to be the Truth.

Why should they prevent him from doing so? It was quite evident that he had no evil intentions. They could safely listen to him, then either forget his words again or retain of them whatever they felt to be good.

Quietly they communicated these views to one another. Then the old man rose to his feet and said solemnly:

"Stranger, since you ask it of us, we will listen to you. You shall be our guest for a number of days, and every evening here in the square tell us of that which fills your heart to bursting. We perceive that you are in earnest."

That was all Zoroaster was able to accomplish that evening. But he was satisfied. Murza, however, grumbled. He admired Zoroaster's composure. He would have preferred to abandon the complacent, satisfied people.

They were taken to an empty hut where a few animal skins lay about, which they could arrange as they pleased. Not much trouble was expended on the guests. But the hut was kept tidy, the animal skins were clean. Zoroaster did not ask for more.

Very early the next morning, Murza set out to fetch food from Marzar for his master. On his way he found some beautiful fruits which he unhesitatingly took with him. As he was approaching the hut again on his way back, a young woman came rushing towards him, screaming, snatched the fruits from him, threw them on the ground and trampled on them.

Dumbfounded, Murza gazed at the frantic woman. He had perhaps taken the fruits wrongfully, but that was surely no cause for their instant destruction. Indignant, he recounted his experience to Zoroaster, who said thoughtfully:

"You do the woman an injustice, Murza. The fruits are probably poisonous."

Later it turned out that Zoroaster was right. Especially in this region many fine-looking, extremely poisonous fruits flourished. Children often fell prey to their craving for them.

During the day, the men went hunting. Zoroaster was not invited to accompany them, so he, Murza and Marzar rode far out to see the really beautiful countryside.

Of inconceivable beauty, the lake nestled among the forests. Today the people were absent, but it was not lifeless. The three men enjoyed the merry play of the little water-sprites, who appeared not to notice that they were being watched.

Not until evening was approaching did Zoroaster return to the huts, and as he brought with him a hearty appetite, he was welcome at the meal.

Afterwards the people settled themselves comfortably again, and invited the guest to speak. During the ride, however, Zoroaster had begged for help. He was most anxious to grip the souls, and he began with the Peris.

"You say that the Peris have to atone for their sins? Are your women really as bad as you think? Are you so much better than they?"

A veritable storm broke loose, from which the Forerunner gathered that the men deemed themselves virtuous, but thought the women capable of any sin.

"How is it that you are so much better? After all, boys and girls are born into the same families. Why do the girls become bad?"

"They are of weaker build, therefore they also have weaker souls," came the reply, to which Zoroaster for the moment could raise no objection.

160

"Why do you unite with these wicked women? Simply send them all away!" Zoroaster suggested.

"We have no one else, and they are good enough for preparing our meals and bearing us sons."

"I have been to many regions of the great realm," the guest now began, "but nowhere have I found such wicked women as here among you. On the contrary: I have seen women whose purity was almost as great as that of the first women, issuing from God's thoughts."

The men could scarcely credit that. But he told them about Madana and Yadasa. Murza, who had sat there in silence, suddenly began to join in the praise of Yadasa.

Then, however, Zoroaster asked how the men had arrived at the opinion that there was an after-life only for the women.

They said they did not know. They had been taught that at death everything is over. But they had also been taught that the women had to serve as Peris. Only when talking with the guest had they realised that the two do not tally.

"You see, friends," Zoroaster established, "thus there are many of your beliefs which are not in agreement. You do believe in Ormuzd. You know that He is a wise, benevolent God. Can you imagine the kind God simply letting Himself be deprived of authority?

"We have learned that he whom you call Ahriman arose from the depravity of human beings. Is that a *god* – something engendered by evil?"

Murza was startled at Zoroaster's audacity, but the men were so taken aback that they accepted the attack on their master quite calmly.

For the stranger was indeed right! If Ahriman were the stronger, Ormuzd would have relinquished His dominion to him. There would be no more need to believe in Ormuzd. But something stirred in them: they would not surrender their belief in Ormuzd, the beneficent One.

Suddenly the chieftain said:

"You speak of Ahriman as being our master. That is not right. We are only afraid of him. Our Lord is Ormuzd."

"You dear friends," exulted Zoroaster, "you need have no fear of the Dark One. If the Light One is truly your Lord, you stand in the protection of God and can laugh at the Evil One!"

He told them more and more of the Goodness of the One God, of the protection that He granted, of the strength that He bestowed. Not until late in the night did the men disperse.

Thus it continued for several days. Every evening Zoroaster won another small part of the souls that had been entrusted to him. But still he had not been able to convince them that neither were the men infallible nor the women altogether corrupt. Whenever he tried to bring about a change in the firmly-rooted views, he encountered obdurate resistance.

Again he asked and implored for enlightenment, so that he might find the right words at last. He returned home from his ride earlier than usual, and went at once to the square in which they met at night.

Suddenly he heard loud screams not far away; at first he took no notice. But they grew louder and sounded so horrible that he jumped up and tried to make his way towards the forest whence the cries came.

When he got there he saw two men running away, while a third lay on the ground covered with blood. The poor man had been so roughly treated that he was unable to help himself.

Zoroaster hardly dared to lift him for the man might bleed to death in the process. Then Murza came and helped him to carry the dying man to the hut of the chieftain. They knew the man, who had always listened intently whenever the discussion was about matters of eternity.

The screams had also summoned others; soon a dense circle of men was standing round the hut. Zoroaster saw that he could be of no further help there, and withdrew.

When the men later gathered in the square, he asked about the injured man, and was told that before he died he had still been able to describe his assailants. Zoroaster verified the statement of the departed one, for he too had recognised the men. The chieftain was pleased by the evidence, since the men had denied it.

"Why did they assault the man?" the guest wanted to know.

"Nasur was not able to tell us that, his strength did not hold out long enough," was the reply.

But the chieftain had secretly ordered both men to be brought in. When they came, he confronted them with Zoroaster, so that he might tell them himself that he had seen them.

But now the Forerunner saw even more. He saw how envy had consumed one of the men. The other appeared to have been only his helper.

Calmly he turned to the two miscreants:

"You are after all men, and you say that you can do no wrong," he began. "But now you have committed a grave offence. You," and he turned to the envious man, "have slain your neighbour Nasur out of sheer, loathsome envy! You," and he gazed at the other man who stood before him, white as a sheet, "have aided him. Thus one of you has perpetrated one crime, but the other at least two. If now you still deny it, you add a further crime to it.

"What do you think will happen to you now? Since you will not become Peris, you will – according to your belief – immediately have to serve in Ahriman's following?"

"I do not want to go to Ahriman," blubbered the accomplice, trembling all over. "I held Nasur down while Dursa struck him."

Astonished, the chieftain stared at Zoroaster, who with so few words had elicited the confession to the crime.

"What had Nasur done to you, that you had to strike him?" asked Zoroaster calmly.

The answer took them all by surprise:

"I do not know."

They looked at one another. It was certain that the man was lying. But why? He must have something to hide.

Then Zoroaster's calm voice rang out again:

"Where is the green stone that you took from the man's hut?"

Terrified, the miscreant stared at the questioner:

"What do you know of the green stone, stranger?" he asked without considering that he was thus giving himself away.

But Zoroaster did not answer his question; instead he repeated his own. Then the wrongdoer stammered:

"I have buried it beside my hut."

At a sign from the chieftain, several men went to look, and found a green stone of rare size, wrapped in a piece of cloth.

"See now, because of this stone you succumbed to envy, became a thief, a murderer and a liar? Can there be anything worse? And you became an accessory to Dursa's crime," said Zoroaster, turning to the other man, who was still blubbering.

"Now that you have the information, men, take the murderers away, lest the evening be spoiled for us by the sight of them," Zoroaster demanded. They willingly complied.

And then the Forerunner established for them that men also can be evil. In view of what they had just experienced they were more willing to concede than usual. Of course they would make this case appear to be an exception, but Zoroaster would not accept that.

They had to admit that they too had secretly committed many an action that was not in keeping with God's Will. He had quietly observed all kinds of things which he now brought forth against them, and the evening's benefit lay in the men's admission that they could not pass before the eyes of Ormuzd.

"That is why you describe Ahriman as the stronger god; because you fear Ormuzd, not Ahriman. You know in your innermost being that one day you must step before the Judgment Seat of God, in the same way as your women. Then every one of you will be brought to justice. How do you hope to pass?"

Again it was late when at last they dispersed. But the chieftain went to Zoroaster and asked:

"Stranger, what is to be done with the two wrongdoers?"

"What is the usual practice here in such cases?" Zoroaster asked in reply.

"We throw the murderer over the cliffs that rise up behind the forest," came the ready answer.

The old man was unaware that his admission demonstrated this case to be no exception, and Zoroaster did not draw his attention to it. He merely requested:

"Let me speak to the men tomorrow."

That was agreeable to the chieftain.

But the following morning the murderer had removed himself from the reach of earthly justice by taking his own life.

Shuddering with horror, the accomplice crouched beside Dursa's corpse.

"Soon I too will be dead," he whimpered to himself. "The stranger has said that then comes the Judgment!"

Zoroaster called the man outside. He himself shuddered at the fearful sight of the corpse.

Then he spoke earnestly to the trembling man:

"Do you feel now that everything cannot be over with this life? Do you know what awaits you if you are to step before the Judgment Seat as you are at this moment?"

The culprit wailed still louder and nodded.

"What do you want to do now?"

"I do not know. Help me, O good man!" implored the terrified man.

"Why did you help Dursa?" Zoroaster wanted to know. Rather vaguely he related that Dursa had threatened to kill him also if he refused to assist him. Nasur intended to report the theft; that is why he had to die.

For a long time Zoroaster spoke to the man, whom fear had so confused that he was unable to absorb anything. They had to wait until he had calmed down. He was permitted to return to the room from which, in the meantime, the dead body had been removed. Zoroaster went to the chieftain to discuss the murderer's accomplice with him.

"The best thing would be to throw him over the cliffs," said the old man placidly. "It would set a bad example if we let him go unpunished."

"Consider, friend," warned the Forerunner, "that he is still unrepentant. He only fears what is to come. Can you find no other punishment for him?"

"I will think it over," decided the chieftain, but Zoroaster perceived that he did not really mean it.

For the present he could do nothing to change the old man's mind. He could only hope that the sentence would not be carried out immediately.

But in the evening he discussed the case with the men, for it gave him a welcome opportunity. They had to admit that men can also sin, although they had no idea what would happen to them afterwards. There were no male Peris. Their belief included no life after death for a man.

In view of the two deaths, which had been so violent, they realised the absurdity of their previous way of thinking. Certainly Zoroaster still had enough trouble, but he spoke untiringly, and proved to them how wrong had been their way of thinking until now. After many evenings they were convinced.

If, however, there was a life after death, they understood quite well that it could not be the same for good and bad people. Since they all deemed themselves good, they shrank from the thought of later having to live with the bad.

Now at last Zoroaster could speak of the great Judgment, and when they had understood that, he slowly guided them to the thought of repeated earth-lives.

He had feared that this would cause the greatest difficulty. However the opposite was the case. Just this was joyfully received by them. In view of their great self-satisfaction, it simply could not be otherwise than that they must be born again to a glorious life!

They pictured it to themselves, were carried away, and suddenly had no further need of Zoroaster's explanations. He even became irksome to them with his constant admonitions.

They left him in no doubt that their hospitality had now come to an end. And he had really accomplished nothing with them. Should he nevertheless depart? He decided to await instructions from above and go to his tent nearby for the present.

Naturally they had long since noticed that he had horses and a servant with him, but they pretended otherwise. That too he did not understand. In the beginning there had been good reasons for his leaving Marzar to wait some distance away. He would have spoken of it long before now, but the men avoided him.

THAT VERY night he slept in his tent with his two loyal helpers, who were happy to have him to themselves for once to answer their own questions. Murza had witnessed and heard so many things that were unclear to him. Above all he did not understand the cautious way in which the otherwise so impetuous Forerunner proceeded.

Zoroaster told him that he had been instructed to this effect. But only in explaining did it become really clear to him how necessary the restraint had been.

"Will you go to the square again tomorrow evening?" Marzar asked, but received no definite answer. Zoroaster himself did not know.

During the night he prayed for an answer to this question. As he was about to rise from his bed in the morning, he realised that his limbs were aching and almost stiff. That was also an answer: he was being detained in the region, unable to visit the people. This went on for some days. Through the discussions with his companions he gained clarity, vistas opened out, and his understanding of eternal things deepened. Not a moment of this painful time would he have wished to forgo.

He was still practically immobile when one midday the chieftain came to the tent, pretending to be out hunting. He was about to express his surprise, but did not succeed under Zoroaster's clear gaze. Therefore he interrupted himself in the middle of the sentence, asking instead whether the stranger was ill.

"It would appear that you have eaten of the berries that grow in abundance around here," he said, after Zoroaster had described his pains to him.

Murza was summoned, and admitted that he had plucked some of these beautiful berries, and because of their pleasant taste, had crushed and added them to Zoroaster's drink.

"The poison is not fatal," the old man reassured the frightened Murza. "Within a few days your master will be able to make use of his limbs again. But you must beware of picking fruits or berries here, however harmless they may appear to you."

Zoroaster told him of the fruits that Murza had brought the first morning.

"I have heard about it," said the old man. "It was my daughter who snatched the dangerous fruits from Murza. They would have brought you instant death."

"It is strange," he went on after a brief interval, "that the plants here have changed so much. I can remember that as a child I ate some of the fruits that are now so fatal.

"A wise old man who once visited us attributed that to the dominion of Ahriman, under whose influence everything becomes bad."

Zoroaster wished to reply, but the old man had not come to discuss plants. Impatiently he waved his brown hand, asking to be heard.

"Stranger, I do not know what to do with the criminal," he said, hesitating a little, as if he was ashamed of asking. "Your words have made me think, and now I can no longer consider it right to kill him. We must give him the opportunity to make amends, if that is possible."

Zoroaster looked at the speaker with ardent joy, and fervent gratitude welled up in him. Thus had God's Goodness softened this obstinate heart!

"I think so too," he said kindly. "Have you thought of some way in which the man could atone for his deed?"

"Nasur has left behind a young wife and six children who are unprovided for. If the bad man, whose name is Wunad, would marry her and provide for her children as well, the damage she has suffered through her husband's death would be redressed."

"But will she want the man who helped to kill her husband, in her hut?" asked Zoroaster in disbelief.

"Where you live, do you ask the women whom they want to marry?" retorted the chieftain angrily. "With us the man decides. The woman must be content if she finds a provider. Therefore Nasur's wife, too, will be happy if Wunad comes to her, for then she need not starve."

"If that is the case, then I also think that it would be a good atonement for Wunad," Zoroaster admitted. The chieftain laughed:

"Indeed, it is almost too easy, for Nasur's wife is young, pretty and as good as a woman can be. He will fare well with her."

"Will his companions not despise him if he works among them again?" Zoroaster enquired.

The old man's answer was no.

"If someone has done wrong and realises it, no one speaks of the past any more."

With that the chieftain had again admitted that wrongdoing was nothing unfamiliar to them. But that the others did not make things difficult for the wrongdoer was a very noble trait in these men. Would that this were so everywhere!

"You will be able to walk again in a few days' time, stranger. Will you come again to us in the square?" the visitor asked hesitantly.

Joyfully Zoroaster promised to do so. But the old man had one more request:

"May I send Wunad to you so that you may speak to him, and make him rightly understand the mercy shown to him by us, and be in earnest about providing for the children? He is very stupid, but he will still understand something," the chieftain assured him. Relieved, he made a move to go.

Zoroaster promised that as well. Now he had trouble in consoling Murza, who came rushing in after the old man's departure, lamenting over the suffering he had caused Zoroaster.

"Do you not realise, Murza," Zoroaster calmed the distressed man, "how your lack of caution ultimately served a good purpose? Without the pains caused by the poison, I would probably have ridden away disheartened. Now I have been permitted to experience how the chieftain came to me seeking advice, and called me back. Let us both rejoice at what the benign God has done."

After three days Zoroaster was able to get up. He forced himself to mount Ray, and tried to ride a little. He still felt unwell. Just as he was about to turn round, he saw a man standing watching him. It was Wunad.

"Have you been standing here long?" asked Zoroaster, surprised.

"I come every morning and go every evening, Sire," came the unexpected answer.

"But why did you not come to me, Wunad?" Zoroaster saw that the man was still afraid. "After all, I only want to help set you on to the right path again."

"Are you saying that I would have been permitted just to enter your tent? Our chieftain said: 'The gracious gentleman, the stranger, will allow you to speak with him.' I have been waiting for this permission every day."

Without explaining his error to the man, who was really stupid, Zoroaster offered:

"Come along then."

Willingly Wunad followed, willingly he let himself be questioned, and replied to the best of his ability.

"If you are allowed to redeem a small part of your great guilt already here, Wunad," Zoroaster admonished him, "do not forget that you must take the place of their father, their provider, for Nasur's children."

"Yes, but also that of the woman's husband," said Wunad with a broad grin. Evidently he was pleased with his punishment.

"You must do everything that lies in your power to atone, my friend. You must forget your own self completely; you may live and work only for the others, whom you have deprived of their natural protector. Will you do that?"

"Certainly, I will gladly do it," said Wunad with conviction. "I shall surely be a better father to them than Nasur was."

Zoroaster realised that the man's limited intelligence would make any discussion of deeper matters impossible. He hoped that perhaps later on he would come to an understanding. For the present he dismissed him, and Wunad ran off as if relieved.

After a few days Zoroaster had made sufficient progress to allow him to go to the open square in the evening. He found all the men assembled as though expecting him. How did they know that he was coming today?

When he asked them, he learned that they had already been awaiting him for three evenings.

"The effect of the poison usually lasts that long," they explained, "but with you it took a little longer, probably because your constitution is different from ours."

They candidly admitted that their thoughts about future lives had misled them. They had believed that each of them must become something very great in future earth-lives. But then they had realised how wrong this was.

Now they wanted to know if they had already been on earth before. Zoroaster said that they had, though he did so reluctantly, for he feared that now as before they would begin their speculations all over again. But they had learned from experience, and were careful not to fall into the same error.

As they now kept silent, reflecting quietly on what they had heard, they began to understand various connections. They understood why one had to live in poverty, another in illness. Previously this had seemed to them unjust. Now they suddenly saw that they were to blame for everything. And again they said:

"It is all so simple!"

This time Zoroaster spoke, pointing out that indeed it was all very simple, but that they would realise how difficult it would be for them when once they sought to put it into effect.

"If you try to lead a spotless life, you will experience how much it takes to give yourselves up."

They willingly absorbed what he told them. It was obvious that they had missed him.

When he parted from them for the night, they escorted him to his tent, and he had to promise to return the following evening.

He did so, and with the firm intention of speaking about women on this occasion.

"You have demonstrated your resolve to act prudently," he began, praising them. "You have absorbed so much which at first seemed impossible for you to understand. Continue in this way, and you will soon have done away with all that is wrong in your views."

They looked at him, pleased. His praise was new to them. Now they would strive doubly hard to be worthy of this praise.

"Tell me what faults you find in your womenfolk," he wanted to know.

They were silent. What should they say? They had nothing to complain of, but they had been taught that woman is worthless. They adhered to this because it was convenient.

Zoroaster read these thoughts, and when no one spoke he repeated aloud what he had seen.

"Is it not so, my friends?" he concluded.

They admitted it. Not one of them had concerned himself about his wife, for to all she was merely a servant and worker.

Then he told them how Ahuramazda had conceived of the woman. Equipped with the finer intuitive perception, she was meant to go before man everywhere, to mediate to him the connection with the higher world. For this reason the man was to protect the weaker one and help her on her earthly journey, so that her finer abilities could remain intact.

"So it was meant to be, my friends, and so it still is in some places," said the speaker, looking at them all. "And how did I have to find things here? Subdued and timid, your women slink about. They slip away at the sight of you, for they never know what to expect from you. I have observed that you beat them when you are in a bad mood. I have yet to hear a kind word.

"You yourselves give heed to your clothing. You dress up as women do elsewhere. But you allow your wives and children to go about in dirty rags. Don't you think that they too would like to dress well?

"The women have to prepare your food, and they are wonderful cooks. At mealtimes you let yourselves be served by them. I have not found this anywhere else before. And then the women and children are given what is left. You do not care whether they have enough to eat or not.

"These are outward things in which you fail to contribute to your women's well-being. Where is your solicitude? Just look for once at their souls. Do you let them participate in your discussions about sacred things? Do you pray with them? Who teaches them while they are still small? I wanted to speak to them, but they shrank back. Have they no need of it? Or have you so restrained them that they are fearful if their souls for once desire a breath of fresh heavenly air?"

When he was silent, the men sat there like scolded children. They looked at the ground, but not in defiance. At last one of the younger men raised his head:

"Master," that was their new new way of addressing him, "Master, I say to you that every word you have just spoken is right! We must be ashamed whenever we think of Ormuzd. Our women are worse off than our animals, for these we tend, and deny them nothing.

"But now tell us, how are we to bring about a change? Our women simply would not understand if we were to change our behaviour towards them. Nor would they understand us if we tried to give them explanations, for we are not so eloquent as you are."

"Not much eloquence is required to explain what is in question," said Zoroaster, who was delighted with this young man. "You must do as I have done with you, and begin at the beginning. Establish a link with what they have known from their earliest years, then they will go on asking."

Embarrassed, the men looked at one another. It was bad that the Master did not know how it was with their womenfolk, that they had to explain everything to him. They were ashamed of themselves.

172

Finally one of them took heart:

"Master, there is no beginning with which to make a link. From olden times our women have been kept in ignorance so that we should remain in control. When they asked us about Divine things, we would say: that is not for you, see to your work. They know as little about Ormuzd as – as your horse," he concluded in embarrassment.

Zoroaster was horrified, and clearly showed it. Why should he conceal the fact that he considered the treatment of the women the most shameful thing he had ever encountered?

But that was of no avail. If he were to send for them and speak to them, out of shyness they would not even listen to him. Nor did he understand anything about women. He did not know how to awaken the finer intuitive sensing which no doubt slumbered also in these wretched, demoralised souls.

He pondered passively, directing his thoughts upwards, imploring help. All at once he knew what had to be done: Yadasa must come. Here was a great, beautiful task for her. Here she could work with her hapless sisters. A great feeling of bliss rose up within him at this good solution.

He told the men about Yadasa, of whom he had previously spoken to them. He described how lovely and pure she was, and how willing to help all women.

"Tomorrow I will ride out immediately with my companions and fetch Yadasa," he cried happily.

"Will she be willing to come with you?" the men asked, unable to believe in such good fortune.

But he had not the least doubt that Yadasa would instantly recognise this task as of the utmost urgency.

"When can you be with us again?" they asked anxiously.

"I will come as soon as it is at all possible, but I cannot say exactly when," was his reply.

He was not at all clear how far it would be to Yadasa's village, but he trusted in the guidance of the little ones.

So HE rode forth the next morning with joy in his heart. He delighted in nature, which at this particular time was unfolding gloriously; he rejoiced in the stillness which gave him so much that was beautiful, and his body delighted in the healthy movement.

One evening he sat before his white tent; his companions had retired to their own, but their quiet whispering could be heard from time to time.

He paid no attention to them, for he was too absorbed in his own thoughts. Suddenly Marzar appeared to have forgotten all discretion. Louder than before his voice rose to ask:

"How can Zoroaster imagine a woman accompanying us? He must not expect that of her."

"I believe he will take other girls on the journey as well," replied Murza indifferently.

Again Marzar's voice rose:

"Does it not occur to him that all three of us are unmarried? He will dishonour Yadasa before all people if he simply takes her with him."

"Remember he is not like other human beings. He is the Forerunner, and therefore he is permitted certain things."

Murza had spoken sharply. But Marzar would not yield.

"Forerunner or no, if he wishes to take Yadasa with him he must marry her!"

Marzar had spoken so loudly that Murza cautioned him abruptly, and the conversation continued in a quiet whisper.

But Zoroaster had heard enough. As though cut with a knife the veil that had hung before his soul parted. All kinds of thoughts assailed him. To think that he had not realised what was obvious to the simple groom!

How could he endanger the noble Yadasa? But he had promised help to the women, they needed her. Should he take Yadasa to the people, and ride away immediately? But then he would be leaving her alone and unprotected among strangers.

She had said at the time that she stood in the protection of purity. But then her father had made the journey as well. And even as all these thoughts went through his mind, the most obtrusive one he pushed furthest away, giving it no chance whatever to be heard.

174

How could he, the Forerunner, marry? His life belonged to God, Whose servant he was.

The whisperers, whose voices had roused him from his unconcern, had long since gone to rest. He sat, as he so loved doing, under the shining starry sky. But the peace that usually filled his soul was not there.

Then he cast himself on the ground and poured out his soul in prayer. What he dared not admit to himself he uttered to the Most High. He would hide nothing, every emotion should lie exposed before the Eye of God. Then he grew calm. And in the calm he heard again the voice of the Luminous Messenger: "Zoroaster, hear me! It is the Will of Ahuramazda that you take Yadasa for your wife. You need a partner to complement your work by teaching the women. A better and purer woman you cannot find. Take her to your heart, and protect her from all adversity.

"She will bear you a son whom you are to call Vishtaspa. Hafiz will not marry. Your son is to inherit the realm. He is to become King. Under his reign Persia will blossom into a blessed land.

"Such is the wise Will of Ahuramazda!"

The voice fell silent. What he had not dared to desire was to become reality. He was to be permitted to call wife and child his own!

Now his prayer was transmuted into praise and thanksgiving. He could hardly wait for the sun to rise in order to continue their journey.

They had to ride another three days, the little ones had said, and they were not mistaken.

At noon of the third day they saw the familiar village emerge. How much had he experienced here! Now he was to be allowed to meet again the people who had so richly rewarded his efforts. That in itself was joy.

They rode to the hut of the chieftain, who looked out from it in surprise. When he recognised Zoroaster, he called in a loud voice to the neighbours. They should all come, the Zoroaster had returned.

Within a few minutes the square was teeming with joyful and excited people. They all hailed the Forerunner, each one wanted to greet him, to thank him, to tell him what he had experienced in the meantime. It was a babel of voices that made it impossible to understand a single word.

Zoroaster greeted them all while his eyes sought Yadasa. Suddenly he heard Murza's voice:

"Sire, over there!"

Yes, there stood Yadasa, a delicate blush spread over her lovely features, looking with radiant eyes at him who had returned. When she felt his gaze upon her, she stepped forward to greet him. Then she went into the hut to prepare a meal.

Slowly the excited people calmed down. They begged Zoroaster to speak to them in the evening, and he promised to do so.

Meanwhile he listened to accounts about the welfare of the village-dwellers, enquired whether there had been any illness, and if they adhered to what they had recognised as truth.

The old man, whose facial expression had markedly changed, said proudly:

"I do not think that there is a single one among us who will forget the experience that you have brought us. We have all become totally different human beings, as you will see tonight. We have also been spared disease. Yadasa told us one day that our suffering was the result of our sins. What we regarded as unbearable torment was in reality the greatest grace of Ahuramazda, for through it so many of us have come to our senses."

Zoroaster's eyes sought the maiden, who had kept away from the men's meal. When he did not see her, he asked her father:

"Is it given to Yadasa to see truths?" The old man confirmed that she had that ability.

"From an early age there was something special about her, which became still more pronounced through her stay with the priestesses. Since you have been here and made us servants of Ahuramazda, she often tells us things which she is given in the night. Now and again I have asked her how these truths are communicated to her, but she does not like to speak about it. Perhaps you know?" he added with childlike curiosity.

"No, I do not know either," the Forerunner replied. "It is different with every human being who is deemed worthy of it. The main thing is certainly not the 'how', but the 'what'. If it be truth, nothing else should be of any concern to us."

"I could even imagine," he continued after thinking over it for a short while, "that such enquiry would hinder the pure reception of tidings from above. You may harm Yadasa by asking how the truths are given to her."

"How can that be?" enquired the old man, who was impressed by Zoroaster's words.

"I told you once," the Forerunner began to explain, "that all human thoughts take on forms. Naturally forms that are invisible to the human eye," he added quickly, as he saw how the old man's eyes widened.

"These forms strive towards the object that has evoked them. Thus if you ponder over the way in which Yadasa receives a truth, this pondering will give rise to a great many forms which immediately surround Yadasa. But thereby you envelop your daughter with a fine cloak, which makes it difficult, if not altogether impossible, for her to receive the rays from above."

The old man marvelled, then all at once understanding, he said:

"Yadasa has often said: 'Do not think of me so much, Father, for then I cannot hear.' The meaning of that is probably the same as your explanation today. But I have understood you now, and Yadasa's words were incomprehensible to me."

The man then enquired about Sadi, whom he particularly liked. Zoroaster told him how completely the servant had changed, which prompted the old man to comment:

"Well, I do not have the gift of seeing truths; but I did perceive that there was a fine kernel in Sadi. Let me tell you something.

"Your horse is quite special. That must be obvious to all men. Here too we have white steeds that are big and strong. Now it happened at the very beginning, before you had taught us, that one of us offered Sadi his best charger in exchange for your Ray. You would certainly not have noticed it. In return, however, Sadi was to receive many precious stones. He did not hesitate for a moment, but threw the man out of the horses' paddock, so that he was in pain for days afterwards."

Smiling, Zoroaster answered:

"Ah, was that why you limped at the beginning of our acquaintance?"

The old man nodded without embarrassment. After all, these were things of the past, of which he was no longer ashamed now. But Zoroaster asked:

"Did you observe Marzar at the meal? Would you dare to approach him with the same unreasonable request?"

177

Startled, the chieftain disclaimed this.

"No, even if I were still as I was then, I would not dare!"

"Hence you see that at the time Sadi was not yet a true servant of the Eternal God, otherwise you would not have dared to approach him. But now he has become one."

"What you are voicing there, Zoroaster, is something glorious," the old man reflected. "When we belong to Ahuramazda no temptation from the Darkness will dare to approach us! That is so reassuring."

They went on talking about various other things, but the Forerunner said nothing about why he had come. He knew that the right opportunity for it would be shown to him from above. He was able to wait, he had learned that.

But the old man could hardly wait to take his guest to the assembly-square. With great joy, the men had carried out changes which truly gave evidence of the earnest striving that inspired them.

They had enclosed the square with stones, and planted all kinds of shrubs behind them. In the centre they had erected a pile of stones similar to the seven on the Mountain of the Festival. It could be seen that the square was more to them than merely a place where all sorts of things were discussed.

"We even have a flame-bowl," said the old man with pride. "If you wish to hold a festival for us in the next few days, we will use it."

Zoroaster liked the idea of the festival. He was also delighted with the symbolically arranged square. Certainly the stone-pile they had erected would remind the people that this was not the place for arguments and earthly matters.

"Do you always gather here?" he enquired.

"What do you mean by that?" asked the old man, uncomprehending. "After all, it is our holy place. We are always here when we want to speak of Ahuramazda and matters of eternity."

"And what about when you have to discuss other things, surely that can happen also?"

"We now have another square for that purpose. When we invite the people to come here, they know in advance that they must leave behind all earthly cares and thoughts. He who cannot do so must stay away."

178

"Do your women attend the gatherings?"

"Of course; Yadasa sees to that. I would have no peace if I were to do it differently. But they come only to the discussions in the holy square, they are not admitted to the others."

The men came from all directions, not boisterous and unruly as before, but calm and dignified. How much indeed the short period of self-discipline had accomplished here!

Zoroaster was amazed, and glad to have been given the opportunity to see this. It would benefit his work with others. There was no crowding on the square itself; every man seemed to know the place where he was permitted to sit.

In this way a dense circle of men was gradually formed. When all were seated, the women and older girls arrived in a long procession. There was something indescribably solemn in the manner in which they approached their "sanctuary". Yadasa led them into the circle of men, where they seated themselves to form the inner circle.

The chieftain and Zoroaster had remained standing by the stones.

"You all know," began the old man solemnly, "that we have the Forerunner once more in our midst. It is a great blessing for us all. Let us give thanks for it to Ahuramazda."

They all rose as one, their arms reaching upwards. It was a gesture completely natural to all, not something they imitated. Thereafter the old man said a few fervent words of gratitude. When he had ended the people dropped their arms, but they remained standing, deeply absorbed, for another few moments, after which they seated themselves again.

"Let us ask Zoroaster to speak to us now," the leader decided; then he too seated himself.

"I am happy that I can be with you again. But still deeper is my joy in recognising how all the good that was placed in you as a tender seed has increased.

"In the meantime we have all experienced a great deal, outwardly to be sure – but still more inwardly. In the process all sorts of questions will have arisen within you. If that is so, I would ask you to put your questions to me today. They will show me what additional knowledge you still need which I am able to give you."

Without shyness the men began to ask. The joy of having the Forerunner in their midst loosened all tongues. And the questions demonstrated that they truly had not wasted their time. They had reflected deeply, had been permitted to discover much.

After many things had been discussed, a woman asked:

"If you may tell us: why must the Saoshyant come as a child, as you once said. I would indeed like to be the mother who is permitted to bear Him, but I would find it a thousand times more glorious if He were to descend in the clouds in all His Might."

"So will He appear when He stands before men as the World-Judge. Ineffable will be His glory then. But the hearts of men will tremble and quake, they will bow down, and yet know that this is not enough. In His greatness, in His incorruptible justice, He will appear majestic to them."

Zoroaster's eyes spanned enormous distances. He stood before the people like a seer. Never before had he spoken thus to men; for he was transported, and unconsciously proclaimed what he beheld.

"Men will perish before His Holy Countenance, before whose radiance none can endure. But those who were His servants, and strove to be faithful, He will summon to Himself. They will be permitted to walk by His side through the Judgment, in order then to serve Him in bliss for all eternity.

"Do you realise, my friends, what is meant by eternal? If you understood it, you would strive still more to keep every thought within the Will of Ahuramazda. To be cast away for all eternity, or to be eternally blest: choose!"

For a moment Zoroaster was silent, though he had not yet returned from his state of transport. The people, who intuitively perceived that they were allowed to experience a very great happening, listened as though spellbound.

"But my friends, the Saoshyant comes not only as the World-Judge. He comes also as the 'Helper', for that is the meaning of His Holy Name. But He can help only if He knows what we human beings feel deep within us.

"What does Ahuramazda know of that which stirs the human soul? He is much too exalted for that! He does not know what temptations and urges approach the wretched human beings. Although He is familiar with the diversely intricate paths of men, He does not know what they feel as they tread them.

"But the Helper will know, for He will relinquish His place beside His Father for a period of time. He will be born as a child like any other earth-child. As He grows up He will proceed in the Golden Ray of Divine Grace and Divine Love. He will live with and among human beings, for only thus can He gain a knowledge of their weaknesses and faults. He will help them, He will bring them the forgotten Truth, the lost Purity. He, the Helper, the Radiant Hero!

"Then He will stride upwards in the Golden Ray. The Saoshyant as earth-man will be no more; the World-Judge, the Son of God will remain!"

Drawing a deep breath, Zoroaster fell silent. His face was turned upwards, as if he were still seeing what he had just proclaimed.

The souls of the people, however, were filled with holy awe. But the awe was on its knees before God, not before the human being who had just conveyed to them a faint idea of Divinity.

No further word was spoken that evening. Silently the people departed, taking the deep impression of the experience with them into the stillness of the night.

On the following day Zoroaster felt unable to remain in the busy village. All the people seemed to be pursuing some work or other; he alone had nothing to do. Yet he longed to reflect in solitude on what the evening had bestowed also on him.

He had received more than any of them. He had been permitted to see, and this seeing had deepened and strengthened in him the knowledge of future events.

Beside it his own wishes paled, so that he had nearly forgotten them. Quietly within him the words of the Luminous Messenger vibrated, but they would fall silent before the glory that had lived in his soul since yesterday.

Not until evening did he return to the village. He became aware that he had eaten nothing all day. Now he was looking forward to the meal. Although it was not so well prepared as the food which had been placed before him recently, it was certainly clean and nourishing.

Men served it, and waited on the diners. That was the custom.

Nazim, the chieftain, had been anxious because Zoroaster had gone away on his own. But Yadasa had comforted him. She knew that he was seeking Ahuramazda in solitude, and therefore could come to no harm.

After the meal they all went to the holy square. They came in the same way as on the previous evening: the men individually; the women assembled at Yadasa's hut and then walked in procession to the square. After the meeting they left in the same way.

Again Nazim said a short prayer, and then invited the guest to speak to them. To this request he immediately added the question of whether he had met any particularly good people on his journeyings.

Zoroaster was happy to be able to confirm that he had. He spoke of the shepherds who lived scattered about in the mountains, and whose souls were completely filled with eternal things. And he spoke of those in the beautiful valley of flowers. Without meaning to he then began to speak about the last tribe he had visited. He described his experiences, and was frequently interrupted by the shouted exclamations of the listeners. Then he began to speak of the wretched, scorned women.

There was a mixture of compassion, indignation, and concern among the intent listeners. Especially the women and girls bemoaned the plight of their sisters, and asked whether there was no help at all for them.

"That is why I have come," confessed Zoroaster. "I hoped to win over some of your women to come with me in order to improve the lot of these others. They would need to live there for a time and instruct the women, fire them by their example, thus compelling the men to show respect.

"Only in that way can help be given. I myself am powerless in face of the old prejudices!"

When he fell silent many different thoughts moved the listeners. Some women and girls were prepared to make this sacrifice, for leaving their familiar surroundings and giving up their present security in order to journey to a people who regarded women in the same way as they did animals, was indeed a sacrifice.

The men were indignant about so much brutality in the customs of these others. They also understood that help must be given, but it seemed hard to them to be without their wives and daughters.

Zoroaster, who saw all these thoughts, knew that he must not voice a question now. He concentrated his whole mind on one single appeal to Ahuramazda for help. Then he rose to his feet, for today he had spoken while seated.

Realising that Zoroaster was about to pray, the people stood up also. But they did not raise their arms, for it was his entreaty that he wanted to place before God's Throne. They sensed this unconsciously.

And he prayed with deep fervour that the Eternal One might fill their hearts with His power, to enable them to hear His call. That He might inspire the spirit of self-sacrifice within those women whom He would entrust with the great, glorious task of pulling other human beings out of the swamp of immorality.

Now everything suddenly appeared in a quite different light. If it was a task to be accomplished for the Most High, then they all wanted to co-operate. No one wished to remain behind. He had hardly ended his prayer before offers to go and pleas to be taken with them came from all directions.

He told them that he would take with him only the women who could be spared here for a short time. Those with small children must devote their attention to them. He would speak with Nazim, and then a decision could be made.

One of the men pointed out that it was better to ask Yadasa than to speak to Nazim. She knew who among the women would be suitable for this work. She knew them all. Women who could be spared could not simply be engaged in this great work if they were perhaps unable to do it.

Those women designated by Yadasa must be taken. If one who had small children were to be included, help would be found in the neighbour-hood. If a sacrifice was demanded by Ahuramazda for the sake of strangers, it must also be done in the right way, and without regard for one's own comfort.

These words pleased everyone. They cheered the speaker. Zoroaster expressed the opinion that anything else should be discussed in the council-square, where they would therefore meet the following day. Today he wanted to tell them something.

They liked best of all to hear again about the Saoshyant. That pleased the Forerunner; elsewhere he had had to clear away so much rubble that he hardly got down to preparing the ground, whereas here he was already permitted to build up.

With an overflowing heart he gave the people what they were thirsting for. They asked about the embroidered sign that he wore on his breast. Some of them had heard the exclamations of the priestess at the Festival. They knew that it was the Cross of the Saoshyant. The others had heard it from them. Now they all wanted to know the meaning of this sign.

Zoroaster told them that he had often reflected upon it. He had found an explanation; he did not know whether it was the right one.

The Cross had four arms of equal length, extending to the four quarters of the world. To him this seemed to signify that the Saoshyant reached out His arms with equal love to all, in order to help them. It was immaterial where men lived or to what people they belonged. He would help them all.

But the fact that four rays broke forth between the arms meant that the indwelling Power of the Sign was so immense that it could not be held back. It must radiate outwards.

The people liked that, and they reflected on it quietly. Then Yadasa raised her voice. So far she had said nothing but a few words pertaining to outward matters.

Her face was turned heavenwards, and Zoroaster gazed spellbound into the purity of those fine features.

"This Sign is to be an admonition to us human beings," she said in a vibrant voice. "We are to stand firmly on the earth that gave birth to us, but we are to look up to Heaven, to the Dwelling-place of Ahuramazda whence all power and all good flow upon us.

"Once we have drawn strength from there, we should look about us in solicitude for others, and with our love embrace everything that is in need of it.

"But brothers and sisters, give heed to the fine balance: there is to be symmetry in all things. As high as we strive towards heaven, so firmly are we to grasp the earth.

"Let the holy proportions pervade all your thoughts, all your deeds; then from you too will break forth rays of power that will kindle flames in other human beings!"

184

Then a youth called out:

"Yadasa, you are interpreting the sign for us human beings. Do you not see that it holds good to a far greater extent for the Saoshyant? From above He comes, downwards He goes, lovingly He inclines towards humanity, and spreads His helping arms out towards them."

Thus the sign had something different to say to each one, and yet it all conveyed the message. Zoroaster was the last to speak that evening when he said:

"As with this sign, so is it with every truth. Every race interprets it as they see it. The one discovers this, another yet a different Law of Ahuramazda. Thus is it willed."

He noticed that they were about to say more, but he referred them to the following day. –

Early the next morning, Nazim came to see him.

"I have come so early because I would like to speak to you," he began somewhat hesitantly. "If you want to be alone with Ahuramazda, then tell me when you will have time for me."

"I am glad that you have come. I too would like to talk with you," Zoroaster said obligingly.

He knew that now the hour of decision for his further earthly life had come.

The two men walked out into the garden, which appeared indescribably fair in the morning freshness.

"Listen, Zoroaster," began Nazim, "Yadasa has spoken to me. She wishes to go with you to the alien people in order to give help to the women. She says that it is the task assigned to her from above. In recent weeks this has been indicated to her repeatedly. Let her tell you about it herself.

"I know that I must let her go; for it would be ingratitude towards the kind, wise God if I were to refuse. But my heart is heavy. Who will give her outward protection?

"Even if you were there at the same time, you know that it is not right for a maiden to leave her father's house by herself. I would like to ask you to encourage her to marry our neighbour's son, so that he can accompany her."

185

Now that it was said, Nazim breathed a sigh of relief. He knew that he was thwarting his child's wish, but his fatherly concern had become too strong within him.

Zoroaster gazed kindly at the old man.

"I can take Yadasa with me only if she goes as my wife," he said calmly.

"As your wife, Zoroaster?" the old man cried, thinking that he had not understood him aright. "What are you saying: as *your* wife?"

"I know I have nothing to offer her except myself, but I think she will not refuse me."

"Refuse you? The Forerunner of the Helper?" The old man was like one out of his mind. "You must tell her this yourself."

With that he hastened away as fast as his old legs would carry him.

Zoroaster stood alone amid the fragrant blossoms. Around him was a ringing, singing and exulting, and his heart took up the resonant tones.

Yadasa was approaching from a garden further away, where healing herbs were grown. Zoroaster called out a greeting to her, whereupon she came nearer.

"Has my father spoken to you, Sire?" she asked, going up to him.

"Yes, he has told me of your wish to go to the poor women yourself. I am happy about that, Yadasa, but I can only take you if you will go with me as my wife. Can you decide to do this?"

"Shall I not be an obstacle to you on your path?" she asked softly.

"Indeed not, but rather the companion who complements my work, the helper whom the goodness of Ahuramazda has ordained for me!"

"Then I will joyfully go with you."

It was said quite simply, but Zoroaster knew that he had gained the best that his earth-life could bring him.

Hand-in-hand they went to the hut of Nazim, who was still in a complete daze. At one time he had pictured Yadasa's marriage quite differently. Then he had given up all mundane plans in order not to distress his child. Now he was getting the best son that he could wish for! It was inconceivable. –

After the morning repast during which Zoroaster told his two companions that he was going to marry Yadasa, he asked the maiden to tell him of her visions, so far as she was permitted to do so. She readily consented.

Often she had seen a lovely white figure. On each occasion she had received the instruction to take care of the despised, ignorant women.

On the last occasion she had been promised that the Forerunner himself would take her to the most wretched of women. Smiling, the speaker had added:

"He will demand something of you. Do what he asks. It will bring you blessing."

"Do you have special customs when two people are joined for life?" enquired Zoroaster, who wanted to be on his way as soon as possible.

"Hitherto we have always followed our forefathers in this respect. The couple would take up their position amid their tribal companions, and promise to belong faithfully to one another. Then the father of the maiden would pray. With that it was all over."

"Let us do likewise," said Zoroaster.

That same evening Nazim prayed with them both before all the people of the village. There was great rejoicing when they heard that the Forerunner of the Saoshyant had chosen a maiden from their midst to be his wife. But they understood his choice. There could be no better, purer maiden than Yadasa. After the short ceremony, at which the flame-bowl had not even been lit, they all proceeded to the other meeting-place so that the women whom Yadasa had selected to accompany her could be named.

All the women and girls would have liked to go with them. Now that Yadasa herself was setting out, it would have been a joy and an honour for them to accompany her. However she had not made the selection through using her own judgment, but had been guided by the voices that whispered so many truths to her in the night.

This time the women had also been allowed to come to the meeting-place, since the deliberations concerned them above all.

Here too Nazim prayed first that Ahuramazda might bestow His blessing on their decisions, and prevent them from acting wrongly.

Then Yadasa went into the centre of the circle, and called out the names of the five women who were to go with her. They were older, strong women, whose homes and children were kept in an exemplary way. Thus it was to be expected that they would also be able to show the neglected women what was right.

It was decided that they should depart at the next full moon, which they considered to be particularly auspicious. And much as Zoroaster felt urged to get on with his task, he acquiesced in this delay of about seven days, because he intuitively sensed that for some reason he was still needed here.

Yadasa and the women then left the circle of the men, to make all the arrangements for what had to be done during their absence.

But the men still discussed in detail the changes which they wished to make in their village. There was some anxiety that through Yadasa's departure the connection with the Light would be lost.

"I am not afraid," said the man to whom this thought had come, "that we shall not all continue striving to the best of our abilities. But Yadasa worked among us like a priestess and seeress. If you now take her from us, Zoroaster, we shall not have the answers to many a question which Yadasa used to draw for us from the Light."

"It is surely not Ahuramazda's Will that you should be without help," said Zoroaster, reassuring the troubled people. "I am not taking Yadasa from you of my own accord. God Himself has decreed that she should be my helpmate. But I cannot remain here, as I should not be fulfilling my task."

"But you will continue to regard our village as your home, to which you will always return, Zoroaster?" asked Nazim, and the Forerunner promised that he would.

"I believe," he then said, "that Ahuramazda has already provided for you. It will be made manifest in one way or other within the next few days. I will ask Him that help may come to you even before we ride away."

In the night the Forerunner left the hut in which he lived with his two companions, and as was his wont, he sought to gain connection with the higher worlds under the starry sky.

Although the moon was visible only as a semicircle, the night was clear. It seemed to Zoroaster that the stars had never sparkled so brightly.

There was so much that he wanted to bring before the Throne of the Most High: Gratitude for the benevolent guidance of his life, for the gift of the companion who would help him with his work. Gratitude also for everything that had taken place in the souls of these human beings.

From this arose quite spontaneously the fervent entreaty not to leave these souls without guidance. Nazim was an upright man, but he was old; moreover it was with difficulty that his thoughts moved beyond the accustomed range of ideas.

Whoever would guide these open human beings had to forgo any self-will completely. Whatever he told them he must draw from deep sources, pervaded by the power from above.

And Zoroaster implored Ahuramazda to awaken a leader for these people. Then he sat down before the hut in quiet inner absorption. He knew that the help for which he had prayed would come.

And while his body was thus seated, his soul went its own way, as it sometimes did. It seemed to be standing in a luminous structure shining with gold and light. Nothing could be seen but this radiance. And the soul stood all alone in the midst of it.

In the solitude it sensed that it was surrounded by celestial power. And it was filled with shivers of holy awe.

Then it seemed that it no longer stood within the room, but began to float, as though borne upwards, gently and easily, always in a straight line upwards. But there was no end; the higher the soul rose the higher the structure arched above it.

The soul could perceive nothing else, although it was undoubtedly surrounded by other things. Then every intuitive perception seemed to cease, only reverence, worship, remained.

And a voice, as powerful as the raging of a storm, and yet as gentle as the whispering of the wind, sounded through the structure. And the voice spoke:

"Forerunner, hearken: "You are to bring the Commandments of God to the human beings who are ready to receive them, so that they will have a firm guideline to which they can hold on their way.

"He is the Most High. Beside Him there is nothing.

"All that you do, do in His honour, then it will bring the greatest benefit to yourselves.

"Consider yourselves no higher than anything else that is created. Plants and animals have kept themselves more pure than you have. Do not forget that. You are to protect and look after them; in return they will help you.

"Do not forget that this small visible world that was given to you is but an infinitesimally small part of that great invisible world which you can only divine. Remember that every step of yours also leads through the invisible world, and take it in such a way that you can pass.

"Keep the connection with the servants of the Most High undimmed at all times. They will guide your petitions to Him, if you ask in the right way. But above all let there be gratitude, and let gratitude be transformed into joyful deed!"

The voice ceased. But the words were engraved in Zoroaster's soul for all time.

His body awoke. Deeply shaken by the experience, Zoroaster went to his bed, and reflected again and again on the stupendous words and their significance for mankind.

Help had been given for those who had begged it of him. Although it was different in nature from what they had expected, it was nevertheless powerful, so long as men kept to the Commandments in absolute purity. In that case they needed no leader to tell them what they should or should not do. –

The next day the Forerunner visited Yadasa in her herb-garden, to tell her of his experience. With bright, radiant eyes she looked towards him.

"I know what you are bringing me, Zoroaster. My soul was also permitted to hear the Holy Commandments in the night, so that we may both know and never forget them. How infinitely great is the mercy of Ahuramazda, that He has permitted His Holy Will to become Word for us human beings."

"His Will become Word!" Zoroaster repeated in happy reflection. "Do you really know what you are saying, Yadasa?"

She did not know, she had had to say it, and it was right. This often happened to her: she said what she perceived intuitively, when a higher one had spoken through her.

And again Zoroaster thanked God for the companion whom He had given him.

In the evening the Forerunner went before the gathering to proclaim his experience. It went far beyond their understanding. They were unable to imagine that the soul could lead a life of its own apart from the body.

But they did not brood. They absorbed as much as they could grasp of what Zoroaster told them. They did, however, understand the Holy Commandments.

First he conveyed them all. Then they decided that he should speak to them about one Commandment at a time during each of the following evenings. That same night they started at the beginning, and Zoroaster tried to place the tremendous significance of the "I Am" before their souls.

Their thinking was too childlike to be able to grasp it fully. They could not understand the need for Ahuramazda to say: "I Am", for they felt that every human being must intuitively perceive Him and know of Him.

And whereas Zoroaster was deeply shaken by the Divine greatness of these words, he had to experience that the others took them as something commonplace.

"Would you wish it otherwise, my friend?" asked Yadasa when he spoke with her about it the next morning. "Let us be glad that the people view everything eternal without doubts.

"Remember what they were like under the influence of the evil one. We experienced terrible things with them at the time. It is like a miracle that they now strive even more eagerly towards the good. Sometimes I do not comprehend it myself. It must be a special grace from Ahuramazda."

In the evening he explained the Second Commandment to the people, and they recognised how much it demanded of them. Each could give some instance to illustrate how often they had transgressed this Commandment.

They told it freely, despite having to admit the great wrongs they had committed. The moment they could add: "that was before you came", it seemed to them obliterated.

Before parting that evening one of the younger men asked whether it would be possible for some of them to accompany the Zoroaster, just as the women were doing in Yadasa's case. They had talked it over among themselves, as they wanted to learn and to be of help to him.

He promised to place the petition before his Luminous Helper. He would do nothing without approval from above.

During the night, under the starry sky, he asked and was given the

191

answer that he should not yet take the young men with him. But when he went on to another people he was to send for them. In the meantime they were to prepare themselves inwardly and outwardly.

This he told them in the evening, and their joy was great, even though having to wait was not easy.

"How long do you think it will take for the wretched people to learn what they have to?" they wanted to know.

He said that it could take months, perhaps even more than a year. But he reminded them once more that he had received the command from above. So they acquiesced.

The days and evenings passed uniformly. Yadasa, who was still living with her father as before, made her own preparations for the journey.

Nazim wanted to give her one of his white horses, but Zoroaster took it for himself, and gave Ray to his wife.

As he did so he remembered that a considerable number of horses must be awaiting him in his native place. Perhaps there were some among them that he could make use of now. But when would he get to his home again?

THE SEVENTH day had dawned. Everyone was happy and excited, although sorry that Yadasa was leaving; for whenever she came back from now on it would always be just for a short time.

Never before had a girl married outside her village! But Yadasa had always been different.

To make the parting easier for her father she bade him a quick farewell. Then she rode side by side with Zoroaster into the fresh morning, followed by the merrily chatting women.

Murza and Marzar, each of them leading a laden pack-horse beside him, brought up the rear.

They had just passed beyond sight of the huts when the little ones appeared.

Full of joy Yadasa regarded the helpers. Zoroaster had not known that she too could see them. It was a great reassurance to him, for now he knew that his wife would never be completely helpless.

In the evening three tents were pitched. Marvelling, Yadasa entered the white tent, which was now to be her home for a long time to come. She was permitted to rest beneath the Sign of the Saoshyant! It was both a miracle and a joy.

The days spent riding together were precious. They had much to discuss. Zoroaster told Yadasa all he knew about the people among whom they would now work together.

On one occasion he warned her against picking fruits there. She reassured him.

"Since I can see and understand the little helpers, I am also protected among plants, as everywhere, Zoroaster," she said cheerfully. "When I see a plant that I do not know, some little voice immediately whispers to me whether its effect is good and healing or bad."

"What was your mother like, Yadasa?" Zoroaster asked, as he thought about Yadasa's nature. The question appeared unmotivated, but she understood him at once.

"Since she died at my birth, I had to rely on what strangers said about her. They all praised her sunny, helpful nature. She had knowledge about many things that others did not know. Wherever someone was ill she was sent for."

When they rested at night the women prepared the meal, while the men pitched the tents and looked after the horses.

They ate separately; Yadasa stayed with her women. Then however they all sat together on the fragrant mossy floor of the forest, and listened to what Zoroaster told them. These conversations were always instructive, also for the women.

Murza and Marzar were almost sorry when finally the village came into view after several days. Now the intimate time together was over, now Zoroaster and Yadasa would have their work, and pay but little attention to them.

As if she had seen these thoughts, Yadasa addressed Murza:

"Now you will have to assist Zoroaster vigorously, while I devote myself to the women. Many things will need to be done, certain matters will have to be discussed. He will not be able to do without you."

Their reply was interrupted by ear-splitting noise.

Watchmen who had been on guard announced Zoroaster's arrival in this tempestuous fashion.

When the Zoroaster stayed away for so long, great dread had seized the people. They feared that Ahuramazda was too angry with them, and would not permit Yadasa and the Forerunner to come and help them.

A few men reassured the others and had undertaken to keep a constant look-out and give the signal as soon as they saw the horses.

Now all the men came rushing up to demonstrate their joy. Zoroaster's tent was again erected at the place where it had stood before. For the present Yadasa stayed behind under the protection of the escorts, while Zoroaster went into the village to greet all those who had remained by the huts.

Some women peered with curiosity and longing from the doorways. They were disappointed not to see Yadasa. But the Forerunner cheerfully called out the good news that his wife would come to see them tomorrow.

And the next morning she came, sunny and ready to help.

With a smile she entered the low, incredibly dirty huts, and the women began to be ashamed of the rubbish all around.

They looked at Yadasa's simple garments, whose sole ornament was cleanliness. They gazed at her slender, clean hands, which did not shrink from making themselves useful everywhere. And in these women, who had never seen anything better, arose the fervent desire to become like this woman.

Nevertheless Yadasa had great difficulty in overcoming the women's shyness at first. She could hardly obtain an answer from them, only their eyes spoke, looking up to Yadasa beseechingly or gratefully, or beaming in admiration.

Many days passed without even the least outward change.

She still had not dared to bring her women to the huts to help. She took all sorts of work to them, above all she had them wash things at the forest brook which flowed along so merrily.

Then it became clear to her that she must not proceed too diffidently. She called the daughter of the chieftain, and asked her for assistance. No doubt she had a great influence over the women, which she must now put to use.

Yadasa told her that she too was the daughter of a village chieftain, and therefore she could understand how much the girl would like to offer her help.

Anara was astonished. What did this strange woman think of her? Should she tell her that all this did not apply to her? Oh no; she would rather try to prove it true.

Brimming with eagerness, she promised her staunch co-operation, and asked to be shown what was to be done.

Yadasa suggested that they should try to clean one hut after another. Should they start with the dwelling-place of the village-chieftain?

"Oh no," said Anara with apparent modesty, while inwardly she had resolved to wait and see first what was done at the others'.

Yadasa laughed. She knew very well what the girl's motive was.

"Well then, let us start at the other end of the village," she said accommodatingly. "Go into that big hut and ask the people to come out so that we can clean it. In the meantime I will send for my women."

Anara disappeared into the dwelling. Yadasa sent Murza to her women, who were only too glad to come. They were all full of curiosity.

But over there by the hut a clamour arose, growing ever louder. The women and children were apparently unwilling to leave their dwelling, in whose filth, which had been accumulating for decades, they felt at ease.

So Anara proceeded with force.

So it must have been, for suddenly a child about two years old came flying out of the hut; the little one was so frightened by the brusque manner in which it had been dispatched that it stopped howling. But the noise inside persisted, and while Yadasa came rushing up to see whether the child was hurt, there followed a second and a third. After that came two young sheep, and finally a screaming woman was pushed through the doorway.

"One of you women must help me," Anara called out in cheerful fighting spirit. "The grandmother is still inside and does not want to come out!"

Laughing, two women ran inside, and rather roughly carried into the open a struggling old woman, whose facial contortions evidenced that she had not seen the light of day for a long time.

195

Yadasa resolved to instruct her helpers to proceed a little less violently in the future. But for the present she was glad that the hut was empty. The women and children had calmed down at the sight of the many neatly dressed women, and were staring at them curiously.

Yadasa now courageously entered the evil-smelling hut. Had she not been present, her women would have lost heart. It was too horrible inside.

"Shall I call men to remove the worst?" Yadasa asked, thereby seeking to arouse her helpers' personal pride.

She had calculated rightly: none of the women would allow the men to help them. They could deal with the task by themselves.

They worked and laboured as never before in their lives. But in working their joyousness grew, so that they began to sing.

Suddenly women arrived from the nearby huts, wondering who was so cheerfully at work there. When Anara saw the other women appear, she remembered that she was to set an example. She began to work eagerly, and was delighted at the admiration that she evoked.

How much there still was to be changed and improved upon in every respect!

Suddenly a girl disengaged herself from the ever-growing band of onlookers, hurried into the hut and began to work eagerly with the others.

"Mirna," cried Anara violently, "you do not belong here. There will be enough dirt to remove from your own hut."

The girl looked sadly at Yadasa, who said pleasantly:

"Let Mirna help, Anara. We are glad of any help. When it is the turn of her hut later on, others will also help her. The more women work instead of merely looking on, the sooner we shall have this work finished."

Mirna cast a grateful glance at her and set to work. Now two other girls followed her example as well, while some of the onlookers hastened in the direction of their own huts.

Lo and behold! Suddenly the same brisk activity began in the other dwellings.

Yadasa observed it with joy. She signalled to her helpers to distribute themselves through every hut so that the work should be done

196

thoroughly and properly. But she called to the owner of the hut that they were just cleaning, and asked her whether she too would not give a hand. After all it was her own dwelling-place that was being improved.

"No, I will not help!" the woman retorted angrily. "I did not send for you. You have no business in my hut. Finish by yourselves what you have begun."

"We will gladly do so," said Yadasa calmly. "I only thought that looking on must be tiresome for you. But I know what you can do: just as we have entered your hut, so you go into another and work there."

The woman liked the idea. Leaving her children with the old woman, who had become quite lively with amazement, she walked with a grin into the neighbouring hut, seizing the children there and dispatching them even more roughly than hers had been.

Then a noisy brawl developed with the occupant of the hut, ending in both women peaceably clearing out dirt.

It was much more than Yadasa had expected. She looked forward to telling Zoroaster about it in the evening.

Meanwhile the latter had not been idle either. On one of the first evenings he had told the men about the sacred square in Yadasa's home village, and had awakened in them the longing to have one of their own like it.

And since the men here had a distinct sense of beauty, and also knew how to cut and embellish stones skilfully, the square promised to become very beautiful. But in addition to the physical work, Zoroaster taught. He instructed the men how to behave in a more civilised manner, he spoke about eternal things, and devoted himself completely to the service of this degenerate tribe.

The serving of the men by women and girls at meals had already ceased, since Yadasa had voiced her displeasure about it. Now they also adhered strictly to the separate meals, in order to set an example.

While Yadasa then retired with her women, Zoroaster went to the meeting-place of the men, in order to speak to all who came.

It seemed that he never grew tired. Murza often warned him and reminded him of his grave illness. But Zoroaster laughed at all the warnings. He felt his powers constantly growing.

In the midst of his most zealous activity the Luminous Messenger of Ahuramazda appeared to him one night, warning him:

"Zoroaster, the time of the Festival on the Mountain is approaching. Because of your work you have already missed one Festival. That was intended, so that human beings should long for the true proclamation of God. But to stay away again would destroy many paths to their souls for you. Already the Atravan boasts that you avoid the Mountain through fear of him.

"Leave Murza behind here to protect Yadasa and her women, and ride to Hafiz with Marzar by the shortest route. Betake yourself to the Atravan and consult with him.

"You will receive further instructions as soon as you need them. But do not delay a single day!"

It was quite incomprehensible to Zoroaster that he could have forgotten the Festival. When he told Yadasa about it in the morning, she comforted him. "It was willed, my friend. In your diligent work you forget the passage of time. You will have difficulty with the Atravan, I feel that. My thoughts will surround you, and remind you to be calm."

"If only you could ride with me yourself, Yadasa," Zoroaster said regretfully.

"The time for that has not yet come. I cannot go away from here and leave the women to themselves. Too little has yet been achieved. Outwardly much has changed, but now I must begin to teach the ignorant souls, so that the women may recognise and experience why everything has happened.

"Also, it is much better for you after your absence to arrive on the Mountain without your wife. In the meantime Murza will see to the men. I believe he needs this for his growth, for his soul is developing wonderfully."

There was great lamentation when Zoroaster announced his intention to ride away, and at once prepared to depart. Their minds were put at rest only when he explained to them that he would definitely return, since he was leaving his wife with them.

Without any special farewell he hastened to his destination with Marzar, after Murza had promised him to take care of everything.

198

"By the shortest possible route," the Luminous Messenger had said.

The words were repeated by the little ones, who led him across upland and swamp on unbeaten trails. They did not even allow him sufficient sleep at night.

The horses had barely had adequate rest before they continued. And neither Zoroaster nor Marzar complained,although their fatigue was often great.

IN SPITE OF all their haste they had to ride for six days before reaching the capital. They rode to the Palace without delay, and Zoroaster went at once to the apartments of the Prince.

He was welcomed joyfully. Hafiz had been expecting him.

"How many days have we before the Festival?" Zoroaster cried impetuously, when they had barely exchanged salutations.

"We must leave in five days' time; you have come at the right hour, my friend," was Hafiz's reply.

"Then I will go at once to the Atravan," Zoroaster decided.

The Prince felt that this time the priest could be sent for. But within the Forerunner sounded the injunction of the Luminous Messenger: "Betake yourself to the Atravan." That he would follow.

Much as he longed to ask after Dshayava, he did not take the time for it. He would neglect nothing. Inwardly composed – for the whole ride had been an inner preparation for this hour – he set out to speak to the Atravan.

He found the priest already awaiting him, for although Zoroaster had been in the city only a very short time, the news of his arrival had already spread everywhere.

Thus the priest had time to compose himself, and to summon up all the resistance which his soul could muster. He greeted his visitor with deference, for he was struck by the natural nobility that emanated from him.

Zoroaster appeared to have grown, he seemed to tower above all men, not only spiritually, but also physically. And from his forehead shone forth the Sign of Ahuramazda. Although unable to interpret it, even the Atravan could not help noticing it.

After greetings had been exchanged, both men were silent. Each waited for the other to begin. Then the Atravan, uneasy at the silence, decided to break it.

"Do you intend to participate in the Festival on the Mountain, Zoroaster?" he asked furtively.

The guest confirmed his intention.

"You missed the last Festival. I thought you would come here for that."

Zoroaster was silent. What was he to say in reply? Again the priest began to speak:

"We would like to see you at the Festival, but do not forget that you come as a visitor, like all the others."

"What do you mean by that, Atravan?" Zoroaster asked, calmly but surprised.

"I mean that you must not speak. You are a visitor, not the priest of the Festival. Only I will speak. This time the priestesses will not be allowed to speak either, because of having given you the opportunity to speak before, without my permission."

"At the behest of Ahuramazda I have something to proclaim to the people," the Forerunner replied firmly. "I will speak. That is why I have come to you, because I wish to discuss all that with you quietly.

"Atravan, consider: we are both servants of the supreme God. Let us teach the people hand in hand. Only in that way can our work be blessed."

"You are mistaken," interrupted the Atravan caustically. "I am a servant of Mithra, in whose honour the festival takes place. I will speak of Mithra and the gods whether you like it or not."

"Surely you know, Atravan," Zoroaster attempted to placate him, "that all gods stand under the Will of Ahuramazda, that they themselves are servants."

Then it burst forth from the Atravan, who saw his position and influence threatened:

"You wish to deprive Mithra of the Festival as you have taken from him the worship of men, and as you are taking away still more. You only wish thereby to elevate yourself before men. Go back whence you have come, and do not disturb us here. Perhaps you too are an impostor, like the false Zoroaster of whom you spoke!"

Without entering into the accusations, Zoroaster said firmly:

"Atravan, I command you to stay away from the Festival! A person with your attitude can no longer be priest."

The Atravan burst into shrill laughter.

"And how would you prevent me from appearing at the Festival if I nonetheless wish to come?"

"That is not my concern, but that of the One Who has just commanded me to dismiss you," Zoroaster said coldly.

Without another word he left the enraged man and returned to the Palace. In his apartment he struggled to regain his composure, for despite his outward calm he was in turmoil inwardly.

Had he done the right thing? He thought he had distinctly heard the voice indicating to him the words he was to say. He called for the Luminous Messenger.

"You did what was right, Zoroaster," he was told. "One must have no patience with people like the Atravan. He could cause too much harm if he were to be present at this Festival, for his heart now belongs only to his own self. His insistence on Mithra is also falsehood. He has renounced the gods as well, because he is aware that they no longer help him.

"The office of Atravan will become unnecessary as soon as the Festivals are conducted in the right way through you.

"Send for the priestesses and the Mobeds, and instruct them in what they have to do."

Zoroaster continued to pray for a long time after the Messenger had left him. Then he went to see Hafiz.

The latter was not in the least surprised at the Forerunner's account.

"I knew that it would come to this. The last Festival was hollow and empty," he said earnestly. "Let us go to Dshayava; he will want to hear how you fared."

Great joy filled Zoroaster at the news that the old man was still alive. He must be very, very old!

"Zoroaster, my son and master," he greeted them as they entered. "It

201

was revealed to me that you would come. Now truth and clarity will make their entrance with us."

Zoroaster spoke of his conversation with the Atravan, and the significant turn it had taken. Dshayava too considered it quite obvious that an Atravan could be dispensed with as soon as the Forerunner had entered upon his office as the highest Priest of the people.

"That you will do at this Festival, Zoroaster," Dshayava said, deeply happy. "The years of journeying around the land are coming to an end. Others will have to do that for you, whom you will carefully prepare here for it. I see a stream of blessing pour forth from this city across the land!"

He spoke prophetically, with his eyes turned inwards.

A servant announced that the priestesses had come, on receiving Zoroaster's message. So the conversation was ended for the present, without Zoroaster's being able to speak of his wife.

He found the four women waiting for him in a beautiful room. They were delighted that he was going to conduct the Festival, and promised that they would follow his instructions in all things.

In reply to his question whether they had anything to report, the oldest of them said that they would prefer not to speak at the Festival. It had never been easy for them. Now that they had been permitted to be silent at two Festivals, they preferred to continue in this way.

That suited Zoroaster, who knew quite well that later Yadasa would address the people.

Now they wanted to know whether flames were to be lit, even though the Festival would no longer be celebrated in honour of Mithra. Zoroaster was in favour of retaining the outward form as much as possible. He would say that the flames were blazing heavenwards to the glory of Ahuramazda.

Afterwards the Mobeds came, and the priestesses left.

When the youths entered Zoroaster saw at once that they were not of one mind. While two of them gazed at him with bright, happy eyes, the others made a gloomy impression, casting sullen glances at him.

"You sent for us, Zoroaster," the oldest among them began, "and we have come, although we are not accustomed to taking orders from anyone but the Atravan."

"I sent for you at the behest of Ahuramazda, as Whose servant I stand before you. The Forerunner, not the person, summoned you.

"You can imagine that this year the holy Festival must proceed rather differently from before. It will be held to the glory of Ahuramazda, the flames will rise for Him!"

He paused for a moment and looked at those standing before him. One of the five reluctant youths had already changed his expression. He gazed intently at Zoroaster, but with an expectation that no longer had anything antagonistic about it.

The oldest, however, availed himself of the pause to speak:

"You can spare yourself the trouble of explaining that to us. We have come from the Atravan, who has described to us the colossal presumption with which you confronted him. My friends and I have merely come to tell you that we will remain with our master, whatever happens. We will go to the Festival with him and perform our duties."

He had expected Zoroaster to flare up in anger, but the Forerunner calmly replied:

"It redounds to your credit that you wish to keep faith with him who has hitherto been your teacher. He never was your master. So long as you have not yet grasped what is at stake here, you cannot but stand by him who has been the Atravan until now.

"But it was precisely to explain this that I sent for you. Consider: as Mobeds you are not servants of the Atravan, but servants of Ahuramazda. As His servants you must submit to His Will. With the coming of the Forerunner we have entered a new era, which naturally brings new things with it.

"A great spiritual upsurge will come over our realm. Whoever among you wishes to join in it is welcome as a helper. Whoever thinks that he cannot do so is free to leave. I will see without resentment the departure of those who think they cannot serve Ahuramazda in the right way."

He looked around.

"If that is the case, Zoroaster, and I feel that you speak the truth," said one of those who had been wavering, "then we are grateful to be permitted to go on serving. Take us with you to the Mountain of the Festival, and rest assured that we will give you no cause for complaint."

"How can you be so impudent as to speak for us all," the oldest among them snapped. "Here each must decide for himself. He must be uninfluenced in saying whether he wants to keep faith with the Atravan, or adhere to the new."

"Again you are right, my friend," Zoroaster commended him. "The decision is so serious as you may not even yet realise. It extends far beyond your present life. For that reason each must make the decision uninfluenced, for himself. This is why I ask you: do you wish to have time to think it over until tomorrow?"

He looked around enquiringly.

"For myself there is no need," said the youngest in the circle. "I ask you, Zoroaster, to accept me as your pupil and servant of Ahuramazda."

"I ask the same," said another. "I will submit faithfully to the supreme God, and to you as His servant."

"I too have no need to think it over," the oldest was heard to say. "I do not acknowledge you. You dared to commit an outrage against the Atravan. I will stand by his side when he triumphs over you."

Not waiting for an answer, the man left the room. Another followed him silently.

The others seemed to breathe freely. The remaining three promised to serve Ahuramazda faithfully, and Zoroaster saw that they were in earnest about it.

He then discussed with them their service, which hardly differed from what had been practised before.

"We shall miss the two Mobeds who have left," one ventured to say. "There have always been seven of us to see to the tasks."

"There will be seven this time too." the Forerunner assured them. "I already have two new pupils who know enough about what I proclaim to fit in at once."

"Then they will know more than we do, Master," the youngest said modestly. "You must have patience with us."

Zoroaster promised that he would, and then invited the youths to come to him for instruction every day until their departure. They looked forward to it. –

In the evening when Hafiz and Zoroaster were sitting with Dshayava, the Forerunner was able at last to speak of the outward events of his life. He spoke of Yadasa, and how she was working among the depraved people. Thereupon Dshayava said kindly:

"You will have to fetch her soon, Zoroaster, so that she can train women-helpers here, just as you are teaching priests. Your wife must stay by your side, so that she can be a companion to you in the right sense."

Astonished, Zoroaster looked at the aged man.

"How do you know that she has become my wife, my father?" he asked, surprised.

Both men laughed and Hafiz said:

"Dshayava was always so connected with you that he could tell me what was happening to you. For we had to know whether you were threatened by danger, so that I could come to your aid. In this way we knew that you had married and we were happy about it. She is the right complement for you. Your gentle wife will bridle your fiery spirit."

For a long time they continued to speak about all the things which the Forerunner had experienced in the two years. But the Atravan was not mentioned at all. This unpleasant affair must now run its course.

The following morning, Zoroaster sent for Marzar and Sadi. Although the latter had recovered, he would probably never be able to ride again. This weighed on him like a burden, for he himself had been at fault; he thought it would now keep him away from Zoroaster for good.

Great was his joy when the Forerunner told him and Marzar that he wanted to take them as pupils, as Mobeds. They were to be allowed to assist even at this Festival. But later they were to go to other villages to work there as priests.

"And who will ride with you, Master?" asked Marzar, in spite of the joy that filled him.

"I will no longer ride away so often, at least not for long periods. I do not yet know who will then accompany me."

The five Mobeds arrived punctually. Zoroaster perceived that the Atravan had spoken to them, but he had not succeeded in influencing them. Firmer than on the previous day, they gazed at him.

Now Zoroaster began to teach the seven men. The instruction was different from that to which the Mobeds were accustomed. Zoroaster said nothing about his high office or the respect due to his own person. What he said was filled with the worship of Ahuramazda.

In the afternoon Prince Hafiz said that he wanted to show his guest something. Together they walked out of the city to a paddock situated at the edge of the forest.

White horses of all sizes were exercising there. The spectacle was a joy to behold.

"These are your horses, Zoroaster," Hafiz explained with satisfaction. "A short while ago your uncle, Sadif, let me know that your horses were taking up too much of his space. He wanted to know if you were still alive, or whether he should sell them. So I had them brought here, because I think you will soon have need of them."

In everything Hafiz did, Zoroaster always felt anew the love he had for him. He thanked the Prince, and looked at the well-kept horses with an expert's eye.

"Once you gave me Ray, Hafiz," he said. "Will you not now choose one for yourself as a gift in return?"

Hafiz had already made his choice. He asked for a fine mare, and it made Zoroaster happy to be able to give.

The next day he asked the Mobeds whether they could ride, for he wanted them all to ride with him. They all confirmed that they could. Each was given a white horse; Zoroaster too replaced the one he had been given by Nazim with one of the noble steeds.

Thus on the sixth day an imposing procession rode out of Hafiz's Palace towards the Mountain. Zoroaster had heard nothing more from the Atravan; so he was hoping that the former priest would have recognised his folly and forgone his visit to the Mountain.

But when Zoroaster's cavalcade had journeyed for a day it overtook the Atravan, who let himself be carried by the two Mobeds, while five others walked behind them to give relief and assistance.

Zoroaster wanted to ride past in silence, but the Atravan called out to him, so that the Forerunner reined in his horse.

"As you can see, your God has not prevented me from coming," he called spitefully. "Beware of thwarting my plans and preventing me from exercising my official function. I will not submit to anything from you, and it will be your fault if the Festival deteriorates into a general squabble. I have asked my supporters to come and oppose yours everywhere."

Zoroaster rode on without saying a word. But Hafiz was appalled that a man who had been priest could harbour such thoughts. Even now, however, they did not discuss the matter further. Each prepared inwardly for the Festival.

In good time they arrived on the Mountain, where Zoroaster had the place and the stone-piles prepared by the Mobeds.

Since the Atravan kept the sacred vessels locked up, Zoroaster had brought others, which were more artistically made than the old ones. He had purchased them from the people with whom Yadasa was still staying.

Each discharged his duties with care, as did the priestesses, so that by nightfall the flames could be lit. There was no sign of the Atravan or his friends.

Instead crowds of people came. The Mountain could hardly accommodate the throng.

They were surprised to see Zoroaster, but it was a joyful surprise. Even those who might have come to support the Atravan held their peace when they did not see their leader.

Instead of praying to Mithra, Zoroaster prayed to Ahuramazda. The prayer came from the depth of his soul, and caused all the other souls to vibrate in it as well.

Then he spoke.

He reminded them that the new age had dawned. God had sent the Forerunner of the Saoshyant, the Helper would follow when the earth had been prepared to receive Him. To this end, however, everyone who would strive to meet the Most Holy in a worthy manner could contribute.

The time had come to make Ahuramazda the sole Ruler over the souls, as He had always been. Now all human beings should know that those whom they had hitherto worshipped as gods were loyal servants of the All-Highest. The worship of the gods must end; the worship of God could take its place.

And since God was so infinitely more sublime than the gods, human beings must also strive much harder to serve Him. Deep earnestness must pervade their souls. They must learn to live in the Will of the Eternal One.

To enable them to do so, however, God had mercifully inclined to them and permitted His Holy Will to become Word. He had formed His Will into Commandments, which all men should inscribe in their hearts.

Then slowly and solemnly the Forerunner uttered the Holy Commandments which he had received.

And he thanked God in fervent prayer for this grace, and sent the people away. But he permitted the women to take fire-brands, as had been the custom until now.

"The flames burn to the glory of Ahuramazda. Think of Him and let your souls shine!"

Later, when the men returned and settled on the ground, Zoroaster told them about the servants of God, great and small, and said that it was the Will of God that human beings also should fit into this wise structure.

Later some of the men asked after the Atravan. Zoroaster said:

"He wanted to come, but something must have prevented it on his way here. Perhaps he will arrive tomorrow."

The following day Zoroaster announced that it was the intention to appoint a priest, perhaps in every larger village, who was to hold meetings regularly, and instruct the people.

"I myself will teach these priests, so that they can proclaim the holy, eternal truths aright," Zoroaster promised. "Anyone among you who has the time, and takes delight in devoting all his powers to the service of the Most High, should come forward later, so that I can determine if he is suited.

"Then, when we can hold Hours of Worship everywhere, always at the same time in all places, an upswing will surge through our people, which must sweep everyone along. Then we shall be able to prepare ourselves aright for the glorious time when the Saoshyant will descend from Heaven to live in our midst."

"Master," a man in the gathering asked, "are there still other peoples besides ours? Do the others also know about the coming Helper? Or must you later on go to other peoples across the tall mountains, to prepare them too?"

"Certainly there are other peoples," said Zoroaster, "but God will send other Forerunners to them. To each people the one it must have, at the time which God considers best."

This one question, however, brought the others to life. Question followed on question, and full of joy Zoroaster replied, for it was thus evident to him how inspired they all were. –

That day also nothing was heard of the Atravan. Nor was there any news on the third day, when Zoroaster discussed each of Ahuramazda's Commandments in detail, again allowing questions to be asked.

A prayer of gratitude concluded the Festival, which had proceeded undisturbed and in a deeply moving way.

But the people would not yet take leave. First about twenty young people, wanting to come to Zoroaster as Mobeds, came forward.

Their fathers were present, so that the question of whether they could be spared at home could be discussed at once. Then Zoroaster decreed that they were to come to the capital in six months' time, and ask for him there.

They were disappointed that they were not permitted to accompany him right away. He told them that his first duty now was to a distant region, but that afterwards they would be able to find him.

Then the question was raised: Zoroaster had taught one tribe a song, – could not all the others also have it?

Smiling, he consented. And a singing contest began, which at first was anything but beautiful. The men's vocal chords were not used to singing. But when they finally realised that it was melodious sound and not loud yelling that mattered, there was considerable improvement.

Zoroaster then asked that the square and the Mountain be cleared. The Festival had gone so wonderfully; they should all take with them the memory of the greatness they had experienced, and not spoil it through subsequent, less beautiful days. They understood that and willingly complied. –

When all had departed, Zoroaster had the square returned to its original state. Then he and Hafiz too, with their retinue, set out on their homeward journey.

Just as they were about to leave the Mountain, they heard loud shouting. From the opposite direction came the Atravan with his seven

Mobeds. They had lost their way so completely that they had been searching for the path during all three days of the Festival.

One of the Mobeds recounted this, while the Atravan remained defiantly silent. He realised that Ahuramazda had not wanted him there, and had prevented him from coming in time; but he still would not give in.

Zoroaster asked the Mobed who had given the information whether they had enough provisions. The youth said they had. So the Forerunner saw no reason to tarry; with a friendly shout the train of white horses moved on.

"What if the Atravan now holds another festival on the Mountain?" one of the Mobeds asked.

"What harm will that do?" Zoroaster replied. "Let him pray to Mithra; it cannot touch Ahuramazda."

After a few days they arrived in the capital. Now Zoroaster could wait no longer, he had to go and see Yadasa.

Hafiz promised that in the meantime he would have rooms prepared for him and his wife. To this end he wanted to add to the Palace. The annexe was to include a spacious room, large enough for the instruction of the young people.

"Would it not be better if a separate building were made available for this purpose?" Zoroaster suggested. "It would certainly be no trouble if I had to go to another place for the instruction. But I think that this new building would need to have two large rooms, for Yadasa will also want to instruct the priestesses; and moreover there should be space for holding Hours of Worship."

"We must also erect two other buildings, in which the female and male pupils can live and sleep," Hafiz decided.

He already realised that time would not hang heavy on his hands until the Forerunner's return. But one question still occupied him:

Zoroaster said that Hours of Worship were to be held in the building.

"We have never yet prayed together other than in the open, Forerunner," he said thoughtfully. "Do you really think that it would be agreeable to Ahuramazda if for this purpose we shut ourselves up in a house built by human hands?"

"Hitherto you have, of course, only worshipped together once a year on the Mountain, Hafiz," replied Zoroaster. "But from now on we shall regularly pray together and speak about holy things. That cannot be done in an open square, in a city where all kinds of cattle run through the streets, where messengers from other places come and go.

"Therefore I think that we must have a large room for these discussions, one that can be fittingly decorated."

Now Hafiz also agreed. He even looked forward to the arrangement of the room; but this he would leave until the Forerunner returned.

The parting with Dshayava was heartfelt. Zoroaster was afraid he would no longer find the old man alive upon his return, but Dshayava comforted him:

"I have still to bless your young wife, Zoroaster, then I am ready to go to other realms."

Sadi, who had to remain behind, was to look after the five Mobeds and tell them of what he himself had experienced.

And Zoroaster rode joyfully with Marzar towards the distant region where Yadasa was looking forward to his arrival.

This time he was permitted to ride on good, well-marked roads. Although his impatience would again have driven him up hill and down dale, the little beings could not be induced to show him the shortest route.

But eventually he reached his destination. In the rays of the setting sun lay the village that had become dear despite all the trouble it had caused him.

Soon the two riders had been seen. Men gathered round them. And while Marzar stabled the horses, Zoroaster went to look for his wife.

He found her in the midst of a group of neatly-dressed maidens who sat together sewing. They were well aware of the impression they must make on Zoroaster, and while Yadasa welcomed her husband, the girls continued to sew as if they suddenly had to make up for years of neglect.

He made them happy by admiring their diligence and neat appearance. Then he let Yadasa take him to all the places where anything new was to be seen.

The village had changed greatly. The huts looked spick and span, and here and there he even observed slight attempts at beautifying. A few little gardens had been laid out as well.

Just then Murza returned from hunting with a troop of young men.

The distribution of the game proceeded in an orderly fashion. Now the men – no longer the women – had to drag the pieces of meat into the huts. Finally the chieftain also returned, and was delighted to see Zoroaster again.

"Murza will speak to us this evening in the holy square," he said proudly. "You will come too, I hope?"

Zoroaster promised that he would. He had hardly found time yet to tell Yadasa about his experiences.

This went on for a few days. Then Zoroaster explained that he must now return to the capital, where more important duties awaited him. He would leave with them Murza, who had chosen Anara as his helpmate. They were all well satisfied with that; for they had grown accustomed to Murza and loved him.

Yadasa spoke very highly of Anara. She had changed for the best. Her occasional outbursts of energy did no harm; from time to time the women needed that, so that they would not lapse into day-dreaming and indolence.

Now Zoroaster informed his wife that they would first return to her home to fetch the young men who wished to accompany him as pupils, and to give the women a safe escort home.

And it came about as Zoroaster had planned.

Great was Nazim's joy on being permitted to see his daughter again; it was greater still when he learned that henceforth she would live in the capital in the Prince's Palace.

He had feared that the kind of life she was leading would become too strenuous for her in the long run. But he could wish for nothing better than to know his daughter safe in the Prince's Palace.

The young people were glad that their time had come at last. Yadasa also selected a number of girls whom she wished to instruct. They were to be trained as helpers, not as priestesses.

Even before the six months of which Zoroaster had spoken were over, he was riding back to the capital with an imposing retinue.

With this began a completely new phase in his life. His period of travelling was over, as was his period of learning before that. He was now the supreme Priest in Persia; no longer did he prepare the way, rather he preserved it.

LIKE A SMALL PALACE, THE APARTMENTS of Zarathustra, the Preserver of the Way, as he was now called, adjoined the imposing Palace of Hafiz – a realm apart, and yet connected with the whole.

Here Yadasa worked with her female servants, who were joined by a few men, in separate rooms, who served Zarathustra.

It was a realm filled with peace and joy.

The two halls were already completed, but not yet decorated. Hafiz could hardly wait to show his friend what he had thought of for that purpose.

The two spacious rooms were of equal length and breadth. But they were not adjacent to one another; instead several small rooms lay between them, to which Yadasa and Zarathustra could withdraw for quiet contemplation.

Other similar rooms were intended for the storage of vessels and such things. From the outside the building had the appearance of a regular square; its flat roof completed this impression.

Hafiz had already provided a variety of things which could be used to grace the rooms, but he did not wish to have anything put in place until it had been approved by the supreme Priest of the land.

First the buildings for the accommodation of the pupils had to be inspected; these buildings, which lay to the right and left of the quadrangle in which the halls were housed, were surrounded by gardens. They were also elongated structures, differing little from the usual ones.

They were already inhabited by the maidens and youths who had come with them from Yadasa's home. Sadi, who had also moved in with his Mobeds, supervised the men. For the women, Yadasa determined the one who was to safeguard the well-being of the others.

Very soon a brisk activity developed, swinging in firmly-established paths.

Every day Zarathustra and Yadasa taught in the two halls. Afterwards, while she instructed the women in various feminine activities useful for the adornment of the rooms, for their own clothing or for the poor, Zarathustra visited Hafiz or went to see Dshayava, who always looked forward to his coming.

A close bond had formed immediately between the aged man and Yadasa. He recognised her purity that nothing could dim, her cheerfulness that stemmed from her joy in working, her deeply rooted faith.

Greatly moved, he had blessed her when Zarathustra brought her to him; but he felt that the blessing flowed back from her to himself.

"Yadasa, blessed one, teach our women how they may become like you!" he appealed.

Later he said:

"I had wanted to live long enough to bless your wife, Zarathustra, fortunate one! Now I implore Ahuramazda that I may yet see your son as well. I know that He will grant me this."

In the meantime the youths who had been chosen during the Festival had also arrived, and gathered around their Master with great enthusiasm. "Master" was the name by which they all now called him.

"Since I have found the Zoroaster, I no longer have a name of my own," he once said to Dshayava, somewhat ruefully.

"Be glad of that, my son," was the venerable man's reply. "It is a sign that you have given yourself up. You live solely in your office. May it continue so even when your child's lips call to you in joy."

That gave Zarathustra cause to reflect. The promised son had not yet announced himself. But since he had been promised, he would not fail to come. Would that represent a danger to his office?

A delicate shyness prevented him from speaking about it to Yadasa, with whom he usually discussed everything. But he brought his conflicting thoughts before Ahuramazda's Throne, and the Luminous Messenger helped him to gain clarity.

"You may enjoy every gift bestowed by God's Goodnesss," said the Luminous One, "but you must never let it come between you and God. Remember the Commandments of the Most High, and you have the answer to all your questions."

When the halls had been decorated, Zarathustra asked how often he was allowed to conduct Hours of Worship there, in accordance with the Will of God.

"To begin with, it will be enough if you meet every time the moon is full," was the answer he received, and to this the Supreme Priest now adhered.

At the full moon the pupils – female and male, the royal household of the Prince, and their relatives gathered in the evening in one of the halls, where Zarathustra carried out his duties.

He began the Hour of Worship with a spontaneous prayer in which, apart from the plea for blessing on this hour, he brought before the Most High all those things that presently occupied the hearts of the people.

Then he interpreted the Commandments to them, or told them about the Saoshyant. Again a prayer concluded the first part of this Hour of Worship.

After that the assemblage proceeded to the other hall, where likewise all the seats were arranged in a circle and where Zarathustra, standing in the middle, answered all questions put to him.

It was here too that Yadasa, upon his request, would speak to the people whenever she had something to proclaim. Her spiritual connection with the higher realms grew ever stronger and more luminous. She was allowed to teach many things which had been granted her from above.

She then stood amid the people like a priestess in her simple white garment. Her earthly eyes looked over the people without seeing them.

Her spiritual eyes were opened wide, and wonderful truths flowed through her.

Those were unforgettable moments for all who were permitted to experience them.

It was inevitable that news of the Hours of Worship should spread in the city. One resident after the other came with a request to be allowed to take part. No one who promised to be peaceful and well-mannered was turned away.

The Atravan too had heard how brightly a new spiritual life was beginning to blossom forth beside him. He had always occupied himself only with his Mobeds, and never paid any attention to other people.

His predecessors had ridden all over the country. He had spurned it, saying that whoever wanted to see him should come to him. Now he suddenly remembered this neglected duty.

Although Zarathustra had discharged him, that did not worry him. He now felt that it was right to visit the people in the land.

Since he had no horses, his Mobeds had to carry him. He could easily have walked with them, but he considered himself too important for that.

With this arduous mode of travelling it was obviously impossible to seek out mountainous regions. So they remained on level ground.

They came at first to a village where Zoroaster had already stayed a number of times; that was apparent in the inhabitants. The Atravan had not considered at all how he would approach the people, what he would speak to them about. That would come to him at the right time, he thought. At the door of the most impressive hut he knocked and requested hospitality. It was given to him as it was to every wayfarer. He and his companions were permitted to spend the night in a kind of barn. Sufficient but very simple food was also taken to them there.

This was not how he had imagined his reception. Indignant, he walked over to the hut from which came the sound of cheerful voices. He thought that he would find the family at their meal, but instead he found women chatting and weaving mats.

Full of indignation they showed him the door. He should remain where the kindliness of the housefather had accommodated him.

"Where is the housefather?" he asked more modestly.

He was at the sacred square, was the answer, which he did not understand, since he knew nothing about such a square.

So for the time being he preferred to eat some of the food which the Mobeds had left him. He then went to look for the square; he did not have to go far. In the centre of the village was a circular space marked out by stones, in which apparently the entire male population were congregated, talking animatedly together.

The Atravan stepped into the circle of men. The discussion ceased. All eyes turned towards the intruder.

"Stranger, it is not seemly to enter and disturb a circle," an elderly man censured him. "Return to the place that charity has allotted you for your night's lodging."

"I am accustomed to better things ...," the bewildered man began, but was quickly interrupted:

"Then you should have stayed where you had it better!"

"I am the Atravan," the priest boasted.

But that did not help him either.

"There is no longer an Atravan," the village-chief said earnestly. "The new age has dawned. Zoroaster is the Forerunner of the Saoshyant; more than that we do not need."

The priest wanted to say still more, but two men led him away to his night's lodgings, pointing out to him that he was interfering. He had no choice but to acquiesce.

The following day he no longer sought to convince the people of his worth, but quietly went his way with his followers.

Only two days later he arrived at another village. There he called on the chieftain, informing him that he had come in the name and on behalf of the Zoroaster.

He was received with joy. Both the meal and accommodation provided for the night indicated in what high esteem the Forerunner was held.

Then the people wanted to know what message he had for them. He said that he was to assure himself of their well-being.

"He did not entrust you with anything else?" the chieftain enquired thoughtfully. "Were you given nothing to proclaim to us?"

"Naturally I am to answer your questions," the Atravan rejoined, assuming that it would be easy to deal with these questions.

He was invited to come to the sacred square in the evening. There he found himself face to face with the entire male population, who were eagerly waiting to hear what he would announce to them.

But it was soon revealed that the priest had no knowledge at all of what Zoroaster usually taught. He was unable to answer any questions. When he attempted to do so he failed.

It required little astuteness to demonstrate to the people that they were dealing with an impostor. Full of indignation they ordered him to leave the village the following day.

"Indeed we should send you away tonight," they said, "but we have learned from Zoroaster that we are to deal with people as we would have them deal with us. And we would not like to be without shelter during the night. Therefore stay until morning!"

217

And the Atravan was not too proud to accept.

But he had taken a dislike to travelling. He returned to the capital disheartened.

He found, however, that here too there was no longer any place for him. No one bothered about him. The gifts and pious offerings on which he had lived until then failed to come. What was he to do?

Three of his Mobeds left him and returned to their homes, among them also the eldest Mobed who had promised never to leave him. The journey had shown him that the priest had no connection whatsoever with God or the gods.

In the meantime the number of pupils gathered around Zarathustra had steadily increased. He could consider sending out the first of those he had taught.

They had absorbed much of eternal wisdom; they were well versed in answering questions of all kinds. Moreover they were used to a simple life, and had acquired good manners. They looked forward to their activity as priests.

They were to hold hours of worship in the way they were accustomed to here. A man from Yadasa's village was sent to the place where Murza had stayed behind. He was to replace Zoroaster's one-time companion there for some time, while Murza accompanied the young priests to the other villages.

Actually Zarathustra had wanted to do this himself, but he received instruction from the Light that he must not leave the capital now. –

Wonderful pictures appeared to him again in the nights. Sometimes he saw himself as a tree bearing fruits, which as they ripened rolled here and there, taking root everywhere and growing into magnificent trees.

Then again he saw his pupils like birds pecking at the grains which he scattered before them. Suddenly a strange bird came and pecked with them. His pupils wanted to scare it away, but a voice called out:

"Let it take what it needs. It does not want it for itself. Beyond the mountains others are waiting for the fruits!"

And yet another picture appeared. Zarathustra saw beyond the high mountains in the east, which seemed to separate his country from other realms. And whereas the mountains which were part of Persia seemed almost small, sky-high rock formations appeared behind them, partly precipitous and partly sloping away gently.

And people, many people, lived there! They stretched out their hands beseechingly towards Zarathustra:

"Help us!"

These pictures, which were certainly meant to tell him something, made a deep impression.

He spoke to Yadasa about them; she assured him that at the right hour the pictures would re-emerge before his spirit, and would then have something to convey to him. She was quite certain that now they were only a preparation for some future event.

For some time now Yadasa and her helpers, who were ever again joined by new ones, went to the huts where poverty or disease made help necessary. For these ministrations the girls and women wore the same plain white garments which Yadasa loved. This had earned them the appellation "the White Sisters", of which they were very proud. They were happy to be sisters to all who suffered.

Gradually, from this place and that in the land, priests sent messages and requests for the help of such a White Sister, so that they too began to spread over the whole country.

In the third year of their presence in the capital, Yadasa gave birth to a healthy boy, whom according to the direction of the Luminous Messenger they called Vishtaspa.

Zarathustra conducted the name-giving ceremony in the sacred hall before all the people. It was the first to be celebrated in this way. Later on children were blessed and given their names at every hour of worship if the parents wished it.

Dshayava had actually been able to experience the birth of the child.

His wish to be permitted to bless it had been granted by Ahuramazda. When Yadasa brought the child to the aged man, and at his request placed it in his arms, the spirit of prophecy came upon the sage.

"Ahuramazda, Sublime, Eternal One, I thank Thee that Thou hast deemed me worthy to behold this child!" he cried in ecstasy. "Child, you are called to carry on your father's work! You shall unite the whole of Persia under the teaching which he has been permitted to bring us in accordance with the Will of Ahuramazda. However you will not become Priest, but King of the whole vast realm. As such you will be the custodian of Eternal Wisdom, of the Knowledge of God!

"You will be strong in the faith, pure and true. And the Blessing of Ahuramazda will rest upon you. Your descendants will become great. They will rule the realm with a firm hand and subdue the neighbouring countries.

"Only much later will human arrogance and human wantonness gain dominion over the souls. Then the immeasurably great realm will go to rack and ruin. The Knowledge of God will sink away, false gods will take its place.

"I see murder and fire, smoking ruins and cities that have fallen into ruin. I see the descendants of our people sink down from their height. They will mix with other peoples; gone is their purity. Woe, woe!"

For a moment the old man was silent. His eyes closed, he collapsed, looking as though he had passed away. Suddenly he straightened.

"But I see a new sun rising over Persia!" he said jubilantly, in a completely changed voice. "The white Wonder-Bird flies over the land. The Heir will stand on the Mountain of Ara-Masdah, and invisible servants will bring Him what is His."

Once again he hesitated, only to continue even more jubilantly: "But the Heir is the Saoshyant! I see it! Child, your father is permitted to be the Preparer and Preserver of the Way for the Saoshyant, but you will be His servant on earth and to all eternity!"

They had all listened deeply moved, and while Zarathustra and Hafiz tried to help the seer, Yadasa quietly carried her blessed child to her apartments.

Dshayava passed away that night. His features were suffused with heavenly peace, as if he had been permitted to behold something beautiful. No one was able to say what age he was. People thought he had been there "always".

At his own request they did not bury him, as Zarathustra would so much have liked to do. They carried the mortal remains to the towers of silence, and laid them there for the great black birds.

"Nothing earthly shall remain of me," had been Dshayava's wish.

This they honoured.

All the residents of the Palace missed him. They could no longer imagine a life without the aged man, but gradually they accustomed themselves to it. Prince Hafiz now spent many evening hours in the small Palace with "his successor", as he usually called Vishtaspa. The little one grew up surrounded by love and care.

THEN ONE DAY a man who was still young came to Zarathustra, and asked to be admitted to the circle of his pupils. His features were different from those of the Persians, though his skin was similar to theirs. His black hair fell down smoothly from the crown of his head, and was trimmed all round it. He had very shiny dark brown eyes, which were almost covered by his eyelids, so that his face looked strangely calm.

Zarathustra asked where he came from. Either the man did not know where he had come from, or he did not want to say; at any rate there was no clear answer to the question:

"Why do you want to know where I come from, O wise man? Is it not enough to say that I know of you, and would like to be your pupil?" he asked.

He spoke the language of the country, and yet there was a foreign quality in it.

"You are a stranger in Persia," Zarathustra responded. "Among my pupils I have only Persians from various tribes, and I would like it to remain that way."

For a moment the stranger looked calmly at the man who was refusing him; then he said:

"Zarathustra, do you usually gather all your fruits around the trunk of the tree?"

The wise man did not understand the meaning of the question. Then the stranger asked once more:

221

"Zarathustra, why do you drive away the strange bird that wishes to peck with your pupils?"

Now the Master knew what the youth meant. But he also knew what the pictures, which he had not understood at the time, were meant to tell him. And the stranger continued:

"Let it take what it needs. It does not want it for itself. Beyond the mountains others are waiting for the fruits!"

These words were not necessary to show Zarathustra that the stranger had come here at the behest of Ahuramazda. Willingly the Master accepted the new pupil, who called himself Miang-Fong.

Never had he had such a pupil. Zarathustra often had difficulty in fathoming the questions he asked. A conversation never ended without the teacher too having learned something important.

When Yadasa saw the new pupil for the first time, she was taken aback.

"Zarathustra, he is a Truth-bringer like you," she said with conviction. "He bears the same Sign of Ahuramazda on his brow. Rejoice that you are called upon to teach another Forerunner."

Miang-Fong lived for over two years in the circle of those who thronged round Zarathustra. He lived with them, and yet completely alone. It was as though an invisible wall stood between him and the others. Only to the Master was it given to break through it at times and gaze into the clear, peace-filled soul of the pupil.

Zarathustra loved to ask the pupils questions which they were to reflect on in silence, and then discuss jointly.

So he had once posed the question:

"Is it necessary to establish definite forms for the outward life of those who wish to serve God?"

The answers were in line with the nature of the pupils. They were completely different one from the other. But most were in favour of a middle course: a few necessary rules should be set up, leaving the rest to every individual; for otherwise artificial instead of living plants would be cultivated.

Miang-Fong was the one who demanded quite clearly defined rules. When giving his reasons he explained that human beings were gliding increasingly into the depths. If this trend was to be checked, barriers would have to be set up. Man would not be restrained by rational arguments. Already too much had been neglected through this approach.

"But your method will train jointed dolls, wooden images, like those the children play with and which they have to manipulate themselves," a fellow-pupil interposed.

"That depends on the rules, my friend," replied Miang-Fong in his calm way. "Blind forms are of no avail. You cannot throw tree-trunks across the path of a downward-hurtling vehicle. That would startle the draught-animals, and the headlong crash would come all the more quickly. It will be the task of those who guide human beings to set up the rules in such a way that the people grasp their essence and purpose as they follow them."

"You all know," Zarathustra advised them, "that I too demand a certain outer discipline wherever I wish to proclaim the tidings of God. Think of the daily ablutions, the separate meals, and many other things which have to be strictly enforced."

"These things are self-evident," came the spirited outcry from one pupil.

"That is how they seem to you, who are no longer used to anything different," the Master replied. "But tell us, Miang-Fong, what kind of rules you would establish if you were sent to a country as a Messenger of God."

Without a moment's thought the pupil replied, his eyes reflecting the depth of his intuitive perceiving:

"Above all I would demand silence!"

He was interrupted by a very lively pupil, who called out in horror:

"Silence, Miang-Fong! That would be dreadful. God has given us a tongue to be used!"

Zarathustra was delighted. He signalled that he was throwing this question open for general discussion. Now the opinions tumbled out in rapid succession. Most held speech to be a necessity.

"And yet more harm is done by speaking than by silence," an older pupil interposed.

"Either can cause harm. Both must simply be used aright."

"Until that can be mastered it is better to avoid unnecessary words."

The opinions had followed one another swiftly. Now Zarathustra seized upon the last phrase:

"Unnecessary words!" he exclaimed. "Who among you is really able to determine whether his words are useful? Each will consider them to be so. Truly it is much better to be silent than to speak at the wrong time."

Now they besought Miang-Fong to comment on his point of view. He explained in a kindly manner that he considered silence an excellent exercise.

"Anyone practising it rightly for once will see how much blessing it brings him. Through silence our thoughts go down to the depths, take root and become fruitful."

"You are right, Miang-Fong," Zarathustra agreed. But one of the younger pupils exclaimed in surprise:

"If one day you are sent to a people, do you really intend to immerse the entire population in silence, Miang-Fong?"

The question was asked with such astonishment that the earnest pupil had to laugh.

"You did not let me finish speaking before, my friend. Of course I would require silence only of the learners!"

"What do you think, shall we not also endeavour to practise the power of silence?" Zarathustra suggested. "I think that we should decide upon a certain day in the month when we will say only what is absolutely necessary. Do you agree to that?"

They assented with enthusiasm. The novelty of it appealed to them. Now they asked what day the Master considered suitable.

"I think there are two days that are important: the day before the Hour of Worship, so that it may bring us that composure which is fitting, or the day after it, so that what we have heard may take root. What is your opinion?"

They could not reach an agreement. But one of the older pupils suggested that the two days be taken. The others concurred, and for a long time the days around the full moon were considered as days of silence, dedicated to the spiritualisation of the pupils.

Zarathustra told Yadasa of this decision, and asked her whether she would arrange the same for her women. She reflected for some time, then she said:

"Our work deals mainly with practical things, which most of the girls undertake outside our rooms. In these circumstances, silence would be impossible. But half-measures are worse than no measures at all. I will tell the women about it, and perhaps they will decide to restrict their talking voluntarily on certain days."

One day Miang-Fong asked to speak with the Master. He told him that during the night he had received the call to travel over the high mountains to a land which would be indicated to him.

There a great and gifted people was about to become engulfed in superstition and vice. He was to bring these people the Truth, introduce discipline and morals, and tell them about God. This people was destined for great things.

Unassuming and modest, Miang-Fong stood before his Master, filled only with the glorious nature of his task, and the great Grace of the Supreme God.

"In that case I will bless you at the next Hour of Worship, my son," said Zarathustra, deeply moved. "Thereafter you may journey wherever God leads you."

He attended to many things that were necessary for this very far, very arduous journey, and gave him one of his white steeds. Miang-Fong refused to take a servant with him.

The Hour of Worship which took place a few days later was governed completely by the departure of the new Truth-bringer. They had all sensed that he was something special. But nevertheless they marvelled now that one from their midst had been called to such a great task.

The Master told them that Miang-Fong had been called even before he came to them, but he, Zarathustra, had not known it then. Yadasa, however, had already seen it at that time. It was precisely because he was called that God had sent him here to learn and deepen his knowledge.

And he blessed the departing one, saying: "Blessed are you, Miang-Fong! You will be the helper to a great people. You will save it from ruin. You will build a firm structure that will outlast the ages. From this people will arise such as will bring the Truth to other peoples.

225

"And when the Saoshyant appears, all those of this people who have held fast to your teachings will be permitted to join him. They will bless you for helping to make this possible for them.

"Before you, who are called to carry the Holy Light into the Darkness, false beliefs will flee like grey mists."

The next day Miang-Fong rode far away.

His departure left behind a gap so great as no one had expected. Only now was it evident how much he had given to them all in his quiet way, how often a single glance had sufficed to bring about clarity.

VISHTASPA grew and became a joy to all. He remained the only child of his parents, who taught him everything they knew themselves.

Their example stimulated him, their word guided him. But he was inseparable from Hafiz. The Prince, who saw in him his successor, took him wherever he went and explained to him every measure he undertook.

Even now the people called him "the little Prince", without realising the rightness of the designation.

"Do you know, Zarathustra," Hafiz said one day as they sat together in intimate conversation, "that sending out your priests has greatly eased the task of ruling for me? Now the whole realm, which hitherto could not be surveyed, has been divided into administrative districts, all of which quite naturally have their focal point here.

"I avail myself of all your priests conjointly, as worldly rulers of the districts under them. In that way order and strict discipline have come about throughout the people.

"Just as their belief has now uniformly become the belief in Ahuramazda, so they also willingly accept all edicts issuing from me."

"Must it not be this way, Hafiz?" the Master asked in reply. "When the Prince himself stands in the faith, he can only enact laws which are in accord with the Will of God. Then worldly and spiritual leadership coincide. We can wish nothing better for our people than that it be ever thus."

Soon afterwards Hafiz received news that wild hordes were attempting to invade the east of his country. Up to now the inhabitants had been able to resist them, but the marauders came again and again in ever greater numbers. Would the Prince send help?

"What am I to do, Zarathustra?" asked Prince Hafiz. "I loathe bloodshed, I love peace. But if I stand idly by while the wild horde invades my country, I will trespass against every one of my subjects."

"If a tiger attacks your herd, you will also proceed to kill it, Prince!" the Master said earnestly.

"And what does Yadasa say?" Hafiz asked, turning to the woman, who once again had found the time to take part in a serious conversation between the two men.

"I say: advance against the enemies in Ahuramazda's Name. Protect your country, as your princely duty dictates. God's Blessing will be with you."

Then Prince Hafiz ordered the men in the surrounding districts to prepare for battle. An impressive troop sped to his side. For many decades Persia had been at complete peace with her neighbours. This was a new experience, falling upon the hearts of the people like a great terror.

Before Hafiz set out with his troops, they were all blessed by Zarathustra. Then began the march towards the sunrise.

For the duration of the Sovereign's absence, however, the country was placed under the protection and rule of Zarathustra. Should Hafiz not return, Zarathustra was to be the ruler until Vishtaspa was a man.

But the well-ordered country hardly needed a ruler. Everything proceeded without the least interference, exactly as though Hafiz were in the capital. Zarathustra had no need to withdraw from his actual task.

This became ever more extensive. Now sacred squares had been established in all the places where priests worked.

The larger settlements had copied the building of the halls for the hours of worship, which were held throughout the country at every full moon. Here and there small buildings had appeared, in which White Sisters were settled, in order to work beneficially in their immediate and further surroundings.

But every year at the same time the Mountain Festival was held, at which it had become the custom for the priests of all districts, in so far as they could arrange it, to meet on the Mountain three days in advance, to give the Master an account of their activities, to seek his advice and to submit questions.

From these meetings Zarathustra drew the truths he would give to the people during the days of the Festival.

The previous year a violent storm had broken unexpectedly, disrupting the Festival with floods of rain. Those attending saw a bad omen in this. "Ahuramazda is angry" was the rumour that passed from mouth to mouth.

But the Master had been able to calm his frightened flock. God was not angry with his people. But they should build a hall on the Mountain of the Festival, so that future Festivals should be protected from rain and thunderstorms.

Among his pupils was one who was outstanding through a special aptitude for building. He had repeatedly directed the construction of smaller halls. It always seemed that new thoughts for this flowed to him from above.

Zarathustra appointed the pupil, Darna, as leader of the work of building this most festal of all edifices. With a number of voluntary helpers, this man remained on the Mountain after the Festival had ended, and had the site levelled. Everything had been discussed with the Master.

While some of the men felled trees, dug up roots, and removed boulders, others carried large stones, as uniform as possible, to the site. This had been the plan. But then one of the men brought forth a request:

"Sir," he said to Darna, "here there is only grey stone. In my home it is red with light veins; in other places it is white. Every stone is beautiful. Each of us loves the stones of his home. Please allow us to bring them from our homes too, so that the Tabernacle of God will be built by us all."

Although the man had uttered his request haltingly, Darna understood him at once, and was delighted with the idea. It would be beautiful if stones were brought from the whole realm for the building of God's Tabernacle.

"It is fortunate that the Master has been visiting a sick priest near here," he said. "He will come to the Mountain once more tomorrow, to see what progress has been made with the work. We can then ask him if it meets with his approval."

It did indeed meet with his approval. He was truly happy with the suggestion.

After the permission had been received, the men vied with one another in bringing the most beautiful stones. The building would now take a little longer to complete, but Darna was of the opinion that all kinds of preparatory work could be done in the meantime, so that God's Tabernacle would be standing by the next Festival.

It was to be a large, square hall with as much space as possible for the numerous visitors. To the right and left rooms were to be added for the assembling Priests and for the helping women.

Darna suggested that lodging places should be built at the foot of the Mountain. But the Master would not hear of it yet. A Tabernacle of God was to be raised, not accommodation for men. After all, they had their tents, which had provided adequate protection even during the very violent storm.

Zarathustra rode back to the capital. He knew that the building was in the best of hands. Darna put into this work all the adoration of which his soul was capable.

ONE MORNING Yadasa came to Zarathustra and said:

"Today Hafiz has set out for home. He is returning with a greater troop than he had when he rode away. I have been permitted to see them. The men he is bringing with him can hardly be called handsome."

"Let us thank God that he is coming back," Zarathustra said with joy. "Let him bring anyone he likes. It would have been difficult for me to consecrate the Tabernacle of God on the Mountain without his presence."

About two weeks later the Prince rode into his city.

All the inhabitants converged to give him a rapturous welcome. Many of those who had started out with him were missing; nevertheless the troop looked impressive and cheerful.

In the midst of the soldiers there were about a hundred men of yellowish complexion, with slanting eyes and flat noses. Their black hair was trimmed all round the head, and was heavily oiled. Their clothing consisted of rags; but it was obvious that even in a usable state it was completely different from that worn in Persia.

After the welcome was over and the non-resident soldiers had continued their homeward journey, Zarathustra asked why the Prince had brought the strange men, with whom they could not even communicate.

Hafiz explained that these were the most distinguished of the hostile peoples. After he had repelled the enemy across the border several times, the thought had occurred to him of seizing the leaders in order to safeguard the peace.

Some of them understood the language of the land. With their assistance he had informed the invaders that their nobles would be killed instantly if they dared to cross the border again.

But if they behaved peaceably nothing would happen to their nobles. In this way he considered his realm to be secure.

"What will you do with these people now, Hafiz?" asked Zarathustra thoughtfully. "They are useless eaters, and they must be given clothing," he added.

"I think they will have to work for their keep," the Prince decided.

But the Master did not like it, although he had no idea of how things could have been done differently.

In the night be immersed himself in prayer and asked for clarity. The Luminous Messenger came and said:

"It was wise of Hafiz to seize these men; for this wild people would otherwise have given him no peace.

"It is also right that he cannot support them without their doing something in return. But he should beware of expecting too much of them or asking them to perform duties that others do not care to do. There is a great danger. Make sure that he recognises it."

But Hafiz had already conceived the idea of engaging the strangers wherever there was a shortage of manpower in the very tasks that no one liked doing.

Therefore he was very surprised when the Master brought him the message from above. Not for a moment did it occur to him to oppose it, not even in thought. He pondered how else it could be arranged.

Zarathustra then suggested that the men should be asked what work they were accustomed to doing, and what they were able to do.

Much to everyone's surprise it became apparent that they were masters at forging metals. They brought forth such intricate forms and decorations as no one would ever have credited to these strangers.

They worked joyfully, without any urging to be industrious. But then another difficulty arose.

The time of the Mountain Festival had come, and anyone who could possibly arrange it wanted to be present this year. Who was to guard the strangers in the meantime? No one would stay away voluntarily.

Finally Hafiz appointed an adequate number of soldiers to the task, and Zarathustra promised that they should have a special Festival on the Mountain after the others had returned.

ALREADY SEVERAL days before the Festival Zarathustra repaired to the Mountain with his pupils, to make all the preparations.

The Hall, built of different coloured stones, looked much more beautiful than he had expected. Darna had not allowed the stones to be used indiscriminately, but had arranged them in specific places according to their nature.

To the best of their ability helpers had planted greenery all round the building. Inside, the floor was also made of stones. Colourful woven and embroidered mats of fine wool hung down over the stone walls.

In place of the usual pile of stones in the centre there was one single rectangular white block, upon which stood a metal chalice elaborately decorated by one of the strangers. All around the walls, on projecting stones, were also mounted bowls in which fragrant oil was to burn.

Arranged in a square were several rows of solid stones, where the women could be seated. The men had to stand behind them.

Everything was very simple, and yet it seemed to them exquisite, and they regarded it as holy.

Three days before the Festival, priests from all parts of the country had come together, and were the first to be permitted to admire the Tabernacle. They thought they had never before seen anything so wonderful.

And then the other visitors to the Festival came pouring in from everywhere. In Hafiz's escort rode Yadasa with her women and Vishtaspa, who was to experience a Festival consciously for the first time. All were filled with rejoicing over the Tabernacle of God. Yadasa expressed what most of them were thinking:

"God's Tabernacle seems to give forth melody."

Everyone thought the Festival a thousand times more beautiful than ever before.

Zarathustra told them of Ahuramazda, the Eternal, the All-Powerful God, Who had been so gracious to the people. Then he spoke of the Saoshyant, the Holy Son of God, Who would come as Helper and Judge.

The multitude was seized with enthusiasm when the Preserver-of-the-Way spoke of Him to Whom his whole life was dedicated. They were deeply moved by his descriptions. Then, as he paused briefly, the childish voice of Vishtaspa, who was standing next to Yadasa, suddenly rang out:

"Vishtaspa will be His servant! He will serve Him faithfully and lead all the people to Him."

How did the boy know of the prophecy? His parents had not communicated it to him. But the words of the child had sounded like a vow, so that no one was surprised when the Master said, deeply moved:

"May Ahuramazda bless you, my son, that you may one day be able to keep what you have just promised!"

Then he continued to tell and to teach, and the boy listened attentively without speaking again.

Soon the Festival was over. When the numerous guests were leaving, Hafiz departed from the Mountain also. Only Zarathustra remained with his pupils to await the soldiers.

Then one night they were awakened by a noise, and saw a gleam of light flitting about. Zarathustra came quickly out of his tent, which was pitched between the trees on top of the Mountain. He caught sight of several men walking around the Hall.

Apparently they thought it was deserted, for they made no attempt to be particularly quiet. Behind the Master the pupils also were now gathered, barring the men's way. It was the very aged Atravan with a few companions.

232

The Master quelled the cries of indignation even before they could be voiced. Then he turned to the aged man, who stood trembling before him:

"Welcome, Atravan, were you not at the Festival?" There was no reply.

Then he instructed his pupils to take the Atravan's companions with them, and invited the former priest to accompany him to his own tent. The old man followed reluctantly. Inside, the Master indicated a warm bed and asked him to rest until morning, when they would talk together. But the involuntary guest would not wait till then. Although he seated himself on the bed, he began to speak at once.

"I see, Zarathustra, that Ahuramazda has become too powerful for me. I had heard about the building of the Tabernacle, and came to destroy it. Outside you will find the implements which we brought with us. I thought you had ridden away, otherwise we would have waited a few more days. But now you are here, and again, as always, your God protects you. But as for myself, He is destroying me."

Zarathustra urged him to abandon these bad thoughts. After all there had once been a time when he too believed in Ahuramazda. He should try to remember that, and give honour to God; then he would also be happy again.

The Atravan, however, confessed that the time of which the Master spoke had never been. He had never believed in God, nor ever in the gods either. He had only paid lip-service to them, so that he could perform the duties of his high office. Now he was still unable to find the way to them.

"Do not trouble about me," he cried, embittered. "I want to die as I have lived!"

With these words he drew out a little phial from his robe. But before he could put it to his lips, the Master had snatched it from him. Then he spent the rest of the night showing forth the Divine Power and Glory to the aged man.

When day broke he led him into the Tabernacle, and there at last the crust laid by obduracy and malice around this old heart burst. The Atravan fell to his knees before the Stone and prayed.

The Master kept him on the Mountain while his companions went home. They had shown no inclination to hear about God, but had only been anxious to get away as fast as possible.

But the former Atravan could hardly be separated from the Tabernacle of God, in which he sensed the power. Zarathustra allowed him to take part in the Festival which was arranged for the soldiers, and rejoiced at the deep impression made by the devout and simple event on the old man.

When he learned that the former priest had no home of his own, but had to live on the charity of those who did not know him, he took him back and allocated him a place to sleep in the city, within the pupils' building.

But after a few months this heart, once so wild, stopped beating. Peacefully the former priest left the earth.

THE YELLOW, slit-eyed prisoners had settled down well. They showed no inclination to leave their new home, in which they felt contented. Little by little they learned the language of the people around them, and had many things to tell about their country which astounded the hearers.

They wandered restlessly from pasture to pasture, living always in tents, or during the hottest time of the year, in the shade of big trees. Only here had they learned the meaning of agriculture.

They lived on the meat of their flocks, which seemed to consist mainly of sheep, and in fact they consumed the meat in its raw state. In addition they ate fruit, and fish which they caught in the great rivers of their country.

They knew nothing about God, nor did they know any gods. They worshipped sinister figures which they claimed to see in their country, and of which the Persians, who listened in astonishment, could form no picture. When asked whether they saw these beings here also, they answered, relieved:

"No, the demons have remained over there. It is too bright for them here."

Zarathustra endeavoured to awaken their souls and speak to them of God.

Gradually the effort was rewarded. Some of the men awakened, and began to ask questions which led slowly to their finding the answers. They came regularly to the Hours of Worship and often asked that pupils might come and instruct them. Later they passed on to their friends what they had grasped.

Their proficiency too received fresh impetus. After they had produced and decorated a sufficient number of bowls for all the places of worship, the Master let them try adorning objects for everyday use.

He brought them bluish-green stones like those worn by Hafiz in his crown, and directed them to mount these into belts, buckles, rings and the like. This they did extremely well.

They never set the stones directly on to the metal, but within a border, reflecting some natural form, usually flowers.

These items became very popular. Everyone was happy to obtain one as an ornament for his wife or his home, and thus the strangers not only earned their livelihood, but also achieved a certain degree of prosperity.

Zarathustra had a work-hall built for them, since the metals could not tolerate the prolonged rains. In addition they had been provided with rooms for living and sleeping.

"The yellow ones' place" gradually became part of the town. Those who lived there were no longer regarded as strangers to the land.

Vishtaspa particularly enjoyed visiting the workmen. They loved the friendly lad with the radiant eyes and deft hands, for he had long since ceased to be a mere onlooker.

He felt drawn to the strange implements. Gently he examined first one, then another; and when the men perceived that it was an inner urge that prompted his actions, they showed him how to use the tools.

One day he came running to the Master, beaming.

"Father, look what I have been allowed to make!"

In his hand he held a blue flower on a stem, fashioned of metal, quite true to nature. While his teachers used the metal as a base, hammering or etching the form of the flower into it, and then adorning it with stones, he had joined the stones to form a flower, holding it together with metal bands.

The yellow ones had greatly admired his work. Now he wanted to give it to his mother, but his father was to see it first. His parents were delighted with the skill of their child, who preferred such work to any games.

But soon no more time was left for this work. Although he was still young, the boy was placed by the Master in the circle of pupils, with whom he was permitted to work and study.

Vishtaspa asked to live and sleep with them also. Zarathustra wanted to grant his request, but Yadasa as well as Hafiz disagreed.

"He is to be Prince, and must become accustomed to life in the Palace. He must learn to be waited upon and to regard this as something natural. Then he will always be kind to his subordinates, as is Hafiz," said Yadasa. "But if he claims these services later as something merited by his dignity, he will be at pains to express this 'dignity' also in his dealings with the servants."

"I wanted my son to grow up naturally," the Master explained; but Yadasa was of a different opinion.

"What is natural, Zarathustra?" she asked calmly. "Surely only that which comes about of itself from the circumstances in which a person finds himself. It would be unnatural if the future King were to grow up in any other way than as he is to live later."

Hafiz agreed, especially because he would not be altogether deprived of the lad's company.

Thus Vishtaspa remained in the Palace except during the periods of instruction, and listened to his mother's stories; or he went hunting and rode far away with Hafiz.

For Zarathustra a time had again come when his soul often wandered, seeing things imperceptible to earthly eyes.

First pictures of human beings crying for help appeared to him, then he had glorious visions from supra-earthly realms. He learned to understand what all this had to tell him.

Although outwardly his life became increasingly active and eventful, he sensed it intuitively as but a covering for what he experienced inwardly. There his true creative work and activity now lay. Whatever he learned or received was subsequently of help to all.

With more and more cries for help from alien peoples, the Master spoke with the yellow ones, to find out whether it would be possible to send a few of his pupils to the country of the strangers.

They, who themselves had found their way to God, wished nothing better than for their people to be guided along the same path. But they did not underestimate either the great danger that lay in the uncontrolled savagery of this bloodthirsty people.

Zarathustra placed his thoughts on this as an entreaty before God. The answer given him through the Luminous One overcame any misgivings.

"Let the pupils go to the distant foreign country, trusting in the help of God the Almighty. By arduous labour they will have to loosen the souls and scatter the seed. But blessing will be upon this work.

"To make it easier for them to win the confidence of the wild people, give those of the yellow ones who wish it the choice of returning to their homeland. You can safely let those go who wish to do so; these long-forgotten fellow-tribesmen have ceased to be a protection against predatory raids."

Zarathustra spoke with his pupils, many of whom declared their willingness to undertake this service. There was such an ardent longing in them to be permitted to speak of God to those who still knew nothing about Him that they completely forgot the dangers.

Then the Master asked the yellow ones which of them wished to return to the homeland.

He had expected that they would all want to leave the country, but instead only two came forward. It was not until he had told them what service was expected of them as a gift in return for their freedom, that seven others declared themselves willing to go with the pupils. But they wished to be regarded as emissaries, to be allowed to remain with the pupils and to return with them later.

"Persia is now our homeland," they assured him. "We must be careful not to tell our brothers too much about what it is like, otherwise they will all want to settle here too. That would be detrimental to Persia."

The sending forth of the pupils to the distant, unknown country became a solemn festival. A few White Sisters had asked for permission to travel with the pupils; but Yadasa did not allow it. First the men should blaze a trail; thereafter White Sisters could follow if necessary.

On the long march through Persia, then across the mountains into the foreign land, the pupils learned the language of the yellow ones.

They found everything just as it had been described to them: false belief and delusion, blood-thirstiness and savagery, licentiousness and depravity. But they taught and worked tirelessly, protected by the yellow ones, who never left them. Their own country was less appealing than ever to them. They complained about how terrible it all was, and worked hard to bring about a change.

But the spirit of sacrifice evinced by the emissaries was not to be rewarded with success. Ever again the unbridled mind of the savage people, who would not tolerate any alien influence, gained the upper hand. Rebellion and murder ensued.

After most of the emissaries and six of their protectors had lost their lives, the rest fled back to Persia.

Zarathustra received them lovingly. There were none of the rebukes they had expected. He had already received tidings from his Luminous Helper about the outcome of the undertaking. Now he was no longer to send anyone to the obdurate people.

THEN Zarathustra was given another mission from Luminous Heights: With Vishtaspa, who had grown into young manhood, he was once more to journey across the whole of the realm, and visit all the places where priests held office.

He should allow himself ample time, but arrange things so that he could be near the Mountain at the time of the Festival, in order to hold it himself.

The mission filled father and son with joy. They would have liked to have Yadasa with them, but she dissented: if she were meant to journey with them, she would have been instructed to do so. She wished to remain with the women.

Hafiz debated for a long time whether he should join them. Although he had become an elderly man, he still felt vigorous, and would have liked to see his country once more. But he too decided to stay at home. Various disturbing reports came from the northern border, and he did not dare to leave the capital.

Thus father and son, accompanied by an imposing retinue of pupils and servants, rode together along the route specified for them.

The youth was brimming with joyful anticipation of all that he would be allowed to see. Zarathustra had told him much about the past; definite ideas had formed in the young man's soul. He had forgotten that as many years as his age had gone by since his father's last journey.

Much had changed in the meantime. Little villages with miserable huts had become flourishing towns. Some lay defiantly poised among rocks; others nestled prettily against the banks of a small river, still others crowded close to a forest, as if seeking protection.

But everywhere they found a lively spiritual life, a uniform faith, and an endeavour to act in accordance with the Commandments of God. There was peace and harmony, eager activity and gratifying cleanliness everywhere.

In the mountainous regions long-haired goats and hardy sheep grazed. From their fur and wool men and women were skilled at producing articles of clothing. Here too were spun the coloured woollen yarns with which the women throughout the country knotted and wove heavy mats.

In the plains the men cultivated the fields and tended cattle and horses, while the women wove fabrics and baskets.

On the edge of the desert there was salt-mining and metalwork, as before. Then there was the rose-district, like a single huge flowering garden. Here the people knew how to extract choice fragrant oils from rose-petals.

Vishtaspa had enough to see; he gazed also with his soul. He wanted to become acquainted with his future subjects in all things.

He also took part in everything he saw. He could not watch a craftsman at work without going up to him for at least a few moments. Wherever possible, he asked to be allowed just to try his hand. And the sunny, handsome youth was seldom denied a request.

No one knew yet that one day he was to become the ruler of the extensive realm. Even so his title, "the young Prince", had spread far beyond the confines of the capital.

His grandfather, Nazim, was no longer alive. Zarathustra showed his son the village where his mother had grown up. The people, who were still very attached to Yadasa, were delighted to have her son with them.

Then they came to the village headed by Murza and Anara. The chieftain had died, and the people had transferred that office to Murza in addition to his priesthood.

At the sight of this pretty village it was hard to believe that it was the place where refuse had had to be forcibly removed.

The two riders and their retinue had now travelled for nearly two years. They then returned to the capital satisfied, longingly awaited by everyone.

Prince Hafiz said that he had only wanted to await the return of his successor; now he was prepared to depart this life.

His face, still manly, had become gaunt and transparent. His hands trembled, but his spirit seemed to have matured even more in recent months. He spoke very little, but what he said was of value.

Now he asked for Vishtaspa to be constantly near him to be given any instructions that seemed necessary.

"I would like to bid my people farewell, Zarathustra," he said one day after spending the night in prayer. "Would it be possible for me to speak to them this evening after the Hour of Worship?"

The Master found this appropriate. The news was spread among the people that the Prince himself would speak to them that evening. And even those who from love of ease usually had various excuses for staying away from the Hour of Worship came on this night.

In the evening Hafiz had himself carried into the Hall of Worship.

The Divine Service proceeded as always. Perhaps Zarathustra found words even more fervent than usual to touch the souls. Then he announced that they should all remain assembled, as Prince Hafiz wished to address them.

Hafiz stepped into the centre, supported by Vishtaspa, who was not permitted to leave his side.

The aged man looked dignified in his richly embroidered robe, with the crown on his head.

He thanked his people for never making life difficult for him by disobedience or discord during his long reign.

"The best thing in my life, Persians, was that God deemed us worthy to have the Zoroaster in our midst," he said, full of gratitude. "From him we have learned to find God, the Most High. Through his activity the realm has been united.

"I depart childless. But when I now go from you, you will not be without a leader. I have trained my successor for you; he grew up in your midst. You love the young Prince. Be as faithful to him as you have been to me!"

Deep emotion coursed through the ranks of people. Then Hafiz turned to the youth.

"Kneel down, my son, that I may bless you."

And as Vishtaspa obeyed the command, Hafiz lifted the crown from his head, and placed it upon the bowed youthful one. He appeared to be saying a quiet prayer as he did so. Then he raised his voice once more:

"May Ahuramazda bless you, my son! He destined you to be King of this people before your birth. King shall you be from this day on. Arise, King Vishtaspa of Persia!"

Despite the holiness of the place, shouts were heard. Some hailed the young ruler, others begged the Prince not to leave them just yet.

He smiled wearily.

"Grant me a few more years by the side of the young King, during which time, as his adviser, I can rejoice in what youthful vigour will undertake."

When the Master observed that Hafiz had no more to say, he stepped beside him, and thanked him on behalf of the people for the loving and kind rule which the Prince had always exercised.

Then he prayed that peaceful years of rest might be granted to the retiring Prince, and helping power to the young King.

The latter entered upon his office with joy. Accustomed from early childhood to the thought that he would one day take the place of Hafiz, he had observed all that the Prince did with open eyes. Later Prince Hafiz had discussed every measure with his young successor before carrying it out.

Now Vishtaspa wanted to do likewise, and each day discuss everything with his fatherly friend; however he met with determined resistance.

"You must not make a habit of asking me in all things whether I approve, my son," said the venerable man kindly, "otherwise you will become too dependent. When you have undertaken something, you can tell me about it afterwards, and we will discuss it. That will be better."

THE UNREST in the north of the country, which had abated, once more increased ominously. Again and again there was news of predatory incursions, murder and arson. Action had to be taken to put an end to the raids.

Vishtaspa had been brought up in the thought that bloodshed was against the Commandments of God. But he also knew that at God's behest Hafiz had marched against the enemy in the past.

So he prepared to ride north, and a great troop of armed men was to accompany him. Although the Prince thought to himself that half the number would suffice, he let the young King have his way. He should show what he was able to accomplish.

As before, Zarathustra blessed the departing soldiers, who rode away cheerfully as if embarking on an adventure. But the King had a plan which he communicated to the officers as they rode.

At first they listened in astonishment to what he was trying to explain to them. Then, when they had grasped what it was all about, they were delighted and asked for permission to tell their men about it.

This took place that very evening, and laughter rang out from tent to tent, giving rise to ever new outbursts of mirth.

In this cheerful mood they arrived in the north after many days of arduous riding. There jagged rocks, ragged mountain ranges towering skyward into dizzy heights, formed the border of the country. These were good hiding-places for marauders.

In all the villages through which he came King Vishtaspa heard the heart-rending plaints of the victims. The nearer he came to the mountains, the more signs he found of sword and fire. The people lived in trembling fear of each new day. His kind voice called out to them:

"It will come to an end, I promise you!"

In very small units, he let his men ride into the mountains according to a well considered plan. Guided by one of the local inhabitants, he had personally explored everything, so that he was able to make precise dispositions.

The marauding neighbours were unprepared for resistance.

Men who had ventured across the border into enemy territory brought news of a surprise attack planned at two points. Now they must be on the alert!

And the King's plan, conceived after fervent prayer, succeeded. All night the battle raged, but without bloodshed, thanks to the King's superior forces. In the morning, the armed men brought a hundred bound enemy captives before the King.

The prisoners cast sullen and hate-filled glances about them. At the same time they could not hide their curiosity.

What they saw here aroused their amazement. Vishtaspa had deliberately stationed all his troops round about. The large number was meant to intimidate, and did so. The men began to tremble. They could only believe that they would now be killed.

Vishtaspa stepped before them and asked:

"Who among you understands our language?"

He saw a number of eyes light up, but the men chose to remain silent. Then some of the mountain-dwellers called out:

"Do not trouble yourself, O King. Nearly all of them understand our language; but we too can speak theirs. We will gladly interpret whatever you wish to tell them."

This the King accepted, and then addressed the prisoners:

"You have committed an outrage in not respecting the boundaries of our country. You have not acted out of want, for you were more concerned with killing people who were asleep, burning down huts and abducting women than with the possession of cattle. Perhaps you have not been taught that that is a sin. But now you shall learn it in a way that will make you never forget it again.

"Since you have behaved like hateful children, you will be treated in the same way as they. You will be beaten so that you may know that you have deserved the punishment. But to prevent your forgetting the lesson too quickly, your heads will be shorn. Afterwards you may go home."

The men howled aloud. To be shorn was a great disgrace, even among these depraved people. They would rather die than appear before their own people in that state.

But the King's intention was to deter them once and for all. He kept to his sentence, which was promptly carried out by his soldiers. All were convinced that the young King had acted justly and wisely. They were glad to be permitted to serve him.

He had impressed upon them in advance that they must neither ridicule nor ill-treat the prisoners. They were to feel that the punishment was indeed administered as such, and not because the others enjoyed doing it.

When all the captives had been shorn, Vishtaspa was sent for. The prisoners were convinced that now they would be killed after all. None believed in the possibility of release.

The King regarded them with compassion. It had been difficult for him to remain firm in the face of so much depravity. Now he spoke to them, and the love which he felt for his fellow-creatures resounded in his voice. He said:

"You have received the punishment you deserved, and may now go home. It will no longer occur to any of you to cross the border with hostile intentions. Tell your companions what is to be expected if it should ever occur to them to do as you have done. They will meet with the same punishment. You can see how many soldiers stand ready here for defence.

"Before you go I would like to tell you something else: You know that I am the King of this country. You have seen how great is my power."

The men nodded almost against their will. They liked him. Some were impressed by the sound of his voice, which touched their hearts without their being aware of it.

"I have commanded my soldiers to kill none of you," Vishtaspa continued. "You can see that they have obeyed my command!

"From this you can perceive that great power is given to me. But there is One Whose Power is a thousand times greater. He has given to all mankind the Commandment not to kill! It is at His behest that all of us did what we resolved to do. This one exalted One is also your Ruler. He is the All-Highest, the Eternal God, Whom we worship!"

Apathetic, uncomprehending, disbelieving, astounded eyes were directed at the speaker. Hardly a man appeared to have understood or to want to hear more.

It seemed to the King that a voice prompted him not to say any more today. The seed had been sown, and must be allowed time to take root.

Thus Vishtaspa ordered the prisoners' bonds to be loosed, and once freed, each one shot off swift as an arrow, without waiting for his companions.

But one of them turned abruptly and made straight for the King. The soldiers stationed themselves more closely round their ruler. They were afraid that the man might have evil intentions. But Vishtaspa checked them:

"Look at him. His good volition shines forth from his eyes. Let him be."

The stranger had approached. Now he awkwardly bent his knee before the King and said:

"I thank you for your kindness. Our people cannot yet appreciate it, but I perceive it, and will always speak of it. Not the punishment, but the love with which it was administered will make us your friends, O King!

"You are young, but you are very wise. You are handsome, but your goodness surpasses your appearance.

"Permit me to return when my hair has grown again, so that I may hear more about the God Whom you serve."

The King granted the wish with joy. He was surprised that the man could speak Persian so well; but he learned that all these people at the border had a command of the language.

When all those who had been set free were out of sight, Vishtaspa spoke to his soldiers. He pointed out to them the necessity of being always prepared. The enemy must not be allowed to imagine that the border had again been left undefended.

"Let us build stone huts in these fissures and rifts, many huts in different places, so that the whole border will be safeguarded. Soldiers must then patrol between the huts and keep watch.

"I think we must alternate the soldiers every year, so that others will constantly come to this solitude."

Then those willing to assume the first guard duty were asked to come forward. About fifty men were left behind, with five commanders. Vishtaspa himself set out for the capital with the remaining soldiers.

Sooner than expected he arrived back in the Palace. Great was the surprise that he had brought no prisoners with him. But it was greater still when he told of the measures he had taken.

Even Zarathustra and Hafiz could not help laughing. But then they quickly became very serious. They recognised how wonderfully the young King was guided, how naturally he listened to his guidance.

"I realise that I acted wrongly at the time when I brought the hundred yellow men with me," Hafiz admitted thoughtfully.

The younger man disagreed with him.

"Had you not done so our people could not have acquired their great artistic skill from them. And that it was right, Prince, is also demonstrated in that our country has never since been threatened by an enemy from their direction."

The thought that Vishtaspa had left soldiers behind at the border particularly pleased the old people. It was proof of his great circumspection. But the King had thought further still.

"From now on I will have the strongest men trained in the use of arms, in mountain-climbing and marching. They will be free to ply their trades as well, but they must devote a certain amount of time to the country. All will benefit from what they are doing.

"The larger the number of those whom I can lead against an enemy, the less bloodshed there will be. I have already spoken with the commanders. They agree with me, and would like to undertake the work of instruction.

"But I also hope, Father, that there will soon be work at the border for your pupils. The man of whom I told you will not rest until he can hear more about God. He will, I hope, even induce others to accompany him. Then priests must be available to instruct the seekers. Our soldiers would do more harm than good.

"I would like to ask you, Father, to send several pupils to the north quite soon to live among the soldiers. I feel some concern lest the men up there in the rugged mountains develop rugged habits themselves. It will be good for the priests to live with them, holding Hours of Worship and advising them."

Zarathustra liked the idea, and while Vishtaspa went to greet his mother, his father said to Hafiz:

"The land is truly in the best of hands. We may depart this life in peace when our time comes. Vishtaspa will be King and Priest at the same time."

246

Hafiz wholeheartedly agreed. He admired the young King, whom he loved like his own son. But he disagreed that Zarathustra could yet be spared.

"I am considerably older than you, my friend," he said firmly. "I shall be the first to be called away."

In that he erred. The first call came to Yadasa, who had long been awaiting it, and had made all preparations for her departure.

She had spoken about it to some of her trusted women-helpers, but had said nothing to the men. There was time enough for them when the hour came.

But Vishtaspa, who had been away from his mother for months, had keener eyes than the others. Dismayed, he returned to Prince Hafiz and his father:

"What is wrong with Mother? Since when has she been so ill?"

The two men looked at him quite confounded. They had not been aware of any change in Yadasa. Now upon giving heed, they perceived many signs of insidious disease.

Then Zarathustra decided to talk with his wife. Unhesitatingly she admitted that he had observed correctly. She added how much she was looking forward to being permitted to go to Garodemana.

"I have been allowed to see it in the night so often that I know exactly where the luminous figures will lead me when at last the soul may leave the weary body. I look forward to it, and you too must rejoice. Our separation will not be long. Then you will come also."

Zarathustra gazed calmly at his pallid wife, whose features still seemed to him more lovely than all others.

"I rejoice with you, Yadasa," he agreed. "I am particularly happy that you have already been permitted to behold what is so glorious. Can you tell me about it?"

Yadasa leaned her head against the wall where she was sitting; she closed her eyes, and began dreamily:

"Bright, luminous steps lead upwards into a light which is indescribable. Bright, luminous beings help the souls to ascend these steps, higher, ever higher. On either side there are gardens in which grow glorious, fragrant flowers, tended by lovely female beings.

247

"I see little children playing in pure, sheerest joy. Ever more luminous the figures become, ever more brilliant the light. I see it all, but I cannot describe it. No human being can do so. You will see it yourself, my friend."

Her voice had grown fainter. The listener feared that she was already gone, but after a short time she opened her eyes and smiled at him.

None of her dear ones wished to leave her by herself any longer. Always one was with her, especially when her legs became too weak and she could no longer leave her bed. She did not suffer, but her whole body was growing weary, making any activity impossible.

One evening her son had carried her in his strong young arms to the most beautiful room in the Palace, where Hafiz and Zarathustra were awaiting her. They spoke of the Saoshyant, to Whom the Way-Preserver preferred most of all to give his thoughts. "I shall be permitted to behold Him from afar," Yadasa said with conviction.

"Shall I also be permitted to behold the three Holy Women, I wonder?" she added dreamily after a few moments.

"You should at least look forward to it, my wife," said Zarathustra, in the tender mood affecting him.

They all sensed that something special was wafting through the room. The shared inner experiencing, which they could not put into words, seemed to unite their souls more intimately.

Vishtaspa wanted to know who the three Women were. He had not yet heard about them; for neither Zarathustra nor his wife spoke of their visions. But today Yadasa's tongue was loosed. She had to proclaim the glorious knowledge to her son as long as she could still do so.

"Know that high above in the Heavenly Realms there are three Queens, who are so lovely, so pure, that we human beings cannot grasp it.

"The Queen of all the Heavens spreads her luminous blue mantle over the others. Her crown sparkles in supra-earthly radiance. Her countenance is the most sublime that one can behold."

Zarathustra interrupted her. With bated breath he asked:

"Have you been permitted to behold the holy countenance, Yadasa? Then you were richly blessed! I have never yet seen it. It was always veiled, allowing me only to divine the lovely features."

"I beheld it, and always the Sublime Woman smiled at me, even as she does now," said Yadasa enraptured, not in the least aware of what she was saying. "Beside her stand the Queen of Love and the Queen of Purity. The Love of God lets fall a red rose. Do you perceive its fragrance?"

Truly it was as if the scent of roses drifted through the room, so strong and invigorating as is not possible for earthly flowers.

"The Queen of Purity spreads her arms. How abundantly blessed am I, indeed! I shall be permitted to serve her in the Luminous Realms. O thou loveliest Woman, let me be thine. I desire nothing else!

"She nods Her consent. She beckons. How glorious! Lord, Sublime One, I thank Thee!"

Gently Yadasa sank back into the cushions that were meant to support her. The three men stood around her praying.

In their souls stirred strong intuitive perceptions, filled only with praise and gratitude. Gratitude that God had placed this pure woman on their life's path, that He had called her away so gently and peacefully. A transfigured smile suffused her beautiful features; it did not fade.

For a long time the three men stood by Yadasa's cloak; they could hardly tear themselves away. Zarathustra determined that the body should rest in a grave. The thought of the towers of silence was unbearable to him.

On the following day all was prepared. Amidst a profusion of flowers, the priestesses carried Yadasa to the grave. They suffered no man to touch her save her husband and the King.

Hymns of praise, which Yadasa herself had composed and taught them, resounded while stones were piled up before the grave. Then Zarathustra spoke a fervent prayer of gratitude, admonishing all not to forget this pure life which had been an example to them, so that they could emulate it.

LIFE proceeded on its course. Yadasa herself had determined which of the women should supervise the priestesses and their training. She had charged another one to live with the Helping Sisters and to guide them.

Both women took it as a sacred duty, and did their best not to allow the gap left by Yadasa's departure to become too great.

But the three men in the Palace felt the absence of the woman increasingly with each passing day. They perceived clearly how often a word of understanding, of conciliation, had bridged inevitable differences.

How often, too, had she placed some event described by one of the men in a clear light, so that suddenly they had to view it differently.

And the more they missed her, the more silent they became among themselves. They could sit together for hours, each wrapped in his own thoughts, without clothing them in words. Sometimes one or the other would look up as if about to say something, but then he became aware once more of the emptiness, and relapsed into silence.

This went on for several weeks, and was becoming ever more tangible, when one evening the young King broke the silence.

"Listen, dear ones," he addressed the two others, "we miss Mother, we miss the companion, the complement. Would it not be good if a woman were to come into the Palace again? I do not think that she could replace Mother, but still she would be of help to us all."

Zarathustra gazed at his son uncomprehendingly. What did he mean by this?

But Hafiz had understood him and asked:

"Are you speaking only in general terms, or have you found the woman whom you are looking for?"

"I have found a maiden whom I have cherished in my heart for a long time. I have not yet asked her if she will be my wife, for I wanted first to hear whether you can bear to see another woman in Mother's place."

"You are right, Vishtaspa," Zarathustra now also agreed. "It is time for you to marry. The realm is in need of a successor; you yourself are in need of the wife."

He did not say whether he would be able to bear it. Hafiz understood him as well.

"It is also time for you to take possession of the Prince's Palace, Vishtaspa," he nodded to the King. "Ask the maiden, and if she consents to be your wife, I will move into your father's small Palace. Thus we shall all be helped."

The Prince's words smoothed the way for all three. Brisk work began in the Palace, to prepare all the rooms for the young queen. Soon afterwards Zarathustra blessed the royal couple in the Hall of Worship.

They had asked to be blessed in God's Tabernacle, at the Festival on the Mountain, but his father would not agree to that. He said that the Tabernacle of God was intended only for worship; the Festivals were to be given no earthly character whatever.

So they were both satisfied. The young Queen was very lovely, especially since it was evident that a beautiful soul dwelt in the graceful body. A childlike serenity and unselfish concern for others distinguished her.

For Zarathustra she felt a great reverence, and sought to make life pleasant for him.

Two years had passed since Yadasa's death when Vishtaspa, beaming with happiness, announced to the two aged men that soon the heir would make his entry.

"If it is a son, call him Hafiz," the Prince requested, and the King promised to do so.

"That is good," joked the Prince, "one Hafiz comes when the other goes. May the new Hafiz preserve the peace for the people, and so guide it that he can lead it to the Saoshyant when He comes. When will that be? I sometimes think that the earth will have to wait a long time yet for Him."

With these words the Prince rose to go to his apartment, but fell back in his seat, fainting.

"Thank you, dear ones, you have made my life rich," he smiled at them.

Then he closed his eyes, never to open them again on earth. At his wish he was interred beside Yadasa's grave, without any hymns, with only a prayer of gratitude.

Now Zarathustra waited to be called away. He alone remained of those who had been young with him. At the command from above he had relinquished his duties to his son, who under his guidance was to grow into the twofold dignity of King and Priest.

But this guidance was hardly needed. Vishtaspa was so strongly guided from above that he always did what was right. His father rejoiced at it.

Again several years had gone by. The patient waiting was difficult for Zarathustra, as he was still called. Did Ahuramazda, the All-Highest, want him to learn this too before he was called away? Then he certainly wished to learn it properly, he thought, after providing himself with this answer.

In the Palace two grandchildren were growing up: a vigorous, active Hafiz and an extremely dainty, winsome Yadasa. They were the delight of the aged man, but they were still too young for him to occupy himself with them for any length of time.

He looked around to see what other old people of his age were doing. They lay in the sun and rested from the burdens of life. He asked now this person, then that whether they did not find it tiresome. They laughed:

"Master, it is wonderful!"

Then he wanted to know whether they longed to be permitted to depart this life. They said that they did not.

"We shall wait until our time has come. That will be soon enough for us."

Why was he so different? Why did his weary body refuse to submit to inactivity?

"Lord, Thou seest my volition to possess my soul in patience, but Thou seest also my need. I do not beseech Thee to take me from the earth, but I entreat Thee: send me work!"

Thus the aged man implored many times during the day. Then Vishtaspa came to him.

"Father, are you too weary to undertake yet another great task? Many years ago you wrote down Ahuramazda's Commandments for us so that everyone can now read them. But when you leave us one day, much wisdom will go with you.

"Would you not like to try to write down as much of it as possible? Although our symbols permit of different interpretations, we will remember your words when we interpret them, and the knowledge will be handed down to posterity."

Now Zarathustra had work for a long time to come. To be able to record the Divine Truths he had to increase the number of symbols, conceive new ones whose meaning would be evident. He had to think, deliberate and record. The days now passed swiftly.

And in the night he reflected on what he had to say, and how best to clothe it in words.

The King had thin stone-tablets made, on which Zarathustra could inscribe his symbols. Once he had completed several tablets, he brought them in the evening to his son, who had to decipher them.

Most of the time he could easily read what his father had intended to write. But if he failed to grasp it, Zarathustra patiently made a new attempt to record his words even more clearly.

And as he worked and reflected, his whole life rose up before his soul. How he had been guided! How God's Goodness had watched over his life, so that he had always been permitted to receive one blessing after another.

Now he wished to be allowed to go on living until he had entrusted his knowledge of the Saoshyant to the stones. Long since the symbol for the Helper and World-Judge had been established. It was a Ray descending from the Cross. Whenever he engraved this Ray, he thought he could feel it passing through him. It permeated him like a great power, awaking in him ever new things which he still wanted to proclaim.

The deciphering of the stones had long been transferred to the Hall, so that the pupils and priests could take part, and at the same time learn the meaning of what had been recorded. They were always happy when the aged Zarathustra appeared in their midst. Through great enthusiasm and lively questions they strove to demonstrate this joy to him.

When the proclamation of the Saoshyant was on stone, the reading-out of it was particularly festive. Vishtaspa himself interpreted:

"The day will come when the Saoshyant will descend from Heaven. He will come as a child, He will be the Son of the Most High. He will grow and learn the ways of men. He will bring them the Light from His Father's Realm, so that they may find the way back aloft. He will graze them as a shepherd grazes his flock.

"Thereafter will come the last day: the Judgment. Great will be the Saoshyant, no longer a man, but only God. Men will be afraid, because they have done evil things.

"But the World-Judge will judge them according to their deeds. They must cross the bridge. He who was evil will fall from it, never to return. But those who have walked across the bridge will enter in to the Eternal Realm of the Saoshyant."

The King had read quite simply, just as it was written down. They all were filled by it.

Then Zarathustra stepped once more into the centre of the Hall where he had so often stood, and began to speak:

"I cannot record how immeasurably glorious the Helper will be. He is the Radiant Hero, without equal. He will go among men, outwardly a man like them, but the Clarity of God will radiate from out of Him. His eyes will be like flames, so that nothing impure can exist before Him.

"As He moves among men, one covering mantle after another will fall away from Him. Then the time will have come when He stands above men as God. Then He will judge them, and they will have to answer for every word they have spoken, for every deed they have done, or even only thought of doing.

"Men, keep to the ways of God! Guard against any wrongdoing; for you will judge yourselves by it before the penetrating eyes of the Son of God!

"Persia, blessed land! From you once again the Child once came who will return! In you was it granted that the way for the Saoshyant might be prepared!"

The aged man raised his head as though listening, and spread his arms out wide.

"I see the radiance of Heaven above me! I see the White Wonder-Bird, the Cross in Its Golden Rays! My earthly path has ended. The ascent may begin."

He stood erect for one more moment, then the arms of his son enfolded the lifeless body of the Way-Preparer – the Way-Preserver, whom God had sent to the people of Persia.

Abd-ru-shin

In The Light Of Truth: The Grail Message

The Author was born in 1875 in Bischofswerda, Germany. His given name was Oskar Ernst Bernhardt. After being educated and trained in business, he established himself in Dresden and became financially successful. In the years that followed, he made many journeys abroad, and wrote successful travel books, stories, and plays.

After residing for some time in New York, Mr. Bernhardt journeyed to London, England. There, the outbreak of World War I took him unawares, and in 1914 he was interned on the Isle of Man.

The seclusion of internment brought with it an inner deepening. He reflected continuously over questions connected with the meaning of life, birth and death, responsibility and free will, God and Creation. More and more the desire awakened within him to help humanity. He was released in the Spring of 1919 and returned to Germany.

He began to write the first lectures for *In the Light of Truth: The Grail Message* in 1923. His explanation of the Knowledge of Creation resounded among his hearers.

In 1928, Abd-ru-shin settled in Austria, Tyrol on a mountain plateau called Vomperberg, where he continued writing *The Grail Message*. The seizure of power in Austria by the Nazis in 1938 ended his work there. He was arrested, and his land and property were appropriated without compensation. Abd-ru-shin was exiled to Kipsdorf in the Erzgebirge, where he was under surveillance by the Gestapo. He was forbidden any further work for making *The Grail Message* known publicly.

On December 6, 1941, Abd-ru-shin died from the effects of these measures. After the war his family returned to Vomperberg, and carried on his work.

If you have questions about the content of this Work,
please contact Reader Services at:

Grail Foundation Press
P.O. Box 45
Gambier, Ohio 43022
Telephone: 614.427-9410
Fax: 614.427-4954

IN THE LIGHT OF TRUTH: THE GRAIL MESSAGE
by Abd-ru-shin

Linen edition, three volumes combined
ISBN 1-57461-006-6
5.5" x 8.5"
1,062 pages
Paper edition, three-volume box set
ISBN 1-57461-003-1
6" x 9"
1,079 pages

Original edition: German
Translations available in:
Czech, Dutch, English, Estonian, French, Hungarian,
Italian, Portuguese, Rumanian, Russian,
Slovak, Spanish

Available at your local bookstore
or directly through the publisher.

Grail Foundation Press
P.O. Box 45
Gambier, Ohio 43022
1-800-427-9217

Publisher's catalog available on request

0335

Further Writings by Abd-ru-shin:

THE TEN COMMANDMENTS OF GOD
THE LORD'S PRAYER
72 pages
Linen clothbound
ISBN 1-57461-007-4
Paperback
ISBN 1-57461-004-X

QUESTIONS AND ANSWERS
232 pages
Clothbound
ISBN 3-87860-145-X

PRAYERS
16 pages
Paperback
ISBN 3-87860-138-7

Available at your local bookstore
or directly through the publisher.

Grail Foundation Press
P.O. Box 45
Gambier, Ohio 43022
1-800-427-9217

Publisher's catalog available on request